Communications
in Computer and Informat

CW01560553

Editorial Board

Marco Kalz   Eric Ras (Eds.)

Computer Assisted Assessment

Research into E-Assessment

International Conference, CAA 2014
Zeist, The Netherlands, June 30 – July 1, 2014
Proceedings

 Springer

Volume Editors

Marco Kalz
Open University of the Netherlands
Welten Institute – Research Centre for Learning,
Teaching and Technology
6401 DL Heerlen, The Netherlands
E-mail: marco.kalz@ou.nl

Eric Ras
Public Research Centre Henri Tudor
Service Science and Innovation Department
1855 Luxembourg-Kirchberg, Luxembourg
E-mail: eric.ras@tudor.lu

ISSN 1865-0929   e-ISSN 1865-0937
ISBN 978-3-319-08656-9   e-ISBN 978-3-319-08657-6
DOI 10.1007/978-3-319-08657-6
Springer Cham Heidelberg New York Dordrecht London

Library of Congress Control Number: 2014942077

Typesetting: Camera-ready by author, data conversion by Scientific Publishing Services, Chennai, India

Printed on acid-free paper

Springer is part of Springer Science+Business Media (www.springer.com)

Preface

The International Computer-Assisted Assessment Conference (CAA) has a long
tradition in providing a snapshot of the current state of the art of technology-
enhanced assessment. In its 17th edition in 2014 the conference for the first
time crossed the channel over to mainland Europe. We continued the tradition
of establishing the conference as an interdisciplinary event in the intersection
between, on the one hand, theory and practice, research and application, computer science, psychometrics and education and, on the other hand, between
primary and secondary education, higher education and professional learning.
To make the conference more attractive for researchers from different domains
we arranged for the first time in the conference's history to publish the proceedings with Springer. The best papers have been selected for a journal indexed in
the Social Science Citation Index.

Besides recent trends such as *learnig analytics* or *serious games* as new interactive technologies for assessment, contributions from the the field of medical
education and technology-enhanced assessment in the health sector were also
well represented in the conference program. Three pre-conference activities targeted different groups: A symposium on large-scale testing facilities in higher
education, a practice-oriented workshop on formative assessment for twenty-first
century skills, and a research-oriented workshop on future trends for technology-
enhanced assessment. Interesting demos presented the latest advancements of
technologies for assessment and a poster track provided opportunities to share
practical experiences with the scientific community. We thank all reviewers, contributing authors, and the sponsoring institutions for their support.

June 2014   Marco Kalz
                                                                         Eric Ras

Organization

CAA 2014 was organized by the Welten Institute, Research Centre for Learning, Teaching and Technology of the Open University of The Netherlands in cooperation with SURF, the collaborative organization for ICT in Dutch higher education and research.

Executive Committee

Conference Chairs

Marco Kalz	Open University of The Netherlands, The Netherlands
Eric Ras	Public Research Centre Henri Tudor, Luxembourg

Local Organizing Committee

Marco Kalz	Open University of The Netherlands, The Netherlands
Mieke Haemers	Open University of The Netherlands, The Netherlands
Christien Bok	SURF, The Netherlands
Sandra ter Horst	Kennisnet, The Netherlands
Desiree Joosten-ten Brinke	Open University of The Netherlands/Fontys University of Applied Science, The Netherlands
Annette Peet	SURF, The Netherlands
Lieke Rensink	SURF, The Netherlands

Program Committee

Geoffrey Crisp	University of Melbourne, Australia
Philippe Dessus	University of Grenoble Alpes, FR
Silvester Draaijer	Free University of Amsterdam, The Netherlands
Jan Ehlers	University of Veterinary Medicine Hannover, Germany
Mark Gierl	University of Alberta, Canada
Lester Gilbert	University of Southhampton, UK
Samuel Greiff	University of Luxembourg, Luxembourg
Wolfgang Greller	Vienna University of Education, Austria
Davinia Hernandez-Leo	University of Pompeu Fabra, Spain

George Moerkerke	Open University of The Netherlands, The Netherlands
Peter Reimann	University of Sydney, Australia
Peter van Rosmalen	Open University of The Netherlands, The Netherlands
Venkat Sastry	Cranfield University, UK
Maren Scheffel	Open University of The Netherlands, The Netherlands
Stefan Trausan-Matu	Polytechnica Bukarest, Romania
Bill Warburton	University of Southhampton, UK
Denise Whitelock	The Open University, UK
Gary Wills	University of Southhampton, UK
Karsten Wolf	University of Bremen, Germany

Additional Reviewers

C. Gruber
S. Fazeli
T. Rebedea

Sponsoring Institutions

Turnitin, Newcastle upon Tyne, UK
European Association for Technology-Enhanced Learning (EA-TEL), Hannover, Germany.

Table of Contents

Gauging Teachers' Needs with Regard to Technology-Enhanced Formative Assessment (TEFA) of 21st Century Skills in the Classroom

Ellen Rusman[1], Alejandra Martínez-Monés[2], Jo Boon[1],
María Jesús Rodríguez-Triana[2], and Sara Villagrá-Sobrino[2]

[1] Welten Institute, Open University of the Netherlands,
Valkenburgerweg 167, Heerlen, The Netherlands
{ellen.rusman,jo.boon}@ou.nl
[2] GSIC-EMIC Group, Universidad de Valladolid, Paseo de Belén, nº 7, Valladolid, Spain
amartine@infor.uva.es, chus@gsic.uva.es,
sarena@pdg.uva.es

Abstract. Several trends in society have led to a request towards schools to integrate 21st Century Skills and technology enhanced formative assessment (TEFA) in their curricula. Although there are frameworks defined at an international level, implementation of technology enhanced formative assessment of 21st Century Skills at school level is seldom. This paper explores the underlying reasons for this hampered implementation by consulting and collaborating with teachers. It provides an overview of these reasons and proposes a collaborative professionalization approach to overcome detected implementation barriers and challenges.

Keywords: Technology-Enhanced Formative Assessment (TEFA), formative assessment, 21st Century Skills, teacher professionalization.

1 Introduction

The fast developments in society imply the necessity of being able to deal with growing complexity, ill-structured problems and with uncertainty about the knowledge and skills needed to function competently. Changing professional and societal demands impact significantly on the requirements for education at all levels. It implies that schools integrate new knowledge and skills in their curricula and have tools to assess them. In this paper we discuss three important trends which should lead to approaches to be used in schools, colleges and universities to facilitate the learning process needed for the development of skills to live, learn and work in society: 1) the proposition of 21st Century Skills, 2) the growing attention for formative assessment and 3) the availability of tools for Technology-enhanced formative assessment. Although the key competences and the 21st Century Skills are defined and elaborated in several international frameworks, we argue that the link to approaches to implement them is currently missing. Although these are meant to be applied and

M. Kalz and E. Ras (Eds.): CAA 2014, CCIS 439, pp. 1–14, 2014.
© Springer International Publishing Switzerland 2014

implemented in each member state, several studies [1][2] mention that, although the competences and skills are seen as important by both policy makers as well as teachers and school managers, few countries have developed implementation plans and assessment policies for them.

In this paper we describe these trends, analyse why implementation at classroom level currently hampers and how implementation could be supported. The analysis is based on Spanish and Dutch data gathered amongst teachers. These data were collected in the context of the PREATY project (**PR**oposing modern **E**-assessment Approaches and **T**ools to **Y**oung and experienced in-service teachers)[1]. This project aims to equip teachers in primary and secondary schools with e-assessment strategies and tools to evaluate a number of key 21st Century Skills and competences. Opposite to the traditional test and output-focussed perspective on assessment, the project pursues to promote assessment for learning, therefore focussing mainly on the formative assessment [4, 5, 6, 7] of these skills. To analyse the reasons for the tardiness of implementation of 21st Century Skills internationally we use a framework developed by Surrey and Ely [3]. They define eight conditions that positively contribute to the implementation of instructional innovations in education:

1. **Dissatisfaction with the status quo;** beliefs on the part of the users (teachers) that things could be better or that others are doing better than themselves. Dissatisfaction can be innate or can be induced by external information about alternatives.
2. **Knowledge and skills exist;** people feel confident to introduce an innovation when they feel competent to do so. A lack of required knowledge and skills lead to immobilization and frustration; training is usually a vital part of innovations.
3. **Availability of resources;** all resources that are required to make the innovation work are provided, e.g. ICT or building infrastructure. Without them the innovation is impossible or reduced.
4. **Availability of time;** (company) time needed to acquire and practice knowledge and skills.
5. **Rewards or incentives;** rewards given for meeting an acceptable standard of performance.
6. **Participation;** the involvement of all stakeholders that are contributing to the process.
7. **Commitment;** evidence of individual support for the innovation
8. **Leadership;** support of different hierarchical levels in the organization

In the rest of the paper we first describe the three trends mentioned. Then we describe empirical results indicative for the level of implementation in schools.

In the concluding section we use the scheme proposed by Surrey and Ely [3] to link the different conditions for and their effect on implementation to the empirical data. The discussion section of the paper contains propositions to improve implementation as we explore them within the PREATY project.

---

[1] www.preaty-project.eu

2   Formative Assessment and Technology-Enhanced Formative Assessment

Assessment is a key aspect in any learning process. Formative assessment contributes to achieve learning goals, due to the feedback and feed-forward information it provides to learners about their performance [4,5,6,7]. Moreover, assessment shapes learning, as students tend to concentrate their efforts on those tasks that have a greater assessment weight or on faults that they made, and assessment promotes students' attitudes towards learning, as well as the tactics they employ [8]. In response to this, authentic evaluation approaches emphasize the alignment between learning goals, application contexts and assessment criteria, as well as in the participation of the students in continuous assessment processes [9].

As with almost any activity in our lives, ICT has the potential to support and enhance assessment processes. This support goes beyond the first approaches to the use of ICT technologies to perform on-line tests. The Joint Information Systems Committee defined a broad concept of e-assessment as any electronic process in which ICT is used to present and perform tasks and activities related to assessment, from the perspective of any of the possible stakeholders: learners, tutors, institutions or the general public [10]. This wider concept of e-assessment leaves more space for benefiting from the potential advantages that the use of ICT may pose. As pointed out previously by the authors [11], these benefits range from a larger control on learning by the involved actors, to an improvement of the feedback quality and motivation of the learners. Besides, technology can track, store, process and visualize learners' results and actions, making these processes visible and available for different learning purposes, and more concretely for formative assessment. It also offers opportunities to differentiate amongst learners. Technology can furthermore help to shape learning scenarios with varied authentic assessment designs [18], enabling formative assessment of both products and processes learners produced and experienced.

From this broad perspective, different approaches for the use of technology to support assessment can be identified. One of them is adapting off-the-shelf tools to the needs of a particular assessment process, like the use of spreadsheets to record and calculate grades, or questionnaire-management tools to present different types of tests to students. However, this approach leaves the effort to adapt the tool to their needs in the hands of teachers. A second approach is the provision of tools designed to support specific assessment methods, and that try to implement the principles of these approaches to make them more accessible to their users (teachers, learners, etc.). In the PREATY project we focused on tools for e-Portfolios, learning analytics, enriched rubrics, and self- and peer-assessment [12]. We chose these assessment methods and tools because they are well suited for the provision of enriched feedback, making them suitable for the formative assessment of 21st Century Skills.

We carried out a survey focused on tools supporting the aforementioned assessment methods, evaluating them on criteria deemed necessary for implementation within schools [12]. This analysis showed a wide number of tools in the different categories. However, the current offer of tools did not fulfil the needs of primary and secondary school teachers and schools necessary for implementation. Most of the reviewed tools, especially those related to Learning Analytics, are still only for researchers and positioned mostly in higher educational settings. They are potentially applicable in secondary school contexts, but it is quite difficult to make a translation towards primary schools. Moreover, they do not (yet) provide integrated environments with a usable interface. Many of the tools are at a prototype or piloting stage. Those in that situation do not provide enough stability for implementation in schools. Others are the result of research projects, which have failed to get the necessary continuation after the project lifespan. They currently lack technical support and an active community of users, which is an important drawback for application in school practices. Language is also a barrier. Since most of the reviewed tools are in English, they are not appropriate for their use in schooling contexts where English is not a native language. Exceptions are classes implementing bilingual models, international schools or those oriented to teach English as a foreign language learning.

In summary, the tools that are currently offered to support assessment methods were found to be not fully appropriate for use by primary and (partially) by secondary school teachers.

3   21st Century Skills

The need to specifically define 21st Century Skills is related to changing societal requirements both in terms of knowledge and cognition. But at least as important are the skills that go along with cognition, namely those needed to cope with changes and to be and stay motivated to learn. Several initiatives exist where groups of experts developed lists of competences deemed to be important for coping with the societal changes. Obviously technological-related skills, such as digital or media literacy, are represented in every list, but these skills go along with skills such as being able to collaborate, being creative, critical, self-regulative etc. Two of the most known of these lists are the key competences formulated by the European union and the 21st Century Skills formulated by a business consortium [16,17]. Both the key competences and the 21st Century Skills in these lists are formulated at a general and abstract level, although their aim is to be applied in (national) contexts and to be implemented within school curricula. However, it seems that the leap from the European to the class level is too big to allow for proper operationalization and hence implementation. That means that the skills as they are formulated do not define learning outcomes or levels of performance related to the targeted educational levels (yet). The EU key competencies are: 1) communication in the mother tongue; 2) communication in foreign languages; 3) mathematical competence and basic competences in science and technology; 4) digital competence; 5) learning to learn; 6) social and civic competences; 7) sense of initiative and entrepreneurship; 8) cultural awareness and expression [16]. The list of 21st Century Skills developed by the business consortium (sponsored by Cisco, Intel and Microsoft) covers 4 domains: 1)Ways of thinking - Creativity, critical thinking, problem-solving, decision-making and learning; 2) Ways of working - Communication and collaboration; 3) Tools for working - Information and communications technology (ICT) and information literacy; 4) Skills for living in the world - Citizenship, life and career, and personal and social responsibility [17]. These lists with key competences are partially complementary and partly overlapping.

Several studies [1][2] mention that, although the competences are seen as important, few or none of the countries have developed clear assessment policies for them. This can easily be understood, as different contexts and constellations of national issues and priorities could define other clusters of competencies as the most important ones. Overall, it seems not yet clear whether all 21st skills should be addressed and are suitable to be taken up by primary and secondary schools and if so, how (a selection of) 21st Century Skills should be interwoven in the consecutive curricula of primary and secondary schools and enacted in classroom practice.

4   Working Together on the Integration of Formative Assessment and 21st Century Skills

The analysis of teachers' perceptions and needs regarding the formative assessment of 21st Century Skills is a complex endeavour, which depends on institutional, school, and personal conditions. Besides this, we have shown in the previous section that the gap between existing frameworks and implementation in educational practice still needs to be bridged. We here describe the results of two approaches adopted within the Preaty project to initiate a translation towards school practices: 1) Gauging teacher needs beforehand, to inform the development of professionalization initiatives around TEFA and 21st Century Skills. 2) Collaborate with teachers in workshops towards translations suitable for their practice.

4.1   Gauging Teachers Needs to Inform Professionalization Initiatives in the Netherlands

The Dutch partner employs various means to gauge the need of primary and secondary teachers, such as document analysis, individual and group interviews. In this paper the focus is on the results of a chat log analysis to gain insight in teachers' needs.

Foundation Kennisnet held an online seminar about 21st Century Skills[2] and how to make them explicit in education, in which various models of 21st Century Skills, reasons and manners to make them explicit and some example implementation projects were shown. During this seminar Dutch participants could discuss presented topics in a chat log. We asked Kennisnet permission to analyse this discussion, to acquire insight in participants' needs with regard to 21st Century Skills and current issues regarding implementation (such as suitable learning activities, assessment practices, technology use) in school practice. 37 seminar participants participated actively in the chat, this group mainly consisting of teachers in various educational contexts, next to educational consultants and researchers. They created in total 443 text entries, which were processed anonymously. Entries which were not directly related to the content of the seminar (e.g. more practical, technical and social entries) were filtered out. The remaining 250 entries were then analysed by means of

---

[2] Kennisnet is the public ICT partner for education in the Netherland, providing advice on the use and implementation of ICT s for primary, secondary and vocational education. See seminar (March 2014): http://www.youtube.com/watch?v=cYyZ3UkspyI& list=PLQI9hXCcoK1QZARMTuQ5YJTgWIYJGcQDg

qualitative content analysis. All entries were read and re-read, a coding scheme was derived bottom-up from the chat-log content and the entries were then tagged with the coding scheme. Each entry could be labelled with multiple labels. Table 1 provides an overview of the labels derived from the chat-log entries and their definition, the label frequency as well as some example entries (in *italic*), to provide further insight in the nature of the discussion.

Table 1. Overview results qualitative analysis of chat log about 21st Century Skills and how to make them explicit in education

Label and description	Label Freq.
Implementation: Remarks about how to implement 21st Century Skills at classroom/school level, mentioning the following aspects: - **how to implement relevant learning activities:** learning activities specified top-down based on specified programmes for (integrated/specific) 21st Century Skills or bottom-up by means of teacher-designed learning activities; potential benefits and role of ICT in implementating 21st Century Skills. E.g.: *"when children would get more digital instruction the teacher saves time which can be used to support acquisition of new skills"* - **how to approach implementation:** at what level (at national, school or individual teacher level), how to gain commitment amongst teachers. E.g.: *"could implementation of 21st Century Skills happen at individual [teacher] level or can it only happen at large scale?"; "search for well underpinned information on which means/methods are most effective compared to only instructing. Not a single teacher would object to a means to help their pupils learn in the best way* - **preconditions** (and their relations) for implementation. E.g.: *think of '4 in balans" [a dutch model for ICT implementation at school level with 4 factors]* - **time and planning issues:** estimation of implementation trajectory, time needed for acceptance of 21st skills approaches in schools, how to use time effectively. E.g.: *"what is the time line to accept the concept of 21st Century Skills as a familiar concept within education?"*	86
Understanding and conceptualization of 21st Century Skills: Remarks about : - **definition, models, background/origin, nature, positioning and critics** of 21st Century Skills. E.g.: *"on their own these skills already counted in the 20th century (think about all 'innovative schools'). To me the ICT component provides another perspective with regards to pace, scale and organization" ;"aim of ATCS21 (Microsoft, Intel, Cisco)is to integrate a lot of ICT within education, and their first strategy is to do so with digital tests and assessments (where in the Netherlands Cito is already busy with). I find this a dangerous development."* - **relations between and stress on skills:** which skills are currently stressed/included and which not, how do the skills relate. E.g.: *"21st Century Skills spans more than just media literacy"*	57

Table 1. *(continued)*

Teacher skills, attitude and professionalization: Remarks about the knowledge, skills and attitude that teachers need to have or acquire in order to be able to implement 21st Century Skills in their classroom. E.g.*: "I think something proceeds this, namely the sense of why you would like to do it [teaching] differently (= attitude)" ;"do we, teachers, actually have these skills ourselves? To say it with other words, how can you teach pupils something, that you don't master yourself?" ;"kids need to learn how to solve problems, teachers need to learn to leave this to the kids" ;" many teachers lack knowledge about the digital world"*	39
Relations between 21st Century Skills and curriculum/content/domain: Remarks on: - whether **skills can be learned separately from content** or whether they should be learned interactively/combined with content and with each other. - whether **skills are transferable from one domain** to another or domain-dependant. E.g.*: "these 21st Century Skills are typically presented if they are not about any content. That's quite interesting, as education is just about content."; "several skills, like research skills and collaboration, are definitely not domain specific" ;" domain specific content can as well stay like it is, skills are just another didactic approach"*	34
Outcomes/output: Remarks on the objectives and potential results of introducing 21st Century Skills in schools. E.g.*:" are there already objectives that need to be reached by education?" ; "are these objectives smart [specific, measurable, acceptable, reachable, time specific] ?" ; "core learning objectives are also well achievable by means of different didactics. That we already know decennia from research. Think for example about collaborative learning"*	32
Good practice, examples and guidelines: References to good practices, examples, thoughts, guidelines and tips that are usable or provide background and inspiration for implementing 21st skills. E.g.: *"I lately bumped into the initiative www.jeelo.nl, interesting and 21st century... project-oriented learning"*	31
Policy: Remarks on decisions and developments around 21st Century Skills at policy level. E.g.: *"From the ministry of education and the curriculum institute nothing is fixed yet, isn't it? Differently than in Flanders where by means of the diamant-model several core competences (that show a large overlap with the skills) are in the curriculum"*	26
Assessment: Remarks on objectives, methods of and issues around (formative and summative) assessment of 21st Century Skills. E.g.: *"are there already tools or instruments available that can measure the 21st Century Skills of pupils/schools?" ;"measuring is from the old paradigm. We have to think how learners can picture/capture their own development. This goes more towards portfolio learning" ; "to me it appears useful to assess the state of affairs, so that you can undertake goal-oriented interventions and adapt your teaching. If this is possible with a portfolio it is fine, but then still you need to analyse it"*	22

Table 1. (*continued*)

Target group: Remarks on 21st Century Skills in relation to a specific target group. E.g.: *"I do see many programmes in media literacy for primary education, but not for secondary education!"; "in secondary education it is mainly about learning pupils to recognize self-regulation and that in the long term they can manage this themselves"*	21
Tools/instruments: Remarks on concrete (ICT) tools or instruments that support teachers, students and schools to (start to) work with 21st Century Skills. E.g.: *"maybe a Kijkwijzer (observation indicators/pointer checklist) is a good way to support teachers, but that you further assess pupils by means of a portfolio and competences"*	18
Research: Remarks on scientific research around 21st Century Skills. E.g.: *"is there any sound research about 21st Century Skills available?"*	12
School management: Remarks on the contribution at school management level with regards to introducing 21st Century Skills in schools. E.g.: *"what does it mean as a manager for policy and team development?"*	12

Looking at the most mentioned themes we can see that the participants are, mostly at an individual level, struggling to make sense of 21st Century Skills and how to implement them in their classroom. They state that there are no clear national agreements, policies, guidelines and frameworks (yet) that can be used to guide their implementation at school curriculum level. It is for example unclear whether 21st Century Skills should be taught in combination with domain-related content and learned 'on the fly' or whether they should be taught, practiced, stressed and evaluated more extensively and expressively. Although teachers foresee a role for ICT to support and enable implementation of 21st Century Skills, next to being part of one of the skills in itself, it is not clear what use would be most beneficial. Teachers also wonder whether they have the required competences to guide the introduction and implementation of 21st Century Skills in their class, especially with regards to the ICT component. Also the manner to look upon assessment of the 21st skills, e.g. in a (combination of a) formative or summative way, is yet to be defined, still even at a conceptual level. In short, teachers and schools are still in a searching and explorative phase with regards to 21st Century Skills implementation.

4.2   Collaborating with Teachers to Translate the Needs to Their Practice in Spain

The Spanish partner designed and set up two teacher training workshops. The first workshop (WS1) was conducted at a primary school reckoned for its innovative character, especially regarding the integration of ICT in their classes [13]. The 25 participant teachers attended the workshop in the context of the continuous formative assessment plan of the school. Therefore, they did not volunteer to assist to this workshop. The second workshop (WS2) was organized at the University stances. Seven primary school teachers volunteered to assist to the three sessions, which were organized right after WS1 had finished. The goal of these workshops was to offer teachers conceptual and practical tools that enabled them to reflect on their assessment practices, show them procedures to integrate the assessment of competences, and eventually, help them apply e-assessment approaches presented at the workshop in their practice.

Evaluation Instruments and Methods

The workshops provided valuable initial evidence about teachers' needs regarding the assessment of 21st Century Skills, and the role that ICT tools can play to support them. The evaluation instruments and methods used were initial and final questionnaires, cbservations and group discussions (see Table 2):

Table 2. Instruments and methods used to collect data in the Spanish workshops, with the labels used to refer to them

	Workshop 1	Workshop 2
Initial questionnaire	[Init-Quest-WS1]	[Init-Quest-WS2]
Formal observations	[Obs1-WS1] [Obs2-WS1] [Obs3-WS1]	[Obs1-WS2] [Obs2-WS2] [Obs3-WS2]
Final discussion	[Diss-WS1]	[Diss-WS2]
Final questionnaire	[Final-Quest-WS1]	[Final-Quest-WS2]

Like every needs analysis also this one has limitations. As mentioned beforehand, we adapted the pace and content of the sessions to the needs of the participants, which were not always relevant to our research goals. Time restrictions were also strong. An example of this is the short time we could devote to the final discussions, due to the time we had to dedicate to previous activities. In response to this limitation, we plan to complete the data-gathering phase by organizing further group discussions with a selection of teachers.

Findings

The first two issues we had to face while designing the workshops were related with how to present the participants methods for the integration of 21st Century Skills in the curriculum, and the selection of the most appropriate e-assessment methods and tools to present at the workshops.

The integration of 21st Century Skills into the curriculum of Primary schools in Spain has not been sufficiently developed at the official level. In spite of some efforts [14], teachers have not received sufficient directions about how to integrate these skills in the curriculum, even less about how to assess them. There are very few examples of schools that have carried out this endeavour [15]. While designing the workshops we used the experience of a secondary school teacher as an example. He is an active innovator himself, who had already faced this problem, and had a vast experience as trainer in teacher workshops. He had designed a process that defined how to map these competencies to assessment criteria, and how to include them in the learning activities proposed in his classes (supported or not by technology). At the workshops he explained his experience and how he had managed to bridge the competencies with assessment criteria, and these with the learning activities. Then, the participant teachers were asked to fulfil an activity plan where they could put in practice these procedures.

It turned out that the intervention of this teacher was one of the most valued aspects of the workshop, as recognized in the final evaluation questionnaire ("*I appreciate that everything was based on the experience of a colleague that has already applied it*" [Final-Quest-WS1]. However, being a secondary school teacher, some participants still questioned whether the examples where applicable to their classes. ("*The assessment instruments are too detailed for the application I foresee in the classroom*" [Diss-WS1]; "*Time in classes is very limited, we do not have time inside or outside the class to reflect on the students' advancement*" (this is related to the formative evaluation) [Obs3-WS1]. This calls clearly for the need of documenting yet more meaningful examples, and to the need of adapting the assessment criteria to match the context of primary school teachers.

The process of assessing competencies requires tools that support teachers in the creation of instruments that operationalize the assessment criteria (control lists, rubrics, etc.). The e-assessment approach that best matches this need are electronic rubrics, and therefore, we focused the workshop on this approach.

We chose Evalcomix[3] out of six other tools that had been analysed previously in the context of the Preaty project [12]. Evalcomix was selected based on a set of criteria referring to the usability, stability, support, language, price, user-friendliness and integration in a VLE. Regarding this last criterion, the teachers in the workshop demanded a tool that could be integrated in Moodle, which was their institutional VLE [Init-Quest-1]. Evalcomix supports the design and management of assessment instruments, such as checklists, rating scales and rubrics. It offers English and Spanish versions, and can be integrated in a VLE (Moodle or LAMS) to assess learning activities. The fact that teachers in this school already used Moodle for their lessons added potential value to the choice of Evalcomix. At the workshops, it was employed to show the participant teachers how to define and apply a checklist, a rating scale and a rubric. The participants worked on assessment criteria defined in a previous activity, and used these and the tool to develop assessment instruments.

However, and in spite of the fact that Evalcomix complied with the selection criteria listed above, it showed important limitations for its use by the primary school teachers. As noted by one of the teachers in the final questionnaire "*The product itself, Evalcomix, needs to be improved. These improvements should be done in two directions: on the one hand, making all the system more intuitive, it should not require more than 10 minutes to learn; on the other hand, the labels should go hand in hand with the (educational) design, words like "attributes" are not in our teachers vocabulary*" [Final-Quest-WS1]. Another teacher in the second workshop raised the question of what was the benefit of using Evalcomix instead of another off-the-shelf tool, such as Google Forms. In the discussion that followed this comment it was agreed that these tools are useful if integrated in a VLE used by the students (not only

---

[3] http://evalcomix.uca.es/

by teachers, as it is the case in many primary schools) [Obs2-WS2]. In fact, Evalcomix only exploits its full potential in complex evaluation processes, involving not only the teacher but also the students, in peer-assessment and self-assessment. These approaches to assessment are not normally used, especially at the first courses ("*The main problem for us as primary school teachers, is … that the students cannot use the resources autonomously due to their age*"; "*The lower levels (referring to 6- and 7- years old) are not able to create their own resources*" [Obs2-WS2].

Of course, technology itself is still seen as an obstacle ("*We cannot depend on technology. It may happen that the connection does not work, and my computer is very slow*") [Obs3-WS1]. When asked about which were the main problems to adopt the approaches studied in the workshop, two groups of teachers pointed out this issue: "*Internet access and the command of computer and technical issues*" [Diss-WS2], "[the main problem is] *The lack of technological resources in the school, the fact that we sometimes do not know how to use them …*" [Diss-WS2]. In fact, we experienced this kind of technological hazard in the first workshop, the one run at the primary school instances. Several issues related to the configuration of the lab, and of the access to the Moodle server used for the course, caused us many problems "*We have dedicated 5-6 minutes to explain them how to enrol in the new course*", "*The server* [where the Moodle course with Evalcomix is installed] *breaks down. We try to export the instruments to import them later on, and it does not work either. I phone B. [in charge of the unit that runs the Moodle server] to get a number to call to*"; "*We are obliged to finish the session now* [15 minutes before expected]" [Obs2-WS1]. As mentioned beforehand, this happened in a school that has been acknowledged to have the highest level of ICT-integration[4]. Schools need more reliable resources to enable a more natural use of technology.

Some teachers expressed their concerns that these methods require them to be in front of the computer all the time [Obs3-WS1], which is not the way they usually work. Therefore, an issue for further reflection is to see whether current ICT-based assessment methods are of value for these classrooms, which are not (yet) implementing the one-to-one computing paradigm. In these contexts, most of the activity is still done off-line, with no intervention of computers, and therefore, the role of ICT-based tools is restricted.

In spite of the limitations observed, the teachers also envisioned some of the potential advantages of these approaches. Interestingly, they stated that they are appropriate to assess group learning (The answered "*To assess group learning*" to the question about which possibilities they saw for these methods and tools) [Obs3-WS1, Diss-WS2]. They saw the potential provided by this kind of systems to share evaluation instruments ("*These instruments can be useful to share with other colleagues*") [Obs3-WS1-3], although, as noted by one participant, "*it is difficult to reach consensus about the indicators with the rest of the teachers*" [Diss-WS2]. Some teachers noted the potential for reutilization ("*It takes time to elaborate them, but it is worthy at mid-term. It can be applied in multiple occasions with slight modifications*") [Diss-WS2].

---

[4] The Regional Administration of Education in Castilla y León has established a 5-level certification system to determine the quality of the integration of ICT at schools. This accreditation takes into account the use of ICT according to the resources available, the quality of the didactic proposals put in practice, and the permanent teacher training proposals accomplished in the school.

5   Conclusions

Holding the results of the two studies presented against the Surrey and Ely model with eight conditions (C's) that positively influence implementation of innovations in education [3] we can draw several conclusions regarding what is possible to advance implementation. We see that teachers do in fact **experience a sense of urgency and dissatisfaction** (C1) with the status quo. Many are at an individual level wrestling with the question 'How can I implement 21st Century Skills in my classroom?'. However, this urgency seems to be mainly caused by external factors (namely due to policy and societal influence) to do something with 21st Century Skills in their classroom, and it is yet unclear whether teachers are in fact at an individual level **committed** (C7) to the introduction of 21st Century Skills in their classroom.

Apparently, teachers currently experience that **the basic conditions and resources** (C3) for implementation are lacking or insufficient and the overall guidelines for implementation are absent or vague. No practical, implementable educational models, methods, assessment indicators and instruments, ICT-tools or guidelines were supplied with the frameworks for 21st Century Skills to make the process of implementing learning activities and assessment practices straightforward. Teachers experience this lack of educational methods as a drawback, although they are actively searching themselves for good practices, tools and instruments that they could use. Lack of clarity about implementation is also related to uncertainty about the definition of skills. The lists of skills are not recognized as new or as indispensable for students to learn, except for the realization that ICT is an integral part of being competent in the skills. Although they do realise that it is important to have instruments to assess the skills, no relation is made with technology-enhanced formative assessment as a pedagogical approach that can contribute to implementation of 21st Century Skills. Also the trouble-free use of the ICT-infrastructure at primary and secondary schools (e.g. in terms of secure and stable wireless network access, sufficient number of devices for a 1-to-1 computing approach, the connection with an overarching Virtual Learning Environment (VLE) and the use of a VLE by both teachers and learners) cannot be taken for granted when introducing TEFA for 21st Century Skills.

Teachers are also unsure about their own **knowledge and skills** (C2) and especially outspoken towards the lack of ICT skills; here the duality between their own lack of skillfulness and the need to train students in this field continues to exist. In addition, they do not experience sufficient participation and leadership by either the ministry nor by school management (C6 and C8). In both studies nothing was mentioned with regard to the **availability of time** (C4) to acquire knowledge and skills and available **rewards or incentives** (C5) for teachers.

Despite the detected conceptual and practical challenges teachers stills see the advantage of integrating 21st Century Skills in their classroom practice and at curriculum level. However, they feel that they need to be facilitated on a more practically oriented level to achieve this in the future. Based on these findings, the Preaty project adopts the following approach to support the implementation of 21st Century Skills with technology enhanced formative assessment at classroom level in primary and secondary schools:

— a collaboration/'joint venture' developmental approach with teachers, by means of collaborative professionalization, to develop a translation from overarching frameworks towards practically implementable solutions and to gain further insight in their commitment at individual level. This approach should also result in further exploring and intertwining 21st Century Skills and formative assessment approaches and the use of technology to support and enhance formative assessment practices in schools.

— using formats that connect to and elaborate upon a teachers' experience, that provide tips and guidelines for implementing them in classroom practice, that highlight potential practical benefits (such as sharing with teachers and re-utalization) and that stimulate teachers' own reflection on their practice (e.g. by (multi-media) story-telling of other teachers' experiences and problems, concrete lessons or good practices and case descriptions of schools).

Acknowledgements. We would like to gratefully acknowledge the contribution of the PREATY Project, that is funded by the European Commission's Lifelong Learning Programme, Project Number 526965-LLP-1-2012-1-GR-COMENIUS-CMP, which has part-funded this work.

References

1. Ananiadou, K., Claro, M.: 21st Century Skills and Competences for New Millennium Learners in OECD Countries, OECD Education Working Papers, No. 41. OECD Publishing (2009), doi:10.1787/218525261115
2. Gordon, J., Halasz, G., Krawczyk, M., Leney, T., Michel, A., Pepper, D.: Key competences in Europe: Opening doors for lifelong learners across the school curriculum and teacher education, Warsaw, Poland, pp. 1–328 (2009), http://ec.europa.eu/education/more-information/doc/keyreport_en.pdf (retrieved)
3. Surry, D.W., Ely, D.P.: Adoption, diffusion, implementation, and institutionalization of instructional innovations. In: Reiser, R.A., Dempsey, J.V. (eds.) Trends and Issues in Instructional Design and Technology, 2nd edn., pp. 104–111. Pearson Prentice Hall, Upper Saddle River (2007)
4. Busuttil-Reynaud, G., Winkley, J.: JISC e-Assessment Glossary, Bristol (2006)
5. JISC: Effective Assessment in a Digital Age. A guide to technology-enhanced assessment and feedback. Bristol (2010)
6. Black, P.J., Wiliam, D.: Developing the theory of formative assessment. Educational Assessment, Evaluation and Accountability (formerly the Journal of Personal Evaluation in Education) 21(1), 5–31 (2009)
7. Wiliam, D., Thompson, M.: Integrating assessment with instruction: What will it take to make it work? In: Dwyer, C.A. (ed.) The Future of Assessment: Shaping Teaching and Learning, pp. 53–82. Erlbaum, Mahwah (2007)
8. Chan, C.C.K., van Aalst, J.: Learning, assessment and collaboration in computer supported environments. In: Dillenbourg, P. (Series ed.), Strijbos, J.W., Kirschner, P.A., Martens, R.L. (Vol. eds.) Computer-supported Collaborative Learning: vol. 3, What We Know About CSCL: and Implementing it in Higher Education, pp. 87–112. Kluwer Academic Publishers, Boston (2004)

9. Gulikers, J.T.M., Bastiaens, T.J., Kirschner, P.A.: A five-dimensional framework for authentic assessment. Educational Technology Research and Development 52(3), 67–85 (2004)
10. JISC: Effective Practice in e-Assessment. An overview of technologies, policies and practice in further and higher education, Bristol (2007)
11. Rusman, E., Boon, J., Martínez-Monés, A., Rodríguez-Triana, M.J., Retalis, S.: Towards the Use of New Methods for Formative e-Assessment of 21st Century Skills in Schools. In: Technology Enhanced Formative Assessment (TEFA) Workshop, Paphos, Cyprus, September 17-21 (2013), http://www.kbs.uni-hannover.de/fileadmin/institut/pdf/TEFA2013-Paper_1_Rusman-et_al.pdf at EC-TEL 2013, http://www.ec-tel.eu/index.php
12. PREATY project: D1.1.: State of the art report on modern assessment approaches and tools. Public deliverable (2013)
13. Prieto, L.P., Villagrá-Sobrino, S., Jorrín-Abellán, I.M., Martínez-Monés, A., Dimitriadis, Y.: Recurrent routines: Analyzing and supporting orchestration in technology-enhanced primary classrooms. Computers & Education 57(1), 1214–1227 (2011)
14. CNIIE, Guía para la formación en centros sobre las competencias básicas (2013) (in Spanish)
15. Atlántida project (2014), http://www.proyectoatlantida.net/ (last access: March 27, 2014)
16. European Communities, Key Competences for Lifelong Learning - A European Framework. Luxembourg (2007)
17. Binkley, M., Erstad, O., et al.: Defining Twenty-First Century Skills. In: Griffin, P., McGaw, B., Care, E. (eds.) Assessment and Teaching of 21st Century Skills, pp. 17–66. Springer, Dordrecht (2012), doi:10.1007/978-94-007-2324-5, ISBN: 978-94-007-2323-8 e-ISBN 978-94-007-2324-5
18. Whitelock, D.: Activating Assessment for Learning: are we on the way with Web 2.0? In: Lee, M.J.W., McLoughlin, C. (eds.) Web 2.0-Based E-Learning: Applying Social Informatics for Tertiary Teaching. IGI Global (2010)

Non Satis Scire: To Know Is Not Enough

e-Assessment of Student-Teachers' Competence as New Teachers

Wilfried Admiraal[1], Tanja Janssen[2], Jantina Huizenga[2], Frans Kranenburg[3], Ruurd Taconis[4], and Alessandra Corda[5]

[1] Leiden University, Leiden, The Netherlands
w.f.admiraal@iclon.leidenuniv.nl
[2] University of Amsterdam, Amsterdam, The Netherlands
{t.m.janssen,j.c.Huizenga}@uva.nl
[3] Utrecht University, Utrecht, The Netherlands
f.a.n.kranenburg@uu.nl
[4] Eindhoven Technical University, Eindhoven, The Netherlands
r.taconis@tue.nl
[5] Amsterdam University of Applied Sciences, Amsterdam, The Netherlands
a.corda@hva.nl

Abstract. In teacher education programmes, text-based portfolios are generally used to assess student-teachers' competence as new teachers. However, striking discrepancies are known to exist between the competencies reflected in a written portfolio and the competencies observed in actual classroom practice. Multiple assessments should be used to provide a more valid assessment of student-teachers' competence as new teachers. Technology can support this kind of multiple and flexible ways of assessment. In a Research & Development project, four types of e-assessments were designed, implemented and evaluated in 27 interventions in 13 post-graduated teacher education programs in the Netherlands. Teacher educators reported positive outcomes of the interventions in terms of new procedures, materials and tools. No significant effects were found of the implementation of the four types of e-assessments on the evaluation by either teacher educators or student-teachers. A possible explanation for this absence of effects might be teething problems of the interventions implemented.

Keywords: teacher education, assessment, teacher competence.

1 Introduction

Assessment and evaluation are increasingly important in all educational sectors. In teacher education programs, text-based self-evaluations are generally used to assess student-teachers' competence as new teachers [1,2]. However, this kind of written self-evaluation does not give valid evidence of teacher competencies that are typically used to guide the curriculum of teacher education programs. Consequently, observation of student-teachers' performance are increasingly used for assessment, such as class observations, teaching materials and tests. Simultaneously, assessment is used

M. Kalz and E. Ras (Eds.): CAA 2014, CCIS 439, pp. 15–27, 2014.
© Springer International Publishing Switzerland 2014

for both formative and summative purposes: assessments are not only used to measure student-teachers' competencies, but also to feed back student-teachers which competencies they already possess, in what phase of development they are and how they can acquire teacher competencies. Technology can support this kind of multiple and flexible ways of assessment. The objective of this paper is to provide insight into how multiple e-assessments of student-teachers' competence as new teachers can be designed in an efficient and effective way.

1.1   Student-Teachers' Competence as New Teachers

In 2005, in response to national and international calls for improved teacher education and greater educational accountability, the Dutch Ministry of Education decided to develop a standard for all teachers in secondary education. Subsequently, a standard was developed resembling the Professional Standards for Teachers in England (http://www.tda.gov.uk/), the National Professional Standard for Teachers in Australia (see http://www.nsw.gov.au/), and the Professional Teaching Standards in the United States (see http://www.nbpts.org/). The Dutch Teacher Standard includes pedagogical, interpersonal, organizational, methodological, relational (colleagues, community), and reflective competencies (see the Association for the Professional Quality of Teachers, http://www.lerarenweb.nl/). The first four competencies (i.e., pedagogical, interpersonal, organizational, and methodological competencies) can be assessed on the basis of teacher performance in the classroom. While the relational competencies that pertain to colleagues and the community are important, student-teachers usually gain only limited experience with these competencies during their training. All six competencies refer to the professional role of the teacher in three types of situations: working with students, working with colleagues, and working in the school. The seventh competence is reflection, which is seen as important for a teacher's ongoing personal and professional development [3,4,5]. All of the seven competencies of the Dutch standard are described according to rubrics of key knowledge, skills and attitudes that teachers must have at various levels. Teacher education programs typically use the competencies outlined in the national standard to guide their curriculum design and assessment. The problem, of course, is how to assess the competencies and thereby demonstrate that teachers meet the required standards.

1.2   Assessment of Student-Teacher Competence

In the 1980s, written teaching portfolios were introduced into teacher education to stimulate student-teachers to think more carefully about their teaching practices and subject matter [1,2], [6,7,8,9]. Portfolios are argued to be suited not only for learning purposes but also for assessment purposes as they represent: "a way to define, display, and store evidence of a teacher's knowledge and skills that is based on multiple sources of evidence collected over time in authentic settings" (p. 58) [10]. Student teachers can include, for instance, the following in assessment portfolios: their ideas regarding teaching, summaries of relevant theories, samples of lesson plans, observational notes on their teaching, and reflections upon their teaching practices. While such documents cover a wide range of knowledge and competence, striking discrepancies are known to exist between the competencies reflected in a written portfolio and the competencies observed in actual classroom practice. That is, student-teachers can sometimes present excellent written portfolios while their teaching performance is evaluated by school and university supervisors as rather weak [7] and vice versa [11,12].

When Delandshere and Arens [10] analyzed the written portfolios submitted to three teacher education programs in the USA, they encountered major problems with the evidence submitted for assessment purposes. Most of the written portfolios consisted of meta-data (e.g., statements of beliefs, lesson plans, mentor observations, reflections on teaching experiences). In other words, the data was removed from actual practice and thus indirect; the portfolios showed the student teachers' views on classroom events and their beliefs about teaching. As Delandshere and Arens point out, however, the assessment of teaching performance requires direct evidence and thus data on the teacher's actual work in the classroom.

In contrast to such indirect sources of data, video recording allows direct teaching evidence to be included in an assessment portfolio. The use of video recordings allows direct evidence of teaching to be included in a narrative. Compared to written or oral accounts, video narratives are likely to provide information on a wider variety of teacher competencies and more specific information on the contexts in which the competencies are demonstrated. This rich picture of teacher competencies and practices obtained in specific contexts can be assumed not only to provide highly valid information but also can be used for analytic and varied reflection.

There is much empirical work on the use of video for learning, mostly in teacher education [11,12] and in professional development programs with (experienced) teachers [15,16]. For example, in their evaluation study of the use of video in web-based computer-mediated communication in teacher education, Lee and Wu [17] found that student-teachers reflect more thoroughly on their teaching, pinpointing the areas of required improvement better, compared to situations in which student-teachers had to rely on their recall of their practices only. Likewise, these authors showed that student-teachers were also willing to share their experiences with and learn from their peers. Moreover, the authors found that – compared to micro-teaching sessions in which student-teachers had to rely on their recall only - peer feedback became more concrete and associated with specific points in the video clips. This feedback was also appreciated more by student-teachers. Finally, watching, analyzing and reflecting upon the video-taped practices of *others* enabled the student-teachers to learn from good teaching models and guard against bad ones. Experiences with how the use of video clips can be further integrated into the professional development of teachers confirm these findings (e.g., Video Clubs in [18]).

However, due to the lack of empirical studies on video portfolios with teachers or student-teachers for assessment purposes, it is still unclear if the inclusion of direct evidence about the functioning of student-teachers in the classroom facilitates a valid assessment of student-teachers' competence.

1.3   e-Assessment of Student-Teachers' Competence

The licensing and certification of teachers today is performance-based and thus recognizes teaching as a highly complex, highly contextual, and highly personal activity [7], [19,20]. In teacher education programs, performance-based assessment is often supplemented with other information from portfolios, which can include lesson plans, reflections, feedback from students, and feedback from supervisors, superiors and colleagues [21]. A portfolio should show not only that the student-teacher knows and understands theory but also that the student-teacher can act in accordance with theory and detect discrepancies between what is taught in theory and what occurs in actual practice.

This complex combination of teacher competencies asks for multiple assessment procedures in teacher education. Technology might support these new, complex ways of assessment. Recent years have been characterized by extensive growth in the use of technology in education, such as virtual learning environments, simulation software, virtual experiments, visualization of complex models as well as tools which enables students and teachers to communicate and collaborate through email, electronic forums, and instant-messaging systems. However, the use of technology in assessment procedure (i.e., e-assessment) is an under-researched area. e-Assessments convey practical benefits such as accessibility of practices, flexibility in updating information, and incorporating multimedia resources [22], in addition to efficiency for both teacher educators and student-teachers. As teaching has been recognized as a highly complex, highly contextual, and highly personal activity, e-assessments might be helpful in order to assess student-teachers' competence as new teachers in an efficient and effective way.

1.4   Problem of This Study

The problem of the present study was how multiple e-assessments of student-teachers' competence as new teachers could be designed in such a way that these could be carried out in an efficient and effective way and provide a valid assessment of student-teachers' competence as new teachers. Research questions were:

1. How do interventions on e-assessment affect the use and evaluation of these e-assessments by teacher educators?
2. How do interventions on e-assessment affect the evaluation of these e-assessments by student teachers?
3. How do teacher educators perceive the implementation of the interventions on e-assessment?

2   Methods

2.1   Research Context

Teacher preparation includes certification at three levels: primary education, lower secondary education (pre-vocational secondary education and the three lower grades of senior general secondary education and pre-university education) and all levels of secondary education. The latter programs are mainly based in research universities and the former two programs are mainly organized by universities of applied sciences.

The context of this study is the post-graduate teaching education program in the Netherlands. Students who graduate are licensed to teach at all levels of secondary education in the Netherlands. Teacher preparation for certification to teach at all levels of secondary education usually takes a one-year full time (or two-years 50% part-time) master program as a follow-up of a master program in a particular school subject (e.g. mathematics or a foreign language). This means that teachers who are licensed to teach at all levels of secondary education have two Masters: one in a school subject or related domain and one in teaching this school subject. The curricula of these teacher education programs exist of 50% courses at the teacher education institution and 50% teaching in school. The common goal of these master programs is to connect theory and practice of teaching in secondary education.

In a Dutch national Research & Development project, Non satis scire (funded by the SURF foundation, http://www.surf.nl/), teacher educators and master students of teacher education programs of all 13 Dutch research universities participated. Teacher educators collaboratively design, implement, and evaluate both formative and summative assessments of student-teachers' competence as new teachers. Four e-assessment types have been addressed: 1) knowledge tests on learning and instruction, 2) providing feedback on students' plans for research on teaching practice, 3) providing feedback on students' web-based video clips of teaching practice and 4) digital self-assessments of student-teachers' reflection.

2.2   Design of the Study

In a multiple-case study research design, 27 interventions were carried out, spread over 13 teacher education programs and the four forms of e-assessment (see Table 1). In order to answer research questions 1 and 2, for each type of e-assessment teacher educators and students from the experimental condition (programs that carried out the particular type of e-assessment) were compared with teacher educators and students from the control condition (i.e., programs that were not part of the experimental conditions). In order to answer research question 3, a multiple case study design was used [23] using multiple data sets about each of the programs.

Table 1. Overview of the design

Intervention	Participating TE programs	
	Experimental condition	Control condition
1. Knowledge tests	4	9
2. Feedback on students' research plans	9	4
3. Feedback on students' video clips	11	2
4. Digital self-assessment	4	9

2.3   Data and Procedures

Data were collected of 115 teacher educators and 644 master students from 13 universities. A digital pre-test and post-test questionnaire was administered to teacher educators to evaluate the four interventions on two aspects: 1) the extent to which different forms of e-assessments were used and 2) the extent to which these forms were valued. A similar pre- and post-test questionnaire was administered (on paper) to students from the 13 universities. In addition, observations of work meetings and evaluation reports were used to map teacher-trainers' experiences with the various forms of e-assessment. Finally, all educational materials (study guides, readers, tests, video clips, student reflections, research plan, feedback forms and completed assessment rubrics) were collected and analyzed to support or contradict interpretations from the questionnaire data and work meetings.

Questionnaire for Teacher Educators. In addition to their gender, age, teaching experience and teaching position, teacher educators were asked to evaluate the use of 1) a corpus of shared items of a knowledge test on learning and instruction; 2) digital knowledge tests; 3) peer feedback on research plans; 4) peer assessment on research plans; 5) digital rubrics to support the assessment of research plans; 6) video recording of student-teachers' practices and 7) self-evaluations.

First, we asked teacher educators to indicate the variety of their use of the assessment types. The frequency of use was measured by 2 to 5 yes/no items, with items like, "Did you use the digital corpus of knowledge items?" (Shared test items), "Did students provide written feedback on their research plans?"(Peer feedback) or "Did you provide feedback on the basis of students' video clips of their teaching practice?" (Video).

Second, the evaluation of each of the assessment types was measured using a series of 4 to 7 similar Likert-type scale statements, with *1*= completely disagree to *5*= completely agree. Example items are "The use of digital tests has a positive effect on the time that is needed to feed back the test results (Digital knowledge test), "Peer feedback has a positive effect on the time teachers spend on providing feedback" (Peer feedback), or "The use of web-based video clips of students' teaching practice has a positive effect on students' insight into their own teaching competence" (Video).

In Table 2, the descriptive statistics are presented for the frequency of use and for the evaluation of each of the assessment types. Of the 115 teacher educators, 60 completed both the pre-test and the post-test. The reliability of the seven evaluation scales met our norm of 0.70, for the first scale with only 4 items after using the Spearman-Brown correction for test length.

Table 2. Descriptive statistics teacher-educator questionnaire

	Frequency scale*	Evaluation scale	Cronbach's α	Exp cond N	Contr cond N
Shared test items**	0 – 3	1-5	.58	26	34
Dig. knowl. tests	0 – 2	1-5	.72	26	34
Peer feedback	0 – 5	1-5	.74	52	8
Peer assessment	0 – 3	1-5	.77	52	8
Rubrics	0 – 4	1-5	.82	52	8
Video	0 – 5	1-5	.77	52	8
Self-assessment	0 – 3	1-5	.78	13	37

* 0 = assessment instrument is not used; 2/5 = instrument is used in various ways

** this scale included only 4 items

Questionnaire for Students. In addition to their university, gender and age, students were asked to report their evaluation of 1) digital knowledge tests; 2) peer feedback on research plans; 3) peer assessment on research plans; 4) digital rubrics to support the assessment of research plans; 5) video recording of student-teachers' practices and 6) self-evaluations.

The items of this part of the student questionnaire were similar to those in the teacher questionnaire. For each of the e-assessments types, a series of 4 or 5 statements were used to measure students' evaluation. These statements were answered on a Likert-type scale, with $1=$ completely disagree to $5=$ completely agree. Example items are "I receive feedback about my test results more timely in the case of a digital test compared to a paper-and-pencil test" (Digital knowledge test), "I can learn a lot from provide providing peer feedback on research proposals" (Peer feedback), or "Supervision using a web-based video clips of my teaching practice is better than supervision on the basis of life observation of my supervisor" (Video).

In Table 3, the descriptive statistics are presented for the evaluation of each of the seven assessment types. The reliability of five evaluation scales met our norm of 0.70. The first scale was excluded from the analyses as the reliability appeared to be low. As shown in Table 2, the distribution of participants in both conditions is strongly skewed, which lowers the chance to find any significant differences between both conditions.

Table 3. Descriptive statistics student questionnaire

	Evaluation scale	Cronbachs α	Exp cond. N	Control cond. N
Dig. knowl tests*	1-5	--	--	--
Peer feedback	1-5	.79	131	5
Peer assessment	1-5	.76	126	5
Rubrics	1-5	.84	130	5
Video	1-5	.78	109	25
Self-assessment	1-5	.78	5	125

* this scale is excluded because the reliability was too low

Work Meetings and Evaluation Reports. During the project period of two years two or three teacher educators per teacher education program that participated in the four types of e-assessment interventions attended three work meetings and completed evaluation reports which were used as input for these meetings. The information from the meetings and reports was summarized.

2.4   Analyses

A mix-method analysis procedure was used. For the questionnaire data, repeated measures analyses were used to examine possible differences in evaluation before and after the interventions. In these analyses, each intervention condition was compared with the three other forms of e-assessment (which form the control condition).

The qualitative data in the written protocols of the work meetings and evaluation reports were combined into a thick description [24 of each of the 27 interventions indicating teacher educators' self-reported experiences with the particular form of e-assessment.

3   Results

3.1   Use and Evaluation by Teacher Educators

The results of the repeated measures analyses of variance for teacher educators are summarized in Table 4 (frequency of use) and Table 5 (evaluation).

The analyses did not show a significant increase in teacher educators' use of the particular assessment procedure, compared to the control condition (consisting of programs that did not use the particular e-assessment form). As shown in Table 4, teacher educators in the intervention condition did generally differ in their use of the particular assessment form from the control condition, but these differences already existed à priori (with all Fs< 1.71 and all ps>.20). It appears that teacher educators apparently decided to participate in the interventions that included the assessment form they already used in their regular practice. A marginal trend was found for the use of a digital knowledge test ($F(1,58)= 3.50$; $p= 0.06$) indicating that teacher educators in the experimental condition tended to increase their use of a digital knowledge test after the intervention, compared to teacher educators from the control condition.

Table 4. Results for teacher educators: frequency of use of assessment procedure (means and standard deviations between brackets)

	Experimental condition		Control condition	
	Pre-test	Post-test	Pre-test	Post-test
Shared test items	1.6 (1.4)	1.4 (1.4)	0.8 (1.2)	1.1 (1.4)
Dig. knowl. tests	0.2 (0.5)	0.3 (0.6)	0.1 (0.2)	0.1 (0.2)
Peer feedback	2.2 (1.8)	2.3 (1.8)	0.1 (0.4)	0.6 (1.2)
Peer assessesment	0.4 (0.9)	0.4 (1.0)	0.0 (0.0)	0.0 (0.0)
Rubrics	2.2 (1.7)	2.2 (1.7)	0.1 (0.4)	1.0 (1.9)
Video	1.8 (1.5)	2.0 (1.5)	0.5 (0.5)	1.3 (1.6)
Self-assessment	0.8 (0.4)	0.8 (0.4)	0.8 (0.8)	0.9 (0.7)

In Table 5, the results are summarized for the evaluation of the e-assessment types by teacher educators. Again, no differences were found between the experimental and control conditions, indicating that teacher educators from the intervention condition generally did not evaluate the e-assessment forms differently, compared to the other teacher educators (with all Fs <0.25 and all ps >.62). Finally, no significant correlations were found between the use of the assessment types by teacher educators and their evaluations of the particular form of e-assessment (with all rs < .25).

Table 5. Results for teacher educators: evaluation of assessment procedure (means and standard deviations between brackets)

	Experimental condition		Control condition	
	Pre-test	Post-test	Pre-test	Post-test
Shared test items	3.6 (0.6)	3.3 (0.6)	3.5 (0.5)	3.2 (0.5)
Dig. knowl. test	3.2 (0.3)	3.1 (0.7)	3.1 (0.6)	3.0 (0.5)
Peer feedback	3.6 (0.5)	3.4 (0.5)	3.8 (0.3)	3.5 (0.5)
Peer assessment	3.2 (0.6)	3.2 (0.4)	3.7 (0.4)	3.5 (0.5)
Rubrics	3.5 (0.5)	3.5 (0.6)	3.9 (0.1)	4.0 (0.3)
Video	3.2 (0.6)	3.2 (0.6)	3.1 (0.4)	3.1 (0.6)
Self-assessment	3.6 (0.4)	3.6 (0.6)	3.4 (0.5)	3.4 (0.5)

Note. Scale is *1* =totally disagree, *5* =totally agree that the particular e-assessment has a beneficial effect

3.2   Evaluation by Student-Teachers

In Table 6, the results of the repeated measures analyses on the data of the master students are summarized. No significant differences were found between students from the experimental and control condition on the evaluation of the e-assessment types (all Fs < 1.85 and all ps >18). A marginal trend was found for the evaluation of peer feedback ($F(1,134)$= 3.35; p= 0.07) indicating that students in the experimental condition generally tended to report a negative evaluation of peer feedback after the intervention, compared to students from the control condition. Generally, students from the experimental condition tended to show lower evaluation scores after the intervention with respect to all types of assessment, compared to the pre-test and compared to students from the control condition. It should be noted that the distribution of numbers of students in the experimental and in the control conditions is strongly skewed. In order to decrease this skewedness, students' practice of the particular e-assessment (yes/no) was used to define the experimental en control condition. Although this increased the number of students in the control condition (i.e. students who were part of an intervention, but did not practice the particular assessment), similar results were found as shown in Table 6.

Table 6. Results for master students: evaluation of assessment procedures (means and standard deviations between brackets)

	Experimental condition		Control condition	
	Pre-test	Post-test	Pre-test	Post-test
Peer feedback	3.5 (0.5)	3.3 (0.6)	3.6 (0.3)	3.9 (0.6)
Peer assessment	3.4 (0.6)	3.2 (0.7)	3.3 (0.9)	3.6 (0.7)
Rubrics	3.6 (0.7)	3.4 (0.8)	3.5 (1.1)	3.8 (0.6)
Video	4.0 (0.5)	3.8 (0.7)	3.9 (0.4)	3.7 (0.7)
Self-assessment	3.8 (0.2)	3.6 (1.2)	3.5 (0.6)	3.8 (0.6)

Note. Scale is *1* =totally disagree, *5* =totally agree that instrument has a beneficial effect

3.3   Teacher-Educators' Perceptions of the e-Assessment Interventions

In Table 7, the results of the qualitative analyses of the work meetings and evaluation reports of the teacher educators are summarized. These analyses show the particularities of using the four forms of assessments. One of the results from the analysis of the educational materials was that teacher educators used the assessments in a formative way, instead of or in addition to summative assessments. This result aligns with observations from Admiraal, Van Duin, Hoeksma, and Van de Kamp [25] that teacher educators strongly prefer the role of mentor or coach, guiding students during their learning process, instead of the role of assessor, which includes judging the quality of students' competence. Moreover, many educational and procedural outcomes can be distinguished such as the setup of a digital repository of test items, quality improvement of knowledge tests, and procedures and rubrics for peer feedback on research plans and for feedback and assessment of web-based video of teaching practices.

Table 7. Results from the qualitative analyses of the work meetings and evaluation reports

Shared tests and test items	Sharing the knowledge tests - used in the various training institutes - was evaluated positively by all participants. Participants reported that they reflected more on good ways of testing and how to improve test items
Digital knowledge tests	Participants indicated that they wished to experiment further with digital testing. Digital testing appeared to be especially advantageous for larger training institutes. However, within these institutes organizational hindrances (i.e. lack of large enough computer rooms) were also reported.
Peer feedback	One participant reported that the developed peer feedback procedure had helped to diminish the workload of teacher-trainers in evaluating research plans written by students. Two other participants indicated that the procedure had a beneficial effect on students' study progress. All participants agreed that peer feedback had an added value for the assessment of research plans.
Peer assessment	Participants agreed that (summative) peer assessment of students' research plans was not feasible, because of the extra workload for students and teacher-trainers. Participants also doubted the quality of students' assessments.
Rubrics	Participants agreed that using rubrics for peer feedback helped to make the assessment criteria more transparent for students and teacher-trainers, and helped to improve the quality of the feedback.
Video	Three findings were reported, on which participants agreed: - Much attention needs to be paid to the technological and organizational aspects before video can be adequately used as an instrument to assess students' classroom practices. - According to participants video cannot replace live observation of classroom practice; rather, video is seen as complementary. Usually, video is used for formative and not for summative assessment. - Discussions of video recordings and feedback on classroom practice should take place in a safe environment (teacher-student, or in small groups)

Table 7. (*continued*)

Self-assessments	According to participants students need help to be able to reflect on their classroom practice and competencies as new teachers. (Digital) self-assessment instruments can be used, but need to be properly "framed" in the curriculum.

4   Discussion and Conclusion

Assessment procedures and criteria were developed and evaluated for testing student-teachers' knowledge of teaching, for assessing a written research proposal using peer feedback, peer assessment and rubrics, for judging video clips of teaching practices and student-teachers' self-evaluations. Although teacher educators reported positive outcomes of the interventions in terms of e-assessment procedures and tools (research question 3), no significant effects were found of the implementation and the evaluation of these procedures and tools (research question 1).

Teacher educators did use a particular type of assessment significantly more in the experimental condition than in the control condition, but these differences already existed a priori. So, it seems that teacher educators participated more in the type of assessment they already used before the intervention started. Student-teachers showed a less positive evaluation of the assessment type after the intervention than at the beginning and compared to the students in the control condition, although differences were not significant (research question 2). It might be that most interventions in the teacher education programs involved in this study were in a so-called experimental phase, showing teething problems in the implementation of the assessment procedures, materials and tools. This would explain why teacher educators are quite positive about the educational outcomes of the study reporting new procedures, materials and tools that were absent before.

4.1   Limitations

As this project was carried out as a Research & Development project aimed at the implementation of e-assessments in teacher education, some limitations of the research design should be mentioned here. Firstly, there might be a bias of self-selection. Teacher education institutes chose to implement two to three interventions with e-assessment in their programs, which means that all teacher educators and students of a particular program participated in the experimental condition that was connected to the particular e-assessment form of their institute. So, the self-selection was on the program level instead of the individual level, and therefore we think that potential confounding effects are quite minimal. Secondly, due to this self-selection of teacher education programs, the distribution of participants in the experimental and control condition was highly skewed, except for the self-assessment intervention. This considerably decreased the power of our analyses and might therefore explain why no significant differences were found between participants of the experimental and control conditions. Thirdly, self-reports of implementations and evaluations were used instead of registration measures such as observation or performance tests. Teacher educators could have under- or over-estimated their use of a particular e-assessment form, although no differences were found in their evaluation of the e-assessment forms. It might be that teacher educators over-estimated their implementation of e-assessment forms as most of them knew they were part of a R&D project that had the aim of stimulating the use of particular e-assessment forms.

4.2   Implications for Teacher Education

In the next years, the procedures and criteria that were designed, implemented and evaluated in the current project should be re-designed and re-tested in order to be used as input for curriculum changes in teacher training programs. As we mentioned earlier, teething problems might have explained why the interventions were not evaluated positively. Some interventions were not fully developed at the time of the evaluations and in some programs the infrastructure did not fully support the interventions (absence of a web-video server or no large computer rooms to administer the digital tests). Recent research on the technical infrastructure of teacher education program in the Netherlands [26] showed a quite conventional picture: basic technology such as computers, WiFi, electronic whiteboards, virtual learning environments and presentation software was available, but not commonly used, and more advanced or innovative technology was less available. So, future pedagogical interventions in the domain of e-assessment in teacher education should concur with a supportive technological infrastructure.

References

1. Fox, R.K., White, C.S., Kidd, J.K.: Program Portfolios: Documenting Teachers' Growth in Reflection - based Inquiry. Teachers and Teaching: Theory and Practice 17, 149–167 (2011), doi:10.1080/13540602.2011.538506
2. Winsor, P.J.T., Butt, R.L., Reeves, H.: Portraying Professional Development in Preservice Teacher Education: Can Portfolios Do the Job? Teachers and Teaching: Theory and Practice 5, 9–31 (1999)
3. Day, C.: Reflection: A Necessary But Not Sufficient Condition for Professional Development. British Educational Research Journal 19, 83–93 (1993), doi:10.1080/0141192930190107
4. Hatton, N., Smith, D.: Reflection in Teacher Education: Towards Definition and Implementation. Teaching and Teacher Education 11, 33–49 (1995)
5. Korthagen, F.A.J.: Techniques for Stimulating Reflection in Teacher Education Seminars. Teaching and Teacher Education 18, 265–274 (1992)
6. Bartell, C., Kayne, C., Morin, J.A.: Teaching Portfolios in Teacher Education. Teacher Education Quarterly 25, 23–32 (1998)
7. Darling-Hammond, L., Snyder, J.: Authentic Assessment of Teaching in Context. Teaching and Teacher Education 16, 523–545 (2000)
8. Woodward, H., Nanlohy, P.: Digital Portfolios: Fact or Fashion? Assessment and Evaluation in Higher Education 29, 227–238 (2004a), doi:10.1080/0260293042000188492
9. Woodward, H., Nanlohy, P.: Digital Portfolios in Pre-service Teacher Education. Assessment in Education 11, 166–178 (2004b), doi:10.1080/0969594042000259475
10. Delandshere, G., Arens, S.A.: Examining the Quality of Evidence in Pre-service Teacher Portfolios. Journal of Teacher Education 54, 57–73 (2003), doi:10.1177/0022487102238658

11. Burroughs, R.: Composing Standards and Composing Teachers. Journal of Teacher Education 52, 223–232 (2001), doi:10.1177/0022487101052003005
12. Uhlenbeck, A.: The Development of an Assessment Procedure for Beginning Teachers of English as a Foreign Language. University of Leiden, Leiden, The Netherlands (2002)
13. Bower, M., Cavanagh, M., Moloney, R., Dao, M.M.: Developing Communication Competence Using an Online Video Reflection System: Pre-service Teachers' Experiences. Asia-Pacific Journal of Teacher Education 39, 311–326 (2011), doi:10.1080/1359866X.2011.614685
14. Rosaen, C.L., Lundeberg, M., Cooper, M., Fritzen, A., Terpstra, M.: Noticing Noticing: How Does Investigation of Video Records Change How Teachers Reflect on Their Experiences? Journal of Teacher Education 59, 347–360 (2009), doi:10.1177/0022487108322128
15. Borko, H., Jacobs, J., Eiteljorg, E., Pittman, M.E.: Video as a Tool for Fostering Productive Discussions in Mathematics Professional Development. Teaching and Teacher Education 24, 417–436 (2008), doi:10.1016/j.tate.2006.11.012
16. Rich, P.J., Hannafin, M.: Video Annotation Tools: Technologies to Scaffold, Structure, and Transform Teacher Reflection. Journal of Teacher Education 60, 52–67 (2009), doi:10.1177/0022487108328486
17. Lee, G.C., Wu, C.: Enhancing the Teaching Experience of Pre-service Teachers Through the Use of Video in Web-based Computer-mediated Communication (CMC). Innovations in Education and Teaching International 43, 369–380 (2006), doi:10.1080/14703290600973836
18. Sherin, M.G., Van Es, E.A.: Effects of Video Club Participation on Teachers' Professional Vision. Journal of Teacher Education 60, 20–37 (2009), doi:10.1177/0022487108328155
19. Moss, P.A., Sutherland, L.-M., Haniford, L., Miller, R., Johnson, D., Geist, P.K., et al.: Interrogating the Generalizability of Portfolio Assessments of Beginning Teachers: A Qualitative Study. Education Policy Analysis Archives 12(32) (2004)
20. Schutz, A.M., Moss, P.A.: Reasonable Decisions in Portfolio Assessment: Evaluating Complex Evidence of Teaching. Education Policy Analysis Archives 12(33) (2004)
21. Wolf, K., Dietz, M.: Teaching Portfolios; Purposes and Possibilities. Teacher Education Quarterly 25, 9–22 (1998)
22. Fill, K., Ottewil, R.: Sink or Swim: Taking Advantage of Developments in Video Streaming. Innovations in Education and Teaching International 43, 397–408 (2006)
23. Yin, R.K.: Case Study Research: Design and Methods, 5th edn. Sage Publications, Thousand Oaks (2014)
24. Geertz, C.: The Interpretation of Cultures. Basic Books, New York (1973)
25. Admiraal, W., Hoeksma, M., van de Kamp, M.-T., van Duin, G.: Assessment of Teacher Competence Using Video Portfolios: Reliability, Construct Validity and Consequential Validity. Teaching and Teacher Education 27, 1019–1028 (2011), doi:10.1016/j.tate.2011.04.002
26. Admiraal, W., Lockhorst, D., Smit, B., Weijers, S.: The Integrative Model of Behavior Prediction to Explain Technology Use in Post-graduate Teacher Education Programs in the Netherlands. International Journal of Higher Education 4(2), 172–178 (2013), doi:10.5430/ijhe

The Emergence of Large-Scale Computer Assisted Summative Examination Facilities in Higher Education

Silvester Draaijer[1] and Bill Warburton[2]

[1] Vrije Universiteit Amsterdam, The Netherlands
s.draaijer@vu.nl
[2] University of Southampton, United Kingdom
w.i.warburton@soton.ac.uk

Abstract. A case study is presented of VU University Amsterdam where a dedicated large-scale CAA examination facility was established. In the facility, 385 students can take an exam concurrently. The case study describes the change factors and processes leading up to the decision by the institution to establish the facility, the start-up of the facility, the foreseen optimization of the use of the facility, threats to the sustainability of the facility and possible future developments. Comparisons are made with large-scale CAA practice at the University of Southampton in the UK. The conclusions are that some specific coincidental situations may be needed to support the decision by senior management to establish such a facility. Long-term sustainability of the dedicated facility is expected to be dependent on the payment structure, the scheduling possibilities and on the educational and assessment benefits that can be achieved. Hybrid models of dedicated facilities and regular computer rooms for CAA seem likely to be adopted, thus balancing cost and benefits. The case shows that sustained effort in building up expertise and momentum are needed to result in viable and sustainable CAA exam facilities.

Keywords: e-Assessment, CAA, Computer-Assisted Assessment, CBT, Computer-Based Testing, CBE. Exams, Proctoring, Inviligation,, Innovation in Higher Education, Change Management.

1   Introduction

The promises of Computer-assisted Assessment (CAA) and the uptake of CAA in Higher Education have, to date, not been delivered on the large scales that were anticipated within the last two decades [1, 2] although smaller successes were reported [3]. A long-standing problem is concerned with delivering large-scale proctored exams due to a lack of effective large-scale physical exam rooms to administer these exams. In this paper, a case description is provided of the VU University Amsterdam that installed a large-scale computer based exam (CBE) facility in which 385 students can take a CBE concurrently. It is known from the Dutch situation that only two other Universities have similar facilities [4, 5] at this scale. Comparisons are made and contrasts drawn with the University of Southampton in the UK, which routinely delivers CBEs to large groups of students also. The emergence of these facilities and the impact of having established such a facility will be described and related to

M. Kalz and E. Ras (Eds.): CAA 2014, CCIS 439, pp. 28–39, 2014.
© Springer International Publishing Switzerland 2014

literature about innovation in higher education and the uptake of CAA in higher education. This will highlight the emergence of large-scale CAA exam facilities as a significant innovation and change in higher education practices.

2   Computer-Assisted Assessment

2.1   Forms of Computer-Assisted Assessment

In this paper, the use of Computer-assisted Assessment in the form of Computer Based Exams (CBEs) in Higher Education for summative examination purposes (exams) is subject of study. Such exams typically consist of combination of selected response test items such as multiple-choice, constructed response test items such as short answer or essays [6], multi-media and the use of domain specific software such as SPSS, R, or MatLab.

CBE requires that students take an exam under controlled and physically proctored conditions. This implies that such exams cannot be taken just anywhere (for example at home) or anytime. In particular tests cannot be taken anytime because the rhythm of teaching and examination in Higher Education is primarily group based; groups of students between for example 100 to 500 students have to take the same exam at exactly the same time under exactly the same conditions.

2.2   Controlled, Reliable, Secure, Invigilated Computer Based Testing

Such conditions call for a high quality infrastructure with respect to technical, logistical and procedural organization to prevent failure. And it is more likely that failures occur with CBE when compared to pencil-and-paper exams. There are simply more elements in the process which can go wrong and the weakest link defines the strength of the whole chain. In particular, the risk that computers break down or are unfit (for example screen resolution being too low, or too slow processor speeds), so that the software does not function at the time of examination because of overloading, the risk that schedules and physical arrangements are set wrongly, the risk of losing data, the risk that students use computers to illegitimately communicate or use forbidden information resources and the like. The care with which successful computer based tests are developed and delivered can in that respect best be compared with precision military operations.

2.3   The VU University Amsterdam CBE Facility Set-Up

The VU University Amsterdam is a residential, campus-bases research University in the Netherlands with approximately 28.000 students. The VU University Amsterdam realized their large-scale CBE facility in the already existing exam hall of the University. This hall contains approximately 595 seats and accompanying tables. 2/3 of the tables were replaced by 385 workstations, which are divided in four blocks of approximately 95 workstations. See Figure 1 for a photographic impression of the facility. Four different exams in each block can be scheduled simultaneous. The screen and workstations are combined into one closed unit that can be folded into a regular table when not in use. See Figure 2. The table can thus be also be used for pencil-and-paper exams. The screen is fitted with a privacy screen so that students cannot see each other's screens.

The workstation are powered via Power-over-Ethernet (PoE) and they take up an average of approximately 10-15 Watts. Therefore heat dissipation is minimal and vans in the workstations and air-conditioning in the hall are not needed. This prevents also dissipation of noise. The keyboard and mouse are separately attached to the unit and can be stored on the side of the table using magnets. The PoE cabling system that is used is not permanently attached to the floor and can be rolled on spools. The complete table with computer unit is stackable so the hall is relatively easy cleared out.

For security reasons, the workstations are placed in a separate VLAN and students cannot login with their institution account. The main functionality of the workstations is regulated by Group Policy Object settings. This controls access to the Internet, access to files, network directories and computer programs. The workstations are further fitted with Classroom Management Software (NetControl2) which enable the support staff to centrally start-up and shut-down all workstations, to lock all workstations until all students are seated and then released at exactly the same time, to send and collect files and assignments, to register students, to enable specific access to internet resources or computer resources, to monitor the computers etc. The central IT-service performs the technical management and maintenance of the workstations.

Fig. 1. Photograph of the CBE facility of VU University Amsterdam in use. The picture shows approximately one block of computers that can be scheduled separately.

Fig. 2. Three pictures showing how the computers and screen are folded into the table

Table 1. Mechanisms driving CAA uptake (after Warburton, 2009)

(1) Dissemination of good CAA practice at department level	From 2004 onwards, the institution had a central supported CBT system. The system was installed as a small scale, low cost enterprise. A number of individual initiatives of teachers could be supported by this institutionalized structure for grassroots projects [7] and departmental innovation projects. Support was also provided by central and departmental learning technologists for training and coaching of teachers to design high quality CAA and the delivery of CBT's and CBEs in dispersed computer rooms.
(2) Coordinated dissemination of CAA practice.	A department wide computer-based test format for the whole Bachor phase was established for one department (Medicine), in which students were obliged to take curricular cumulative tests. The central unit provided the infrastructure and support to design high-quality CAA.
(3) Coordinated procedural risk mitigation	The central learning technologist support unit provided the sustained ownership of hands-on risk mitigation procedures and fiats accordingly. But also, training and coaching of teachers to design high quality CAA items and tests. The central learning technologist, in Fullan [8] and Kotter [9] terms, served as a sustaining champion.
(4) Coordinated physical risk mitigation by central L&T specialists	The central learning technologists support were experienced and could enable department-to-department contact to be able to use each other's computer rooms to allow for tests being taking concurrently up to 350 students. The CBT systems performance ability was also expanded to accommodate larger student groups. Large-scale CBT events became progressively more common.
(5) Coordinated strategy for CAA uptake approved by senior management	As three departments moved into more structural development and deployment of CBEs (Medicine, Life Sciences, Arts), trusting the central unit to provide sustained support, awareness at the senior management level of the institution grew. Failures could be prevented and procedures would become more fluent to execute by using both MLE and CBT software for exams, specifically targeted at the purpose of the particular tests and the experience and skill of the involved teachers and departmental support staff. The central learning technologist again served as a sustaining champion and driving force during this period (Fullan [8] and Kotter [9]).
(6) Senior managers provide coordinated resources	The accumulated knowledge and tooling and obvious large scale use of CBT made it possible to show what benefits CBT could deliver for the institution and this influenced the senior management's opinions and decision processes in the idea acceptance of a large-scale facility gradually.
(7) External influences	In the Netherlands, attention has been recently directed towards Assessment and Quality Assurance of Assessment in all forms of Education. In particular, the Accreditation Organization of The Netherlands and Flanders (NVAO). Such national attention for Assessment can effectively drive policies by which CBT can be promoted as an element that can increase quality. Opportunities offered by CBT to give more frequent formative tests and accompanying feedback are examples of this.

2.4   Factors for Successful Change

The establishment of the large-scale CBE facility at VU University Amsterdam can be regarded as a successful change process. The success with which this change process was implemented can be analyzed in terms of characteristics and inhibiting and driving forces for successful change that have been identified by several scholars. We will illustrate how the VU University Amsterdam played on the driving forces and navigated through the inhibiting forces as identified by Warburton (2009) to be able to establish the large scale CBE facility. The illustration is provided in Table 1 and Table 2. This illustration can possibly serve as best practice for other institution to identify at what position they are in their effort or process to scale up the use of CAA for examination purposes. Following that, threats to the sustainability of the facility will be described as the change process has not be completed yet. Some comparisons will be made with the situation in Southampton University. Finally, conclusions will be drawn and discussed.

Table 2. Dealing with some obstacles which inhibit CAA uptake (after Warburton, 2009)

(1) Failures of invigilated CAA tests and fear of these	As there was ongoing central support for CBT at the institution and the performance ability and breakdown risks of the CBT process were gradually being brought under control, failures were prevented. Also, procedures of damage control, both related to the exams themselves, as well as the impact on the perception of risk or failure [10] were developed and could be quickly applied. In particular, managing expectations [11, 12] resulted in more of an emphasis on the institution celebrating successes instead of focusing on failures.
(2) Ineffective dissemination of good CAA practice	When deciding to establish the large-scale CAA exam hall, senior managers required that the facility be used for more than just selected response test item exams. The team in charge of designing the facilities for the computer network and software functionalities therefore integrated the use of Classroom Management Software and specific adaptable network settings in the facility. This enables the distribution and collection of any kind of document, enables or disables access to specific resources and allows for combinations of domain specific software e.g. SPSS, OxMetrics, MatLab, ChembioDraw, Pearson's MyStatLab, video, Word in combination with the institutions LMS (Blackboard, TurnItIn) and CBT system QuestionMark Perception.
(3) Ineffective procedural risk mitigation	Because of the steady growth of the use of CBE in computer rooms, various aspects of procedural risk mitigations were known. It also was quickly acknowledged that a central facility would simplify processes very much and would therefore mitigate these risks.
(4) Fragmented approach to physical risk mitigation	As the uptake of CBE gradually grew, physical risks were easier to counter. For example the central unit invested in simulated load tests to ensure that the CBT system operated fluently under heavy anticipated load.
(5) Institutional strategy shortfall	In general, CBT software is not easy to operate [13, 14]. So, in most departments, it is not the teachers who operate the CBT software but learning technologists who devote part of their time to this task, and they work closely with the central support unit by positively stimulating a community of practice [15, 16], actively exchanging ideas and expertise. Central and departmental learning technologists built up expertise and fluency, efficiency and effectiveness in operating the CBT system. Teacher were advised to focus on developing test items and learning technologists to support them in editing items in the CBT system [13].

Table 2. (*continued*)

(6) Senior managers withhold resources	The first attempts to implement CBT were based on a small-scale effort, with limited resources and limited impact. Using CBT mainly focused on online formative assessment purposes. As the use of CBT steadily grew, resources at the departmental level (departmental learning technologists) and central level (increasing performance ability of the central CBT system, time of central learning technologist support), resources could grow gradually without involving large impact decisions regarding resources by senior management. This implied that senior management control was unneeded. The approval of senior managers was, however, needed to establish the large-scale facility. The senior management however got convinced to provide the resources because of the track-record of success and a business case approved by the senior management.
(7) Widespread concerns about 'dumbing down':	See (2) Coordinated dissemination of CAA practice of Table 1 and see (2) 'Ineffective dissemination of good CAA practice'

It can be argued that institutions that establish a large scale CBE facility have at least been partly successful in the uptake of CAA. Such a facility allows the institution to control most of the risk factors by which CBT can fail and therefore mitigates these risks. However, the benefits for the institution, and hence the success, must also be reached by having faculty use the facility as much as possible and in the best way possible. Also, success can be defined whether this large scale facility will be in operation for a sustained amount of time. This aspect of success will be addressed next.

2.5   Startup Success for the CBE Facility

At a particular moment in time, the large CBE facility was ready for operation. An important factor for the sustainability of the facility is that it is used as quickly as possible to show the ongoing experience of success [9]. Though the need for CBEs had already been established before the facility came into existence, it is quite a big leap between organizing some 10-s of CBEs per year to hundreds or more CBEs per year. Much effort was exerted to make sure that the institution succeeded in administering about 120 exams, comprising about 32.000 exams in year one.

There were four further conditions fulfilled to support this success, building on the capacity that had already been established before the facility came into operation.

Central Funding. In first instance, it was tried to establish a payment structure in which each test taken had to be separately paid-for by the individual teacher or department. In the pre-planning phases of the implementation of the facility, investigations into acceptable levels of costs (and expected benefits) were discussed with departments and pay-per-use was seen as acceptable. However, when push comes to shove, this turned out to be quite a hurdle. In comparison to pencil-and-paper tests, teachers and departments as additional perceived the out-of-pocket costs to regular business and every teacher or department had another (or no) structure for funding. In the months running up to opening the facility, this raised severe difficulties in persuading faculty to use the facility. Therefore it was decided to firstly centrally fund the facility, allowing the departments to administer CBEs without additional out-of-pocket costs and increase an 'installed base' of CBEs administered in the facility. This decision could also be defended as the main fixed costs for the facility are inflexible (computer hardware, computer software, support, redemption) and therefore stimulating demand is defensible in order to lower the cost per exam as much as possible.

Central CBE Support Expert. It was decided that the CBE facility was to be supported by an expert (central supporter for CBEs) who would work closely with the departmental learning technologists, leaving the original support structure intact. For departments without a learning technologist, the expert would provide support on a fee base.

Priority in Scheduling. In the facility, pencil-and-paper exams can still be administered. However, it was arranged that the central scheduling office was to assign placements to CBEs over pencil-and-paper exams and that CBEs with large groups were given priority over small CBE groups.

Information Provisioning and Communication. The central CBT expert and the central support unit in charge of the CBE facility organized 'Road-Shows' to increase the visibility of the CBE facility and the benefits it could have for both the students and faculty members in term of efficiency, speed and forms of assessment. It turned out that the facility was also much needed for centrally organized pre-sessional assessments and other centrally organized entrance and certification test for professional awarding bodies both within and outside of the University.

2.6   Near Future: Optimizing the Deployment of the CBE Facility

Based on the CBEs that were administered before the facility came into being and based on the expectations as laid down in the Business Case of the facility, it was intended that the positive return on the investment would be based on partly transitioning large scale exams with constructed response test item format (short answer, long answer, essay) into CBE administered selected response format (True/False, multiple-choice). The rationale for this being that the lack of marking time for selected response test items would compensate for the extra cost of the facility.

In the phase of securing start-up success, all types of exams however were admitted to the facility. No explicit strategy to persuade faculty to change some of their choice towards selected response item formats in favor of constructed response items was undertaken. In the majority of cases, exams that were already administered as multiple-choice test items were converted to CBEs. However, it was emphasized by the central support unit, to promote the use of the CBT facility for exams with constructed response test items and test aimed at measuring ability to solve problems with domain specific software. This enabled the central support unit to gain expertise in this not much known area and identify efficiency gain.

Efficiency gains can be achieved in two areas. First, gains in marking efficiency turned out to be achievable for short-answer (approx. 5 sentences) or long-answer test items (approx. 20 sentences). For that purpose, these answers needed to be scored via MS Excel tables. Scoring these answers via an extra column in excel along the shown answers is very speedy. No comparative experiments have been undertaken with respect to speed of grading, but all teachers agreed on this point. Second, gain in efficiency was in particular reported by means of preventing time for producing, storing, handling and reordering pencil-and-paper tests. People in administrative roles for pencil-and-paper tests could simply be omitted from the process.

Finally, in order to accommodate for peak-demand for the facility, options are studied to combine both the facility and other computer rooms in the University.

2.7   Threats to Long Term Sustainability of the CBE Facility

As the facility has proven its technical success and beginnings of Business Case success, there are still threats regarding the sustainability of the facility. We anticipate three short term threats.

Adverse Payment Structure. The payment structure of the facility is still in debate. In order to control costs, institutional policy is increasingly geared at damping demand for facilities. Several models are in discussion. One of the threats is that this structure forces individual teachers or departmental administrators to consider the deployment of each individual exam in terms of costs. This is in the VU University Amsterdam strengthened because the cost for pencil-and-paper tests are not known. This would hinder the process of deciding to move to or sustain a CBE procedure. Also, in view of complex central scheduling processes, this could cause the uptake of CBE to slow down or diminish due to over-sensitive scheduling deadlines. It is hoped that the payments structure will be based on prepayment model in which departments pay a fixed fee per year based on their number of enrolled students. This will provide departmental managers and the central scheduling office a clear priority and decision process and that the facility will be used to the maximum amount possible, that every department can use the facility and thus the institution lowers the cost per test maximally.

Institutional Budget Cuts. Ongoing budget cuts, imposed by government and the institution, combined with and reorganization of central support units is a constant threat to the sustainability of the facility. Every time, the existence or set-up of the facility is questioned, strong arguments must be able to be put forward to keep the budget in line with fixed cost and support cost. Being more efficient could perhaps be realized by shifting work to teachers themselves or by deploying working-students, but the main fixed costs are those for the hardware, software and maintenance of the facility. So, little gain can be expected of such operations. Also, budget cuts at the departmental level could diminish uptake.

Adverse Scheduling Possibilities and Experiences. In the Netherlands there is a national tendency for an increasingly uniform semester scheduling structure because of the demand for students to be able to have a flexible curricular programs, even between universities. This causes a peak in demand for computer workstations during a limited number of exam periods. In the Netherlands, this constitutes often 6 so-called examination weeks. Though the facility is large (385 workstations), it is still limited in size compared with the total student population or encountered cohort sizes, for exams in larger departments (such as Business and Law). Only four sessions can be deployed per workstation per day. This leads to the situation where a number of exams that should use CBT cannot be scheduled. This causes uncertainty and possible frustration for teachers, which in turn could lead teachers or departments abandoning the deployment of CBT exams.

For the longer term, different approaches or end-to-end solutions could undermine the grounds for existence for the facility or could lead to other solutions. The most obvious of these is that computer rooms that are already available on campus could be assigned to administer CBEs. As has been described in the previous sections, in the process leading up to the decision to install the large-scale facility, exams were already administered simultaneously in various computer rooms with all risky factors and costly logistics and invigilation practices that the CBE facility intended to alleviate.

Some institutions, however, have explicitly adopted the dispersed computer-room strategy to increase the uptake of CBT. A notable example is the University of Southampton [17], where there is a legacy of workstation provision in a smaller spaces with a total maximum aggregate capacity of c.400, there is a strong and steadily increasing demand for CBEs, in some cases for undergraduate cohorts of more than 500 students. This growth in demand has taken place steadily over the last decade, during which time Southampton University implemented a central Managed Learning Environment (MLE) team staffed with eLearning and eAssessment specialists. The University has in this way exerted sustained effort in building up expertise and momentum with respect to CAA uptake [18], comparable to the VU University Amsterdam. Aggregate volumes are now (2014) running at 10.000 computer-based tests per annum, two thirds of which is concentrated in two two-week exam periods, one at the end of each Semester. Because of budgetary constraints, there was little prospect of funding a large single (300-400) dedicated space for CBT along the lines of those implemented at VU University Amsterdam or the University of Bradford in the UK [19]. Other factors which militate against the provision of single large dedicated CBE space at Southampton include the lack of a large enough existing space and an ongoing increase in pressure on teaching accommodation generally as the University continues to grow incrementally. Warburton and Robinson concentrated on simplifying and making more robust the process of starting CBEs in multiple workstation rooms simultaneously by means of special software ExamStart and special monitoring and authentication techniques. The approach taken at Southampton University shows a strong resemblance to the approach of Wageningen University and Research Centre who developed the Secure Test Environment [20]. The MLE team at Southampton University is proud of the progress made there in running large-scale CBEs in multiple locations robustly and simultaneously, but acknowledges that in their situation 'necessity is the mother of invention'. They acknowledge that such large-scale exams are intrinsically risky and can cause inconvenience. Large numbers of invigilators are required, technical support resources can become thinly stretched - especially during University Exam Periods - and coordinating multi-site CBEs is a time-consuming, stressful and onerous commitment. The Southampton team can see that a single large dedicated CAA space could do much to lighten the administrative burden on the Exams Office and the IT Department. For example, it is estimated that the processes of scheduling, organising of and invigilating (proctoring) each computer-based exam would be reduced by a factor of about four, which is the average number of rooms recruited currently for each CBE at Southampton. Similarly, the number of CBEs taken if a single large dedicated CBA facility were available is estimated as roughly five times greater, because the existing workstation resources are used heavily for teaching and during term-time and for revision during exams (and are therefore – due to policy regulations – not made available for CBEs).

Other developments that could threaten the sustainability of the facility of VU University Amsterdam, or the approach taken at the University of Southampton, are the emergence of complete new technologies in which hard- and software combinations are made with diminishing costs. One could think of new opportunities for a Bring Your Own Device strategy (BYOD) or an online proctoring strategy. A BYOD strategy could be that students take their own device to the institution and in which exams are distributed via a wireless network. The amount of control that should be possible by the institution regarding security and performance for the personal device should be able to be implemented easily and robustly. Another development is that more and more companies offer solutions in which students can take an exam at home with their own device. Such solutions require the student to install special proctoring software and to make recordings via a webcam while taking the exam. Such approaches however are inherently more vulnerable to technical, organizational and invigilation problems. The costs for online proctoring solutions are still too high and these have not yet been shown to be fully robust end-to-end solutions. But perhaps in some future scenarios, such solutions could become viable.

3   Conclusion and Discussion

The comparison between the situation at VU University Amsterdam and the University of Southampton shows the emergence of two models for large-scale CAA. The case of the VU University Amsterdam is shown in which one large dedicated central facility has been established (uni-location) and the case of Southampton University in which several smaller facilities are combined to form one large facility (multi-location). In both cases, a longer standing tradition of CAA was needed to precede the further up scaling of both the facilities and number of exams administered. As the case of the VU University Amsterdam further shows, it takes both a deliberate course of action to build on factors to drive the uptake of CAA and as well as a deliberate course of action to mitigate the inhibiting factors. But also, the VU University Amsterdam case shows that coincidental factors determine whether a single large dedicated facility is liable to be approved by senior management. These are factors concerning the decisions leaders in senior management, factors relating to the physical arrangement of buildings on a campus-based university, factors relating to the physical design of workstations, factors relating cross-institutional trends with respect to accreditation and public opinion regarding the importance of assessment. Without any of these factors, senior management would maybe not have decided in favor of the large-scale facility.

The case study show clearly that scaling up CAA-use in institution for Higher Education is a complex and long-term process. Sustained effort of building up expertise and momentum is required to come to a stage in which the use of computers for examination purposes results in serious volumes of test taken and hence results in serious attention by senior management.

The case of the VU University Amsterdam is a typical illustration of change as it occurs in higher education. As many individuals at various levels within a University are involved and have an influence in leading up to a decisions to establish a large-scale facility, elements of organized anarchical decision making [21] are visible. But also experimentation [8], sustained effort [22], dedicated support and playing on the driving forces and minimizing the inhibiting forces for the uptake of CAA and some specific circumstances form the ingredients of the change at the VU University Amsterdam. It is also an illustration of the phases of unfreezing, changing and refreezing in educational change as described by Lewin [23] and Schein [24]. The unfreezing phase existed of raising awareness in the institution that a move to a large-scale CAA facility was needed and that tough decisions regarding investments and university policies needed to be made. The change phase is currently underway in which the uptake is realized and perceptions regarding planning and costs concerned which examination procedures at the University need to be reconsidered even more broadly. The refreezing phase in the case of the VU University Amsterdam has not been fully completed as the described threats to the sustainability illustrate. So maybe, the installation of the large-scale facility could in future dates be regarded as an intermediate phase that served a tactic goal to raise the uptake of CAA in the short term and create momentum to work prudently and systematically on new technologies and practices to sustain volumes for even longer term effectively and efficiently.

In conclusion however, it has been shown that the establishment of large-scale CAA at institutions for higher education is increasing and turning into sustainable facilities. Effective and efficient combinations of current technologies and organizational power has been shown to be attainable, leading to enriched and multiple-forms of CAA, delivering the promise of summative CAA slowly but surely.

References

1. Clauser, B., Schuwirth, L., Newble, D.: The use of computers in assessment. In: Int. Handb. Res. Med. Educ. (2002)
2. Warburton, W.: Quick win or slow burn: modelling UK HE CAA uptake. Assess. Eval. High. Educ. 34, 257–272 (2009)
3. Draaijer, S., Parsons, R.: Transformatie en online toetsen. In: van Geloven, M.P., van der Wende, M.C., van der Veen, J. (eds.) Van Trend Naar Ttransformatie. ICT-Innovaties in Het Hoger Onderwijs, ch. 13. Wolters-Noordhoff (2005)
4. Jager, S.: Implementation of digital testing at the University of Groningen (2012)
5. Keijzer, M.: SURF: Casusbeschrijving: digitale toetsafname bij TU Delft (2012)

6. Mogey, N., Paterson, J., Burk, J., Purcell, M.: Typing compared with handwriting for essay examinations at university: letting the students choose. ALT-J 18, 29–47 (2010)
7. Gunn, C.: Sustainability factors for e-learning initiatives. ALT-J 18, 89–103 (2010)
8. Fullan, M.: Change forces: The sequel (1999)
9. Kotter, J.P.: Winning at change. Lead. Lead. 27–33 (1998)
10. Van Noort, G , Willemsen, L.M.: Online damage control: The effects of proactive versus reactive webcare interventions in consumer-generated and brand-generated platforms. J. Interact. Mark. 26, 131–140 (2012)
11. Khazanchi, D., Reich, B.H.: Achieving IT project success through control, measurement, managing expectations, and top management support. Int. J. Proj. Manag. 26, 699 (2008)
12. Kopalle, P.K. Lehmann, D.R.: Strategic management of expectations: The role of disconfirmation sensitivity and perfectionism. J. Mark. Res. 38, 386–394 (2001)
13. Hartog, R., Draaijer, S., Rietveld, L.C.: Practical Aspects of Task Allocation in Design and Development of Digital Closed Questions in Higher Education. Pract. Assess. Res. Eval. 13 (2008)
14. Schoonenboom, J.: Using an adapted, task-level technology acceptance model to explain why instructors in higher education intend to use some learning management system tools more than others. Comput. Educ. 71, 247–256 (2014)
15. Eckert, P.: Communities of practice. ELL 2, 683–685 (2006)
16. Wenger, E.: Communities of practice. Communities 22, 57 (2009)
17. Warburton, W., Robinson, G.: Robust Delivery of CAA Exams. In: Whitelock, D., Warburton, W., Wills, G., Gilbert, L. (eds.) CAA 2013 International Conference. University of Southampton (2013)
18. Shephard, K., Warburton, B., Maier, P., Warren, A.: Development and evaluation of computer-assisted assessment in higher education in relation to BS7988. Assess. Eval. High. Educ. 31, 583–595 (2006)
19. Dermo, J., Eyre, S.: Secure, reliable and effective institution-wide e-assessment: paving the way for new technologies. In: Presented at the CAA 2008 International Conference. University of Loughborough (2008)
20. Folkerts, G.: Tool: Secure Test Environment, http://www.surf.nl/en/knowledge-and-innovation/knowledge-base/2013/tool-secure-test-environment.html
21. Kezar, A.: Understanding the Nature of Higher Education Organizations: Key to Successful Organizational Change. In: Understanding and Facilitating Organizational Change in the 21st Century, pp. 59–77 (2001)
22. Miles, M.B.: Unraveling the Mystery of Institutionalization. Educ. Leadersh. 41, 14–19 (1983)
23. Lewin, K.: Quasi-stationary social equilibria and the problem of permanent change, pp. 238–244 (1961)
24. Schein, E.H.: Kurt Lewin's change theory in the field and in the classroom: Notes toward a model of managed learning. Syst. Pract. 9, 27–47 (1996)

Functional, Frustrating and Full of Potential: Learners' Experiences of a Prototype for Automated Essay Feedback

Bethany Alden Rivers[1,*], Denise Whitelock[1], John T.E. Richardson[1], Debora Field[2], and Stephen Pulman[2]

[1] Institute of Educational Technology, The Open University, Milton Keynes, UK
{b.alden,denise.whitelock,john.t.e.richardson}@open.ac.uk
[2] Computer Science Department, The University of Oxford, Oxford, UK
{debora.field,stephen.pulman}@cs.ox.ac.uk

Abstract. OpenEssayist is an automated feedback system designed to support university students as they write essays for assessment. A first generation prototype of this system was tested on a cohort of postgraduate distance learners at the UK Open University from September to December 2013. A case study approach was used to examine three participants' experiences of the prototype. Findings from the case studies offered insight into how different users may perceive the usefulness, future potential and end-user of such a tool. This study has important implications for the next phase of development, when the role of OpenEssayist in supporting students' learning will need to be more clearly understood.

Keywords: automated feedback, essay-writing, software evaluation, case study.

1   Introduction

OpenEssayist is an automated feedback system designed to provide instantaneous support to university students as they draft essays for summative assessment. There are two components to the system: (1) the learning analytics engine (EssayAnalyser) and (2) the web application that provides feedback for students (OpenEssayist) [1, 2]. The rationale for developing an automated feedback tool, such as this one, rests largely on the knowledge that university students find essay-writing to be challenging task [3]. A system that provides immediate feedback, or "advice for action" on students' draft essays could be one way to support learners in the essay-writing process [4].

In September 2013, a first generation prototype of OpenEssayist was made available to students for testing. At this stage of software development, it was important for the research team to understand the answers to three questions: (1) How useful is OpenEssayist for helping students prepare drafts of their essays? (2) How could the prototype add more value to the essay-writing process? and (3) What type of student

---

* Corresponding author.

M. Kalz and E. Ras (Eds.): CAA 2014, CCIS 439, pp. 40–52, 2014.

would benefit from using an automated feedback tool for essay-writing? This paper reports on empirical research that was carried out to address these questions.

2   Computer Based Summative Assessment

The bulk of work in the automated marking of free text has been concerned with essays. One of the earliest marking systems which was put into commercial use is E-rater [5]. E-rater uses various vector-space measures of semantic similarity to determine whether an essay contains the appropriate conceptual content. It also carries out some shallow grammatical processing, and looks for simple rhetorical features (e.g., a paragraph containing a phrase like 'in conclusion' ought to go at the end of the essay).

Other commercial essay marking systems include IntelliMetric and Pearson's KAT engine, based on Landauer's Intelligent Essay Assessor [6, 7]. Both of these systems use a vector-space technique for measuring semantic similarity to a gold standard essay, known as Latent Semantic Analysis. For the most part, these systems focus on assessment alone, rather than feedback. Some of the systems can be used to elicit generic feedback on a final version of a draft essay. However, this type of feedback is not tailored to the essay.

Thus while automated assessment of free text can be thought of as reasonably well understood (although of course current systems are relatively crude compared to a human marker) the process of constructing individualized feedback automatically is much less well established.

3   Evaluating Prototypes for Automated Feedback

Thus far in the development of OpenEssayist, focus groups had been carried out with students to understand how they go about writing essays [8]. This research informed a model of students' essay-writing processes that was used to develop the prototype (see Figure 1).

Additionally, some usability tests, employing a think-aloud protocol, were conducted with a few members of academic staff, and insights from accessibility experts were used to inform the early stages of the design process. However, up to the point of this study, students had not been involved in testing the prototype.

There is an abundance of literature dealing with software evaluation, usability trials and accessibility testing of prototype educational technology. Alden et al. [8] identified two research reports that were very relevant to the empirical evaluation of OpenEssayist. The first was a study by Chandrasegaran, Ellis and Poedjosoedarmo (2005), who carried out user-testing with 29 undergraduate students to evaluate their software called EssayAssist, a computer program that helps students make decisions during the essay writing process. Their study asked students to identify which features of the software were helpful, missing or problematic. Although their paper reported on a relatively early stage of development, the authors were hopeful that, eventually, this software would provide students with a much-needed level of essay-writing support. According to the authors, what set EssayAssist apart from other, similar writing tools was the "in-process guidance" that helped students when they encountered a problem with their writing [9].

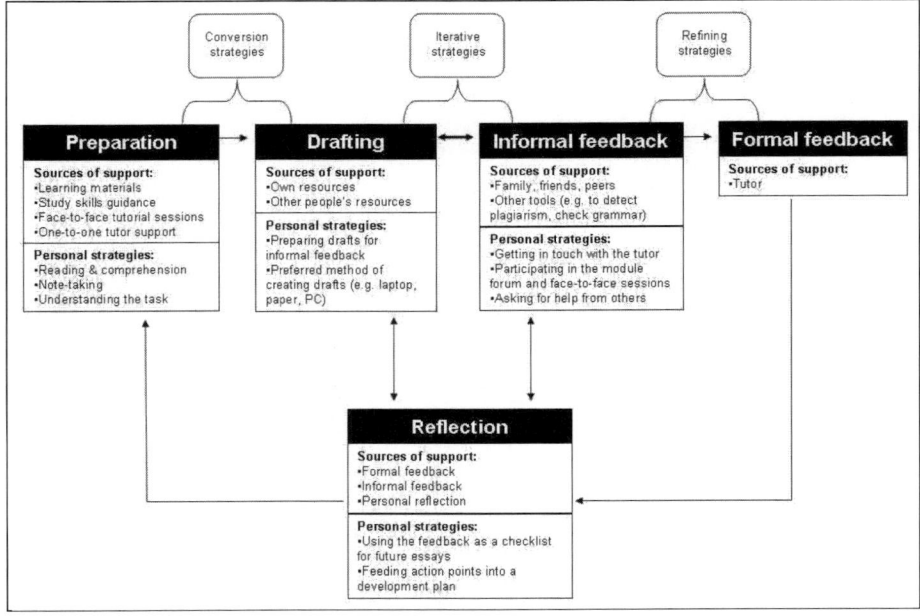

Fig. 1. Processes of essay-writing [8]

A second report by Roscoe et al. (in press) discussed various methods used to test the first version of the 'The Writing Pal (W-Pal)'. W-Pal is an intelligent tutoring system that offers automated formative feedback to students as they prepare essays. Their system uses game based instruction and focuses on the development of writing strategies. This team of authors reported that W-Pal was unique to other 'automated writing evaluation systems' (AWEs) because it had been designed with a pedagogical focus. Other AWEs, according to Roscoe et al. had been designed to rate the quality of essays. Their team evaluated W-Pal using several phases and methods of testing. The first version of their prototype was deployed with different groups of users, each asked to complete usability and perception surveys after using the system [10].

As in these studies, the first generation prototype of OpenEssayist was deployed on a group of student-users. Insights from this testing will be useful in terms of developing the usability and accessibility of the system. However, it is also important for the next phase of development to consider whether students perceive such a system to add value to their learning experience and who, exactly, they believe would use such a system.

4   The OpenEssayist Prototype

The core functionality of the OpenEssayist system can be grouped in two distinct parts: task and draft. The task side relates to the management of the system's activities. These include tasks such as logging in and out, accessing specific essays, submitting new drafts and keeping a record of submissions. The draft side of the system

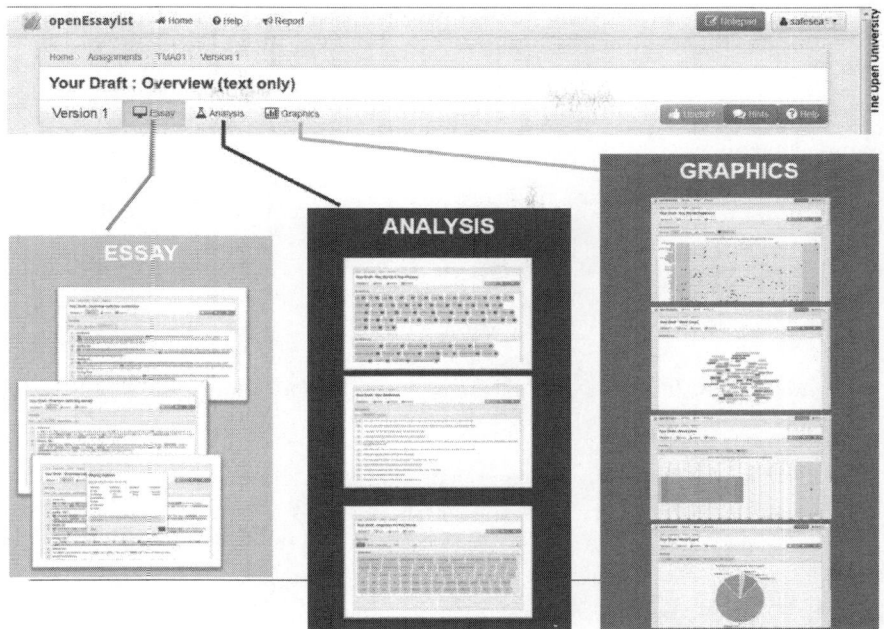

Fig. 2. Draft Overview [1, 2]

relates to the activities around a specific draft that has been submitted for analysis. Outputs from these activities are provided to the user as external representations of different analyses—or "views". Table 1 is a list of these views that were available to users of the first generation prototype of OpenEssayist and Figure 2 is an example of the 'Draft overview' view. See Van Labeke et al. (2013a, 2013b) for a more detailed account of the system's functionality [1, 2].

Table 1. External representations of essay analyses in the OpenEssayist prototype

View	Description
Draft overview	A page showing a structured version of the draft essay in which key words, phrases, and sentences can be highlighted
Key words and key phrases	A page showing the frequency distribution of the most used words and phrases in the draft essay the key words and phrases in the draft essay, including their frequencies
Key sentences	A page showing the most important sentences in the draft essay

Table 1. (*continued*)

Key word dispersion view	A page showing how the key words and phrases are distributed across the entire draft essay
Word cloud view	A page showing a picture of a cluster of the key words and phrases presented in different colours and sizes to visualize their frequency distribution.
Word limit view	A bullet graph showing the number of words within each section of the draft essay and comparing the total words with the word limit of the assignment
Word count view	A pie chart showing the number of words within each section
Organize the key words view	A page that allows the user to group key words and phrases and to then see the groups highlighted in different colours in the draft overview view

5   A Case Study Approach

A case study method allowed the team to explore an "exemplifying case", or one that "provides a suitable context for certain research questions to be answered" [11]. To address our research questions of usefulness, future potential and perceived end-user, the research team employed a case study approach to gain a closer insight by way of three users' 'stories' of OpenEssayist.

Students on a postgraduate module at the UK Open University were invited to engage with the OpenEssayist prototype between September 2013 and February 2014. Of this sample, two students agreed to participate in a more detailed discussion of their experiences of using OpenEssayist and one student in the cohort, who decided not to use the system, also agreed to participate in this case study.

Permission to carry out this research was approved by the University's Student Research Project Panel and by the University's Human Research Ethics Committee. Participants provided informed consent before engaging in recorded telephone interviews, which varied in length from 12 to 35 minutes. Transcriptions of the conversations were analyzed to investigate key themes and to summarize each participant's own narrative.

6   The Case of OpenEssayist

6.1   Maria's Story: "It Encourages You to Think but it's too Bewildering for a Novice Learner"

At the time of sharing her experiences of OpenEssayist, Maria was in her late-fifties, working in part-time employment. According to university records, Maria was a White woman, held a postgraduate qualification and had a disability. She was reportedly enrolled in the present module for career and personal development reasons. During the interview it emerged that Maria had a very strong background in language and linguistics.

When asked to explain her approach to essay-writing, Maria was able to talk about how she took notes, created a plan (using 'something between a mind map and a list') and constructed a structure using headings. The planning, according to Maria, was the most important stage of essay-writing. She explained that an absence of a structure made her feel 'less confident' and that it was 'a bit scary' to forge ahead without clear direction.

Maria said that she prepares drafts of her essays, building on her own reflections after each draft. She has clear strategies for using feedback to improve her performance on subsequent essays, and was able to share a specific example of when she used the tutor's suggestion to demonstrate a deeper understanding of certain concepts within her writing.

There was a sense of excitement as Maria talked about the ways that OpenEssayist could assist student in these early stages of essay-writing. For example, Maria thought that the Key Sentences view could help learners during the planning process because it shows the most important sentences. She explained that if these were stripped out, then it should show the essay structure. When asked to talk about how OpenEssayist would help a student during the drafting stages, she commented that 'it can throw up things that you haven't been aware of.' In particular, Maria thought there was potential for the system to helps students with their writing style, word choice and essay structure.

Maria thought that the Key Word Dispersion view was a useful resource because, as she explained, students struggle to find different words or phrases to mean the same thing. She suggested that the functionality of OpenEssayist would add more value if it also worked as a thesaurus. Maria thought the system could highlight *variety* as a positive feature in one's writing, by offering suggestions for alternative words and phrases.

When asked to consider the type of learner who might benefit from OpenEssayist, Maria was clear that it should not be aimed at a novice student. She explained that the present version is too 'bewildering' and that it would, therefore, be an inappropriate tool for a beginner or for someone who was 'not so familiar with ICT'. (Later in the interview, however, Maria contradicted this notion by suggesting the tool be tested with students on a first year essay-writing module.)

Her earlier excitement endured throughout the interview and flowed into a few ideas of her own for the future of the system. She toyed with the idea that OpenEssayist could be a catalyst for peer support, explaining that 'you are a bit more isolated as an Open University student'. Maria thought it would be a good idea for the system to help students help each other but, when pushed to explain, it was difficult for her to envision how this might work.

Furthermore, Maria saw the possibility for OpenEssayist to help students with other types of assignments, not just essays. She wondered, too, whether the system could help foreign language students with their assessed work.

6.2 Robert's Story: "It Could Be Useful but Mainly for Students Who Are Less Confident"

Robert had declined the invitation to participate in the earlier usability test and therefore, had not provided his demographic data. When asked in the interview to describe his professional and educational background, he explained that he had a background in criminal psychology, anthropology and religious studies. He said that the present module was contributing towards his second Master's degree and that he was also working towards a PhD.

Robert could not understand what OpenEssayist was supposed to do for him and he was unsure whether to use it for his own assignments. He already felt confident with his essay-writing skills. Later in the interview, he admitted that there are still a few areas of essay-writing where he was not so confident (word choice and structure). And, on ending the interview, he explained that, actually, he would have liked to have used OpenEssayist on his second assignment but could not find the link to the software.

Robert explained that he has different approaches to planning and writing depending on the length of the essay. For short essays, he just starts writing and applies a structure later. For longer essays, he creates a structure first and then 'populates'. His activities prior to planning and writing include reading the task and taking notes based on what is required. He said he writes 'many, many drafts'.

Robert does not use other people as sources of support, unless it is for proofreading. His described his approach for using feedback from the tutor to enhance his performance as threefold: (1) analyzing feedback by going through the comments, (2) understanding what they are saying and where they are coming from, and (3) trying to adapt what he has written to compensate for that. A lot of the feedback that Robert receives deals with organization or phrasing of ideas. He was able to describe an example of when he used feedback to improve his performance on a previous assignment, by including more theoretical discussion.

Although he didn't use the prototype, he could see how such a system 'would be very useful.' He thought that students with learning disabilities would benefit from using such a system, such as students with dyslexia, as well as students who are not as confident writing essays. As a learning tool, he perceived OpenEssayist as one that could help a user focus on 'what bits might be important', like 'structure or synthesis'.

Robert confessed that he still 'struggles' with word choice, not always knowing whether he is choosing words that are too colloquial or too academic. He also 'struggles' with structure—'knowing how much to talk about, how much needs actioning'. While it did not seem relevant for Robert to use the prototype to support his own essay-writing, through conversation with him, it seemed that he was rethinking whether such a tool would be useful to him in the future.

6.3 Karina's Story: "Worrisome, Confusing and Fascinating: This System Is for the Younger Generation, Not for Mature Learners"

Karina took early retirement after a 'career in technology'. She had earned a Bachelor of Education and a Bachelor of Science when she was younger, but during retirement decided to enroll on the Master in Online and Distance Education. Even though she is a 'technologist at heart', she was always interested in teaching and mentoring throughout her career. According to university records, Karina was a White woman in her early-fifties. She already held a higher education qualification and was enrolled in the present module for personal development reasons.

Karina admitted that she had really struggled with essay-writing during her higher education experience. The word count was always perceived as a constraint because she naturally had 'way too much to say'. In her professional life, this had not been a problem because she just wrote to whatever length she needed to put her point across, and then attached an executive summary. 'I always found that writing the essay was the hardest thing.'

Karina's approach to essay-writing never felt methodical enough to her, and this used to frustrate her. She continued to feel that she 'ought to be better organized in gathering the scenes and the supporting evidence, but it never seemed to work out that way.' She explained that her pre-writing tasks include: understanding the theory, understanding what points she needed to make, understanding what academic material she needed to include to answer the question, structuring her thoughts around what approach she was going to take to answer the question, and trying to give some structure to the essay-writing process (the last which, she described as a 'challenge'). Her process used to be to write a very long draft, usually spending a lot of time on the first two sections and then less time on the final section. She usually realized that she could have rewritten her first draft again.

Despite feeling that essay-writing was a challenging activity and that she lacked a rigorous method, Karina admitted that she feels fairly confident about writing essays despite experiencing 'the real bad patch about two and a half weeks in'. She starts preparing and writing early. Her career has helped her become accustomed to working to deadlines and just 'getting it done'.

Karina shared that she perceives online learners to be disadvantaged because they do not have opportunities to talk to their peers about how they are going to approach their essays. As an online learner, she found it strange how little dialogue there was around essay-writing. She said she was never told *not* to share this sort of information but rather she believes she was not allowed to do so because of the discourse around plagiarism 'that features so heavily in everything'. Karina suggested that one way to offer peer support around essay-writing could be to talk about essay structures and the use of word count. This would not give away the actual essay, she explained, rather it would offer students the chance to talk about how the essay could be approached.

Karina's first thoughts about OpenEssayist were of fascination and intrigue. She said that, as a technologist, she was interested in a tool that could deal with a variety of written essays. She felt surprised to learn that it was designed to deal specifically with each assignment, rather than as a general tool. She was not sure whether this perception was correct or not. After using the tool, she could see the potential of the system based on what 'was being got at' but she was not sure that she was able to use it in the right way. She questioned whether her use of headings and formatting meant that the system could not recognize new sections or that it could not recognize that her essay was covering a particular point.

Reflecting on her experiences with OpenEssayist, she struggled to understand why, in the places where she was making 10 or 15 points, the system only picked up on her making two or three points. She again questioned whether this was due to the structure she imposed through stylized formatting. This mismatch between what she had understood her essay to achieve and what the system said her essay was achieving caused her to feel worried.

> I think I thought I wasn't answering the question (laughter), so so you
> know it slightly threw me off track and then I made my way back so it
> was a bit of a prompt to make sure that I went back and said 'well am I
> making some faults here?', umm as it was a bit of a checkpoint for me,
> but I ended up worrying that the tool was right and I was wrong.

Karina saw that the system could help students reflect on their essay by encouraging them to think about the essay in terms of the system's output.

> the messages you were trying to put through, you know the weight of the
> argument, the percentage of the introduction, conclusion, so yes, yes I do
> because those are important features as well as what you write in, how you
> write it and how you structure it.

Karina said she was used to incorporating feedback into her further work; doing so was important in her career (in building and designing systems). So, she felt okay about incorporating feedback from her tutor. 'It is sort of part and parcel of the way I work, really.'

Karina suggested that a built-in narrative or preface to using OpenEssayist, would have helped her understand it better.

> I think I would have liked, umm and I think this is true of any technolo-
> gy, is someone to talk me through it, so although it was very easy to use,
> it wasn't easy to understand, if that makes sense?

She thought that this narrative would be best delivered as a tutorial prior to using the tool. Karina reflected on a previous experience of having an hour-long tutorial from a tutor for using an accessibility tool. She remembered that the tutorial 'sort of transformed understanding'.

When asked to comment on what type of learner would be the target audience for OpenEssayist, Karina believed that a traditional-aged student would be best equipped to benefit from this tool. She stated that 'younger graduates are quite a lot much more able [sic] to deal with these tools and so on.'

Like Maria, Karina believed that the functionality of OpenEssayist could be enhanced if it advised students on word choice, as a thesaurus might: 'so here are the alternative words that you could use'. Karina also thought that the system could encourage students' reflection by offering examples, such as an exemplar introduction or conclusion. She felt that she struggles (sometimes) because she has only ever seen her own essays. She suggested that these examples could be specific to the module or general. One idea of Karina's was to have examples of excellent essays that students can input into OpenEssayist and examine the results. The exercise then becomes understanding what output looks like from a good piece of writing.

7   Findings

7.1   Usefulness

Of the three stories, Maria's was the most positive in terms of what the system could already do. She could see the potential of various views to prompt a user to think about their essay structure and the variety of words they had used in their writing. On the other hand, Karina's experience of using OpenEssayist was frustrating and confusing. As a technologist, Karina brought certain expectations of what the system was going to do. When these hopes were not met, this caused disappointment. When the output from the system caused her to doubt its ability to pick up on her key points, she was left feeling puzzled at the root cause, rather than enabled by the system. Despite these worries, Karina was still able to see the possibilities of the system for supporting developing writers. Indeed, it was the participants' ability to look past the system's current functionality that illuminated its potential.

7.2   Potential for Adding Value

All of the participants were able to talk about the potential of OpenEssayist to add value to their essay-writing experience. There were two main themes—structure and word choice—that emerged from each of these narratives. Maria, in particular, was interested in how the system could enhance the essay-planning process. Both Robert and Karina saw this possibility too. All of them, in some way, mentioned that word choice was an issue for students as they write essays. Not only finding the right words to use but also finding a variety of words to use, is an area where they believed students struggle. A built-in thesaurus and mechanism for suggesting alternative words seemed to be a priority that they perceived OpenEssayist could address, with further development of the system.

The notion of peer support emerged as a theme, with Maria and Karina both wondering how or if students could share their ideas for essay-writing. Clear ideas for how OpenEssayist may be able to support this process were not explicated. However, they all saw the potential for peer support to benefit students, particularly distance learners. Karina's suggestion that the system have a built-in narrative to support learners in understanding the various functions and outputs is one way to enhance the value that OpenEssayist may offer students.

7.3   Target User

Interestingly the findings of the case study indicated that, although these three users could talk about how this system might help students, none of them perceived the system as being targeted at them. Generally speaking, there was a sense of 'it's nice—but it's not for me'. Maria and Karina, who actually used the system, agreed that the current prototype would not be appropriate for new students, nor for students who are new to ICTs. It was also suggested, by Karina, that such a tool would be more appropriate to younger learners, implying that mature learners would struggle with OpenEssayist. Robert, who did not use the prototype, perceived the system to be more suitable for students who are less confident. Using these parameters, it would seem that this system is most suitable for a traditional-aged university student in Year 2 or 3 of undergraduate study, who does not feel sure about his or her skills at essay-writing.

8   Discussion

These three stories offer insight into how students might perceive the usefulness, potential and intended audience of OpenEssayist. The current version of the system is somewhat useful in that participants, like Maria, can see the benefit of certain outputs, or views. These three students had several ideas for making the system more helpful, by using it to assist students with essay planning, word choice and by fostering peer support.

When considered alongside other themes in their stories, it seems that what these learners really want is for the processes of essay-writing to be more explicit. Maria prioritizes the planning stages of writing and wants clearer support with essay structure. Robert uses different strategies for approaching his writing but admitted that he struggles with structuring his writing and in choosing the right words. Karina called for a richer, more open discourse around essay-writing in general.

In contemplating the next phase of development, it is germane to question where a system like OpenEssayist fits among systems such as EssayAssist, W-Pal and other AWEs. Perhaps part of the answer will be: *OpenEssayist is unique because it makes the essay-writing process obvious.* Reflecting on earlier research, it is clear that Maria, Robert and Karina followed processes of essay-writing that were already proposed in Figure 1. Maria's approach to note-taking and drafting showed that she employed "conversion strategies" from the outset. Robert's approach included preparing a lot of drafts. Karina, despite her admission that she needed a more rigorous method, actually employed a series of strategies to move her through the process. All of them were able to talk about specific examples of how they used feedback to improve their performance on future pieces of writing.

Moving forward, there is scope for OpenEssayist to be more influential in providing automated assessment *for* learning. Drawing on Karina's suggestion, perhaps, this will be possible by creating a narrative about essay-writing around the system that encourages users to reflect and build on their own processes. In this way, the future of OpenEssayist may still involve scaffolding and skill development, while at the same time will prompt a metacognitive *understanding* of the development of one's approaches and strategies.

9   Moving Forward

Further evaluation studies are running with postgraduate students studying at the Open University, the University of Hertfordshire and the British University in Dubai. One of the interesting challenges that is being pursued by the team is the role of creating meaningful visualizations that promote "Advice for Action" [4].

Visualizations can promote thinking by helping individuals identify patterns in a set of data, and to promote the discovery of emergent properties that could not have been originally predicted. This is key to the team's current empirical investigations where they are seeking to identify and refine a set of visualizations for the OpenEssayist system [12].

Another issue that needs attention is whether the user requires training in order to interpret pictures. Although it has been argued that people can interpret pictures without training, the question is still open. In this respect, it is important for the team to understand how diagrams are able to represent concepts unambiguously. The case studies presented in this paper suggest that the visualizations need to emphasize the personalization of the analysis.

Enabling higher education students to receive timely advice about their draft attempts at essay-writing can provide insights into the generic skills of essay writing. This type of feedback also opens to the possibility of not only self-reflection but also engaging in a productive discourse with peers and/or a tutor.

Acknowledgements. The SAFeSEA project team is particularly grateful to The Open University students who participated in this study and the Module Team on the MA in Open and Distance Education for endorsing the study. This work was supported by the Engineering and Physical Sciences Research Council (grant numbers EP/J005959/1 and EP/J005231/1).

References

1. Van Labeke, N., Whitelock, D., Field, D., Pulman, S., Richardson, J.T.E.: OpenEssayist: extractive summarisation and formative assessment of free-text essays. In: Proceedings of the 1st International Workshop on Discourse-Centric Learning Analytics, Leuven, Belgium (April 2013a)
2. Van Labeke, N., Whitelock, D., Field, D., Pulman, S., Richardson, J.T.E.: What is my essay really saying? Using extractive summarization to motivate reflection and redrafting. In: Proceedings of the AIED Workshop on Formative Feedback in Interactive Learning Environments, Memphis, TN (July 2013b)
3. Bruning, R., Dempsey, M., Kauffman, D.F., McKim, C.: Examining dimensions of self-efficacy for writing. Journal of Educational Psychology 105(1), 25–38 (2013)
4. Whitelock, D.: Activating assessment for learning: Are we on the way with Web 2.0? In: Lee, M.J.W., McLoughlin, C. (eds.) Web 2.0-Based E-Learning: Applying Social Informatics for Tertiary Teaching, pp. 319–342. IGI Global, Hershey (2010)
5. Burstein, J.C., Chodorow, M., Leacock, C.: Criterion(SM) Online Essay Evaluation: An Application for Automated Evaluation of Student Essays. In: Proceedings of the Fifteenth Conference on Innovative Applications of Artificial Intelligence, Acapulco, Mexico, pp. 3–10 (2003)
6. Rudner, L.M., Garcia, V., Welch, C.: An Evaluation of IntelliMetricTM Essay Scoring System. The Journal of Technology, Learning and Assessment 4(4) (2006)
7. Landauer, T.K., Laham, D., Foltz, P.: Automatic Essay Assessment. Assessment in Education: Principles, Policy & Practice 10(3), 295–308 (2003)
8. Alden, B., Van Labeke, N., Whitelock, D., Richardson, J.T.E., Pulman, S., Field, D.: Using student experience as a model for designing an automatic feedback system for short essays. International Journal of E-Assessment (in press)

9. Chandrasegaran, A., Ellis, M., Poedjosoedarmo, G.: Essay Assist—Developing software for writing skills improvement in partnership with students. Regional Language Centre Journal 36(2), 137–155 (2005)

10. Roscoe, R.D., Varner, L.K., Weston, J.L., Crossley, S.A., McNamara, D.S.: The Writing Pal Intelligent Tutoring System: Usability Testing and Development. Computers and Composition (in press), `http://129.219.222.66/pdf/Roscoe2012WritingPalTutor.pdf` (accessed April 14, 2013)

11. Bryman, A.: Social Research Methods, 2nd edn. Oxford University Press, Oxford (2004)

12. Whitelock, D., Field, D., Pulman, S., Richardson, J.T.E., van Labeke, N.: Designing and testing visual representations of draft essays for higher education students. Paper Presented at the Discourse-Centric Learning Analytics (DCLA) Workshop, LAK 14 (March 2014)

Implementation of an Adaptive Training and Tracking Game in Statistics Teaching

Caspar M. Groeneveld

Department of Psychology, University of Amsterdam,
Weesperplein 4, 1018 XA Amsterdam, The Netherlands
cg@dds.nl

Abstract. Statistics teaching in higher education has a number of challenges. An adaptive training, tracking and teaching tool in a gaming environment aims to address problems inherent in statistics teaching. This paper discusses the implementation of this tool in a large first year university programme and considers its uses and effects. It finds that such a tool has students practice with statistics problems frequently and that success rate of the statistics course may increase.

Keywords: adaptive testing, computer adaptive testing, CAT, digital testing, formative testing, statistics teaching, serious gaming, game based learning, learning analytics.

1   Introduction

Statistics teaching in higher education has a number of challenges specific to the field. Students learn best at their own level, dealing with problems that are neither too easy for them, nor above their current skill level (Glynn, Aultman & Owens, 2005; Zimmerman, 2000). Further, students learn best by practicing, with a range of problem types and a variety of contexts (Garfield, 1995). Also, retrieval and reconstructing previously learned knowledge may enhance learning more than studying (Karpicke & Blunt, 2011). These notions run, however, contrary to how statistics is often taught in university courses in the social sciences.

Statistics courses must treat certain subjects and certain problems according to a predictable time schedule and in a specific order. In a course setting, only specific problems are presented in a given week, which makes problems during practice either predictable and creates a false sense of mastery in some students, or will discourage and lose students who have fallen too far behind. Also, students in social sciences generally do not choose their programme for its statistical components and often think of statistics as a necessary evil. Finally, students often consider performance on math and statistics as talents, in which some, gifted students happen to succeed and others are doomed to struggle or fail. Even if an innate talent contributes to success, treating math performance as the result of a malleable skill rather than a fixed talent yields better results (Dweck, 2008; Blackwell, Trzesniewski & Dweck, 2007). This short paper examines the implementation of the Statistiekfabriek, an adaptive training and

M. Kalz and E. Ras (Eds.): CAA 2014, CCIS 439, pp. 53–58, 2014.
© Springer International Publishing Switzerland 2014

tracking system intended to confront these problems, in a large first year university course.

This short paper is accompanied by a demo paper, also submitted for the CAA conference 2014: "Statistiekfabriek: An Adaptive Training and Tracking Game in Statistics Teaching in Practice".

2   An Adaptive Training and Tracking Game

The Statistiekfabriek, or Stats Plant, was delivered in 2013 to address these problems. The Statistiekfabriek was developed with a Surf grant within its Testing and Test-Driven Learning (TTL[1]) programme by the University of Amsterdam, the University Medical Centre Utrecht and the University of Twente, together with Oefenweb.nl, a spin-off company from the University of Amsterdam and a private partner within the project. Built on the same principles as Rekentuin, or Math Garden (Klinkenberg, Straatemeier & Van der Maas, 2011), the Statistiekfabriek offers statistics problems in an adaptive game setting. Students have, regardless their ability level, a 75% chance of correctly solving a problem, which is motivating and stimulating since students always work at their own level. Students receive questions from previous material and later material as well, as items on different topics can have the same difficulty. This means that students may have to retrieve knowledge from previous periods and that they can be confronted with subjects that have not yet been discussed.

The Statistiekfabriek determines difficulty of items in its database automatically through a unique approach inspired by the Elo-algorithm: both items and students are considered players, with students gaining a bit in rating when 'beating' an item with a higher difficulty and the item losing a bit in rating, and vice versa. Within the algorithm, both accuracy and speed of the student's response are taken into account: a faster response leads to a larger change in the student's rating. While the algorithm requires large numbers of students and items to work effectively, it allows for a completely self-organizing adaptive item bank. The system's scoring rule is also known as the high speed, high stakes scoring rule (Dutilh et al., 2011; Klinkenberg, Straatemeier & Van der Maas, 2011).

The algorithm can work with a set of items and students of which there is no information. All would start with a rating of zero. Playing will then quickly affect the rating of both players and items positively or negatively on a continuous scale. Students and teachers are presented with transformed ratings on a 0 to 10 scale, where 0 for a student means that she will answer no item correctly, and 0 for an item means that all students will answer the item correctly, and 10 the opposite. In practice, items in the system are given a start rating: a manual estimation of difficulty by experts, which allows them to converge to their actual rating faster. Similarly, students in higher years do not start at 0, but are given the average rating of the lowest percentile of their cohort as a start rating, again to allow them to reach their skill rating faster.

---

[1] http://www.surf.nl/en/themes/learning-and-testing/
digital-testing/testing-and-test-driven-learning-
programme/index.html

The Statistiekfabriek provides a gaming environment, which is intended to offer extra motivation to practice. Practice time, accuracy and speed of response in the Statistiekfabriek are operationalised through coins, which students can spend in the factory. The limited time for each problem is represented by a number of coins decreasing per second and shown on screen. Students win the remaining seconds of the time they have for a question in coins if they answer correctly, but lose this amount of coins if they give an incorrect answer. Thus, since there is a 75% chance of being correct, the amount of coins will represent the amount of time practiced. Finally, students can see their own development in rating, or skill level, and their frequency of practice (Fig. 1), where the vertical bars are the playing frequency per week, and the line is their progress in rating, and students can compare their own skill level with that of students in the same academic year as they are and see in which percentile they are in the three domains of the program (Fig. 2). Students find which topics proved most challenging for them in their report page, and can link from these topics to elaborate examples provided by Khan Academy.

Besides providing feedback to students on their skill level and problem areas, teachers can access students' information as well and determine which topics are problematic, and subsequently attend to students who have fallen behind, address problematic topics in class or lectures, or adjust their instruction to the student.

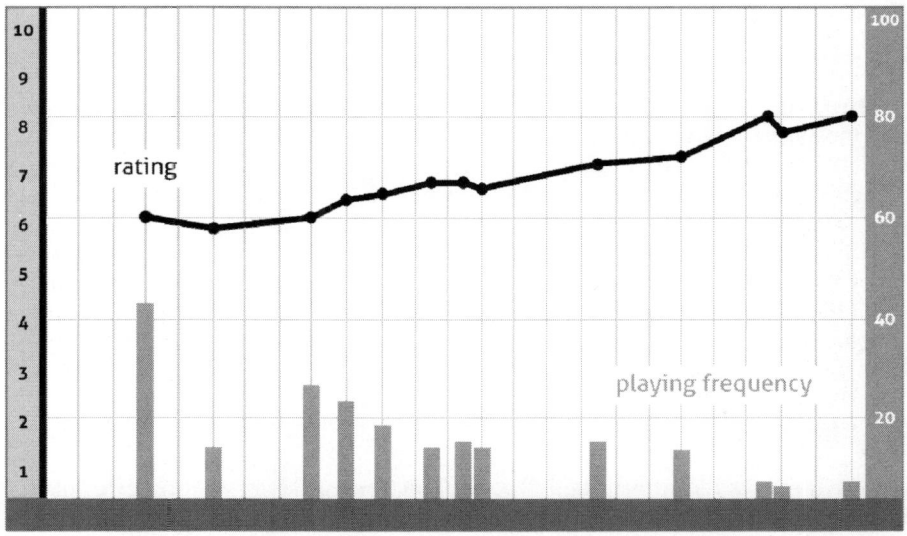

Fig. 1. Playing frequency and rating development over time

Domain Scores

Domain	Absolute rating	Relative rating within group	Last played	Problems solved
Descriptive Statistics	3.72	100 % (very good)	16 days ago	161
Probability	5.29	92 % (very good)	144 days ago	147
Inferential Statistics	2.03	73 % (average)	51 days ago	98

Fig. 2. Student's absolute and relative ratings in three domains

3   Implementation

There are different ways of implementing formative systems. In an ideal world, students are autonomous, intrinsically motivated adults with sufficient self-efficacy. In our experience, first year university students in a large non-selective social sciences programme, such as Psychology, hardly use formative systems at all when they are not either accompanied by incentives or made obligatory and strongly embedded in the curriculum.

In this setting, Statistiekfabriek was offered to all students in the first year statistics course at the University of Amsterdam. A bonus point, constituting roughly 10% of the final mark, was awarded to all students at the beginning of the course. This bonus point would decrease by a seventh every week, during the seven week course, that students would not earn the minimum number of coins. The choice to award a bonus point and have it disappear if students would not play was made to appeal to students' sense of loss aversion. Students are rewarded for the number of coins earned, rather than their skill level, which rewards effort rather than their ability, as students need to solve similar numbers of problems to get a certain amount of coins, regardless of their skill levels. In other words, students are rewarded for the process and for practice, not for the outcome.

3.1   Usage and Evaluation

Students widely used the system: 89% of the 496 students who made the exam also used the system. At the same time, the majority of students appeared to play for the minimum amount of coins required to keep their bonus point. This may well be an unintended consequence of providing an incentive: by rewarding them with a bonus point, students receive an external motivator.

At the evaluation students indicated that the system was intuitive and easy to use. This was confirmed by teachers, who reported no or hardly extra work after implementation. Students reported they would like for all problems to have solutions, though they do understand that the system does not provide these since they are presented with a rapid series of problems.

3.2   Effects

Two clear effects were found in this population. First, students' frequency of playing (coins) and students' rating in the Statistiekfabriek correlate significantly with the final mark at the exam (r=.31 for playing frequency and r=.39 for rating), though a regression analysis with frequency and student ratings as independent variables shows only an effect for student ratings on the final mark. Also, in the year the Statistiekfabriek was implemented, success rate of the course increased. Success rates, or the percentage of students passing the first year courses, were considered for three consecutive years (Fig. 3). While the statistics course, Research methods & Statistics, had the lowest or second lowest success rate in the two years prior to the implementation of the Statistiekfabriek, success rate was highest of all six first year courses in the year of implementation, 2012-2013.

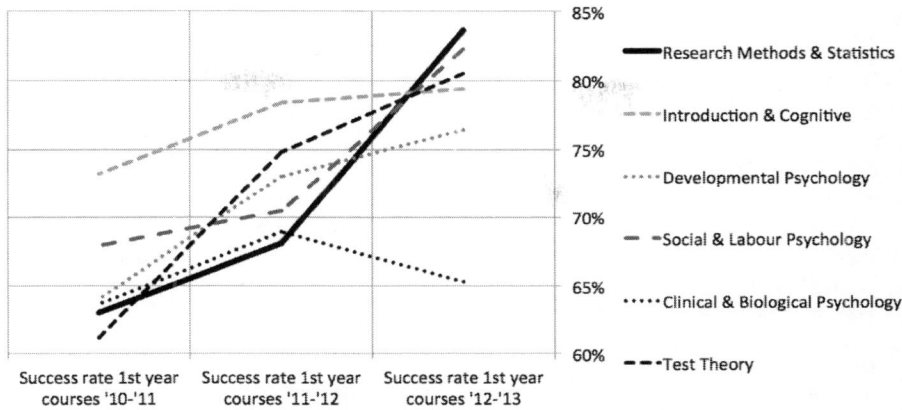

Fig. 3. Success rates of all 1st year Psychology courses over three years

4   Conclusion and Discussion

The implementation of the Statistiekfabriek has strengthened our belief that an adaptive gaming, training and tracking environment can be effectively used in higher education for statistics teaching. Students clearly appreciate the system, though teachers will have to clarify and manage expectations that an adaptive system like the Statistiekfabriek does not primarily serve as exam training. Instead, it helps students over their entire academic career to recognize and solve all types of statistical problems they may encounter in their later occupation. In that sense, the Statistiekfabriek may help create better statisticians rather than help teach to the test. Further, though we have found both correlations in students' skill levels, their playing frequency and the final mark, and found an impressive increase in success rate, we should be wary of drawing strong conclusions. First, in a regression analysis with frequency and ratings as independent variables and the final mark as a dependent variable, only rating proved predictive of the final mark. However, most students solved only the required number of problems, leading to a ceiling effect where low variance in the number of problems solved will not contribute much to the variance of the final mark. Also, with systems like these there is a danger of mistaking a correlation for causality, since better, more motivated students can be more likely to use formative tests effectively and more likely to do well on the final exam. Second, the high success rate in the final exam is reassuring, but can hardly be considered evidence.

Finally, the implementation choice will affect usage. When students were given an incentive, they played massively but most only played the minimal amount of time required to keep their bonus point. In other, voluntary, implementations we have seen that only a third to a quarter of the students use the system, albeit more intensively. Since these students are likely to be the better students, and interventions such as these are aimed at average students, we would argue for having an incentive in the implementation. Using this approach we are confident that statistics in the social sciences can be more accessible to students of all levels.

References

1. Blackwell, L.S., Trzesniewski, K.H., Dweck, C.S.: Implicit Theories of Intelligence Predict Achievement Across an Adolescent Transition: A Longitudinal Study and an Intervention. Child Development 78(1), 246–263 (2007), doi:10.1111/j.1467-8624.2007.00995.x
2. Dutilh, G., Wagenmakers, E.-J., Visser, I., Van der Maas, H.L.J.: A Phase Transition Model for the Speed-Accuracy Trade-Off in Response Time Experiments. Cognitive Science 35(2), 211–250 (2011), doi:10.1111/j.1551-6709.2010.01147.x
3. Dweck, C.S.: Mindsets and Math/Science Achievement. Carnegie Corporation of New York, Institute for Advanced Study, Commission on Mathematics and Science Education, New York (2008), http://www.growthmindsetmaths.com/uploads/2/3/7/7/23776169/mindset_and_math_science_achievement_-_nov_2013.pdf (retrieved March 23, 2014)
4. Garfield, J.: How Students Learn Statistics. International Statistical Review 63(1), 25–34 (1995), doi:10.2307/1403775
5. Glynn, S.M., Aultman, L.P., Owens, A.M.: Motivation to Learn in General Education Programs. The Journal of General Education 52(2), 150–170 (2005), doi:10.1353/jge.2005.0021
6. Karpicke, J.D., Blunt, J.R.: Retrieval Practice Produces More Learning than Elaborative Studying with Concept Mapping. Science 331(6018), 772–775 (2011), doi:10.1126/science.1199327
7. Klinkenberg, S., Straatemeier, M., Van der Maas, H.L.J.: Computer Adaptive Practice of Maths Ability Using a New Item Response Model for on the Fly Ability and Difficulty Estimation. Computers and Education 58(2), 1813–1824 (2011), doi:10.1016/j.compedu.2011.02.003
8. Zimmerman, B.J.: Self-Efficacy: An Essential Motive to Learn. Contemporary Educational Psychology 25(1), 82–91 (2000), doi:10.1006/ceps.1999.1016

Assessment of Collaborative Problem Solving Using Linear Equations on a Tangible Tabletop

Valérie Maquil[1], Eric Tobias[1], Samuel Greiff[2], and Eric Ras[1]

[1] Public Research Centre Henri Tudor
av. J.F. Kennedy 29, L1855 Luxembourg-Kirchberg, Luxembourg
[2] University of Luxembourg
Coudenhoven Kalergi, L-1855 Luxembourg-Kirchberg, Luxembourg
{valerie.maquil,eric.tobias,eric.ras}@tudor.lu,
samuel.greiff@uni.lu

Abstract. Using Tangible User Interfaces (TUI) for assessing collaborative problems has only been marginally investigated in technology-based assessment. Our first empirical studies focused on light-weight performance measurements, usability, user experience, and gesture analysis to increase our understanding of how people interact with TUI in an assessment context. In this paper we propose a new approach for assessing individual skills for collaborative problem solving using the MicroDYN methodology with TUIs. These so-called MicroDYN items are high quality and designed to assess individual problem solving skills. The items are based on linear structural equations. We describe how this approach was applied to create an assessment item for a collaborative setting with children that implements a simplified model of climate change using the knowledge of the previous studies. Finally, we propose a series of research questions as well as a future empirical study.

Keywords: Tangible User Interfaces, linear structural equation, MicroDYN, collaborative problem solving, technology-based assessment.

1 Introduction

For the last few years, the term 21st Century skill has shown up in scientific literature, for instance in the latest reports on technology-based assessment [1] as well as in the Digital Agenda published by the European Commission [2]. These so-called 21st century skills refer to skills, such as, complex problem solving, creativity, critical thinking, learning to learn, decision making, etc. [3]. Several researchers have stated that the acquisition of these 21st Century skills and their development are only marginally investigated [4]. A particular 21st Century skill is complex problem solving which encompasses the ability to successfully deal with untransparent and dynamically changing problems. To this end, complex problem solving is considered key to success in life and was included as transversal domain in one of the most prestigious large-scale assessments worldwide, the Programme for International Student Assessment (PISA) in its 2012 cycle [1, 5].

M. Kalz and E. Ras (Eds.): CAA 2014, CCIS 439, pp. 59–66, 2014.
© Springer International Publishing Switzerland 2014

The fast development of new technologies for gathering data in real settings allows us to assess specific 21st Century skills such as complex problem solving. This is not possible by conventional paper-pencil tests or even by using desktop applications we know from computer-based assessment. More natural forms of interaction such as touch, speech, gestures, and handwriting support assessment researchers to explore new areas of skill assessment. Therefore, the availability of affordable devices motivated us to develop several so-called tangible user interfaces (TUI) for assessment. The use of TUI for assessment is new and therefore knowledge about how to design those systems and how to develop test items for TUI is very limited.

Section 2 summarises research on this research topic. Section 3 describes the overall research methodology and Section 4 elaborates how a test item related to climate change has been developed for the TUI to assess collaborative problem solving. Section 5 proposed the design of the upcoming empirical studies and concludes the paper.

2   Related Work

2.1   TUI-Based Assessment

To date, literature provides first exploratory results on the learning benefits of TUIs. In particular, the additional haptic dimension, the better accessibility (for instance for children), and the shared space that can be used in collaborative situations [6] are claimed to be beneficial in learning situations. According to Klemmer et al. [7], the physical objects and actions of TUIs allow using multiple senses of our human bodies and have an essential impact on our understanding of the world. They encourage rapid epistemic actions (i.e. try and error actions), thus lower cognitive load by simplifying thinking processes [8]. Learning and assessment can be supported by representing problems in a new way, using physical and digital elements. Further, the way the users are solving tasks can be detected and feedback can be directly given. Nevertheless, no TUI has been systematically used and evaluated in the context of technology-based assessment (TBA).

Ras et al. [9] have conducted a series of empirical studies in order to identify harmonies and tensions concerning the use of TUIs for assessing skills of complex and collaborative problem solving. Several items have been developed, two of which are depicted in Fig. 1: The aim of the matching item (left) was to assign the labels of the planets (put on small tangibles) to the images. The goal of the windmill item (right) was to explore the impact of different variables such as wind speed, number of blades, and height of the windmill on the energy produced by the windmill. The output changed real-time according to the manipulations of the input.

The results revealed that the shareability of the space, the non-responsive ("offline") spaces and the versatility of the physical objects are advantages of TUI used in collaborative problem solving. We also observed that users proceed by short experimental units to explore different setting of variables (see also Section 3). A more detailed description of the outcomes of these studies can be found in Ras et al. [9].

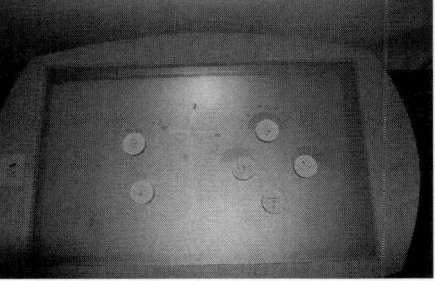

Fig. 1. Match item and simulation item

2.2   MicroDYN

This study is the first to suggest implementing MicroDYN items on a tangible table and to employ them in a group (i.e., a collaborative) setting. Up to now, MicroDYN items have only been used as a computer-based assessment approach towards assessing complex problem solving skills in individuals. In this, the problem solver has to detect the causal links between a set of connected variables and acquire knowledge about these links (dimension of _knowledge acquisition_; [10]) and, in a subsequent step, apply this knowledge (dimension of _knowledge application_, [11]). Several studies have shown the validity of MicroDYN with regard to the assessment of complex problem solving (e.g. [12]).

3   Research Methodology

In general our research has two aims: First, to better understand how users interact with a TUI in a collaborative assessment context and, hence, to better design TUI-based applications for assessment based on the well-established MicroDYN items; second, how, from a psychometric point of view, we can develop high quality test items in general (e.g. valid and reliable) for collaborative problem solving in a TUI setting.

A general principle for scenario selection is that we select a domain of practical relevance interesting for the public (see windmill example and climate change example in Section 4) and at the same time allows us to model the relation of domain variables with linear equations. All TUI-based items are developed to assess collaborative problem solving, meaning that 3 to 6 users interact with the system at a time. Each system provides a simulation environment where variables can be manipulated. Typically, users perform so-called experimental units separated by what researchers in decision making call landmarks.

The overall research methodology is iterative: develop new or improve existing test items followed by empirical studies. All studies gather data with a focus on assessment issues such as assessment performance or psychometric indicators (e.g., difficulty, discrimination index, etc.). Interaction studies coupled with usability and user experience evaluations provides insight into how best to design TUI. This design knowledge is documented in so-called design artefacts. They are derived from literature as well as from practical experience. They are an outcome of the design research methodology [13, 14] we follow.

Each empirical study features research questions and allows us to gather practical experience. Each study follows the same design: First, a debriefing questionnaire is used with a simple pre-test to assess available domain knowledge and digital literacy skills related to user interfaces; second, the users collaboratively interact with the tangible user interface (unlimited time); the users decide when they are ready to stop the exploration of the simulation environment. Performance of the MicroDYN items is assessed in conjunction with the test taking procedure. Finally, participants answer a post-test questionnaire about the simulation environment.

Data gathering is done by video recording of the assessment sessions, logging interactions with the TUI applications (e.g. moves and rotation of tangibles) as well as questionnaires (either paper-based, or using multiple-choice items on the TUI).

4   A Tangible Climate Simulator

4.1   Climate Change as a Complex Problem

Today, scientists agree that the Earth's climate system is warming up and that a significant cause of the change is due to human activities [15]. This is often referred to as *Global Warming*. Global Warming is mainly evidenced by increases in global average air and ocean temperatures resulting in the widespread melting of snow and ice leading to rising global average sea level. The main reason of this warming is caused by increases in concentrations of greenhouse gases, to which the largest contributor is carbon dioxide (CO_2). Certain waste management and agricultural practices aggravate the problem by releasing chemical compounds such as methane and nitrous oxide, which further fuel the warming, trapping ever more heat in the atmosphere.

To allow children to understand the relations between the different variables, as well as to follow the MicroDYN methodology of Greiff et al. [12], a simplified model of climate change was defined. The model's principle is as follows:

- At start-up, the system shows the total amount of CO_2 as emitted today. To simplify the system, it assumes that this prediction is the average across all variables presented to the children. Hence, if the children always choose the average across all variables, the amount of emitted CO_2 will neither improve nor worsen. The variables allow exploring what would happen if we change the CO_2 output of a very specific aspect (e.g. meat consummation). By choosing a value diverging from the average, the output is changed.
- The system shows the effect on the different outputs as given by the system of linear equations.

4.2   Collaborative Widgets for Manipulating Variables

To allow for a maximum of simultaneous accessibility and shareability of controls we designed a collaborative widget which reacts to rotational input. Questions are visualised as different widgets are placed on the interface. For every question, three widgets, corresponding to the respective answers, are provided. The children can manipulate the widgets to provide their inputs on each answer, setting how the group is divided between choices. This allows defining the distribution of the group which can then be translated to the world population.

For each parameter, the system provides feedback related to the parameter value, i.e. the percentage related to its maximum value. Further it calculates the output of the total amount of CO_2 emissions as defined by all widgets triplets.

The widgets can be used in two ways. At the beginning, they are set to a zero value. Children change the value while answering the different questions. The system calculates the CO_2 output and the impact on global temperature in real time as answers are provided. This is the AS-IS situation. Children can explore WHAT-IF scenarios, that is, they can change the value of variables, changing the distribution of the population and influence the CO_2 output.

This approach incites that all children actively participate in setting the values and, in the second phase, allows them to collaborate in small groups to simultaneously manipulate the widgets. Exploring different scenarios will allow children to identify what behaviour has the most impact on CO_2 output as well as identify where they and their parents can have the most impact by identifying what behaviour they are most willing to change if any.

4.3   System Architecture and Design

The system features two main components: the TUI library that allows defining and instantiate all kind of tangibles; and a library that allows for defining complex problems. The TUI library is used to define all feedback and interactive tangibles as shown in Figure 2 provided to the children.

We use the complex problem solving library to instantiate a system of linear equations, one for each question, nested in a very simple linear equation as follows:

$$
\begin{aligned}
Q_1(t+1) &= w_{X_1} * X_1(t) + w_{Y_1} * Y_1(t) + w_{Z_1} * Z_1(t) \\
Q_2(t+1) &= w_{X_2} * X_2(t) + w_{Y_2} * Y_2(t) + w_{Z_2} * Z_2(t) \\
&\vdots \qquad\qquad \vdots \qquad\qquad \vdots \qquad\qquad \vdots \\
Q_n(t+1) &= w_{X_n} * X_n(t) + w_{Y_n} * Y_n(t) + w_{Z_n} * Z_n(t)
\end{aligned}
\tag{1}
$$

$$
CO_2(t+1) = w_{Q_1} * Q_1(t+1) + w_{Q_2} * Q_2(t+1) + \cdots \ w_{Q_n} * Q_n(t+1) \tag{2}
$$

With Q, the question dependent output, t the discrete time steps, w_i the weight of variable i such that $w_i > 0$, and X_i, Y_i, Z_i the input variables for a question i.

This setup allows us to weigh each variable according to their impact on the CO_2 output. While these are all approximations, we believe they are necessary to provide children with interesting questions they can answer based on their experience and their environment and see the effect of their actions even if it would normally be too small to see in a more sophisticated and real life simulation.

4.4   Cycle of Use

The cycle of learning and assessment includes several steps. In a first step, children will be asked to answer questions defined by the widgets lying next to the interactive surface. Each question requires the children to think about their daily life, in particular the kind of food they are eating, or the way they travel. The table then provides immediate feedback about the CO_2 emissions they are creating. In a second step, children can modify the different parameters of the model, in order to explore and understand how they relate to each other. Finally, children will be asked to solve the actual task, i.e. to minimize the CO_2 emissions of the group by modifying only one parameter per person.

The performance of the children will be assessed using a questionnaire on the gained understanding about the relations between the different parameters. Further, the last step of the problem solving activity will be recorded in order to assess the solving strategy of the group.

5   Future Work

The future work defines research questions that will be answered by data gathered from 20 groups of children aged 8 to 10. They will explore and solve the presented issues of climate change on the table. Audio and video logs will be recorded of the sessions and children will be asked to provide information for a questionnaire to measure their gain in understanding on climate change. This future research is motivated by five research questions:

- RQ1: From the perspective of embodied interaction, how do the participants proceed to solve a complex problem? Can solving patterns be described by means of experimental units?
- RQ2: What are the characteristics of an experimental unit? Can experimental units be classified in different categories? How can an experimental unit be defined?
- RQ3: Is there a correlation between the amount and type of experimental units a participant is actively involved, and his/her gained understanding?
- RQ4: How does the mode of delivery (i.e., the tangible interface) change the nature of the test taking process?
- RQ5: How is individual complex problem solving behaviour related to behaviour within the collaborative setting implemented on the tangible interface?

To answer RQ1, the video material will be analysed using the CLM framework [16]. Collaborative learning mechanisms (i.e. making and accepting suggestions, negotiating, joint attention and awareness, and narrations) will be identified and chronologically arranged to describe the solving process. Key scenes will be described in detail using transcripts and screenshots.

To answer RQ2, the experimental units, as extracted from RQ1 will be analysed with a focus on the duration, the use of space (online/offline), formal aspects of speech, gestures, and physical manipulations. This will allow us to propose a first definition and set of categories of experimental units.

For evaluating RQ3, the solving sessions will be segmented and classified based on the definition and categories of RQ2. The amount and type of experimental units per participant will be isolated and compared to their gain in understanding.

Finally, to answer RQ4 and RQ5 the collected data will be compared to data previously collected in experiments with MicroDYN (i.e., individual data) and we will engage into in-depth analyses of the underlying processes both in the individual and the collaborative setting.

By answering the research questions, our research will provide a deeper understanding on how TUIs can serve as tool for assessing 21st Century skills that are inherently hard to assess using traditional approaches. In addition, in inquiry-based learning scenarios simulation play a major role [17]. Outcomes from this research domain can be used to understand the experimentation process in a simulation environment or, for example, to prevent students from 'gaming' the TUI system. In collaborative testing, factors, such as decreased anxiety, good discussions, supported cognitive processes (e.g. retrieving information, thinking through the information better, etc.) have led to a higher test performance [18]. Such indicators will be also of interest in a TUI context in the future.

While preliminary tests are promising, the research data might open up a new venue for future assessment requirements.

References

1. OECD: Better skills, better jobs, better lives. A strategic approach to skills policies. OECD Publishing, Paris (2012)
2. Ferrari, A.: Digital Competence in Practice. JRC Technical Reports. European Commission, Joint Research Centre, Institute for Prospective Technological Studies Seville (2012)
3. Binkley, M., Erstad, O., Herman, J., Raizen, S., Ripley, M., Miller-Ricci, M., Rumble, M.: Defining Twenty-First Century Skills. In: Griffin, P., McGaw, B., Care, E. (eds.) Assessment and Teaching of 21st Century Skills, pp. 17–66. Springer, Dordrecht (2012)
4. Bennett, R.E., Gitomer, D.H.: Transforming K-12 assessment. In: Wyatt-Smith, C., Cumming, J. (eds.) Assessment Issues of the 21st Century. Springer Publishing Company, New York (2009)
5. OECD: PISA 2012 assessment and analytical framework mathematics, reading, science, problem solving and financial literacy. OECD Publishing, Paris (2013)
6. Marshall, P.: Do tangible interfaces enhance learning? In: Proceedings of the 1st International Conference on Tangible and Embedded Interaction, pp. 163–170. ACM, Baton Rouge (2007)
7. Klemmer, S.R., Hartmann, B., Takayama, L.: How bodies matter: five themes for interaction design. In: 6th Conference on Designing Interactive Systems (DIS 2006), pp. 140–149. ACM, University Park (2006)
8. Esteves, A., Van den Hoven, E., Oakley, I.: Physical games or digital games?: Comparing support for mental projection in tangible and virtual representations of a problem-solving task. In: 7th International Conference on Tangible, Embedded and Embodied Interaction, Barcelona, Spain (2013)
9. Ras, E., Maquil, V., Foulonneau, M., Latour, T.: Empirical Studies on a Tangible User Interface for Technology-based Assessment - Insights and Emerging Challenges. International Journal of e-Assessment (IJEA), CAA 2012 Issue: Pedagogy and Technology: Harmony and Tensions 3 (2013)
10. Mayer, R.E., Wittrock, M.C.: Problem Solving. In: Alexander, P.A., Winne, P.H. (eds.) Handbook of Educational Psychology, pp. 287–303. Lawrence Erlbaum, New York (2006)

11. Novick, L.R., Bassok, M.: Problem solving. In: Holyoak, K.J., Morrison, R.G. (eds.) The Cambridge Handbook of Thinking and Reasoning, pp. 321–349. University Press, Cambridge (2005)
12. Greiff, S., Wüstenberg, S., Molnar, G., Fischer, A., Funke, J., Csapo, B.: Complex Problem Solving in educational settings – something beyond g: Concept, assessment, measurement invariance, and construct validity. Journal of Educational Psychology 105, 364–379 (2013)
13. March, S.T., Smith, G.F.: Design and natural science research on information technology. Decision Support Systems 15, 251–266 (1995)
14. Hevner, A.R., March, S.T., Park, J., Ram, S.: Design science in information systems research. MIS Quarterly 28, 75–105 (2004)
15. IPCC Working Group I: Climate Change 2013: The Physical Science Basis (2013)
16. Fleck, R., Rogers, Y., Yuill, N., Marshall, P., Carr, A., Rick, J., Bonnett, V.: Actions speak loudly with words: unpacking collaboration around the table. In: ACM International Conference on Interactive Tabletops and Surfaces, pp. 189–196. ACM, Banff (2009)
17. Van Joolingen, W.R., De Jong, T., Dimitrakopoulou, A.: Issues in computer supported inquiry learning in science. Journal of Computer Assisted Learning 23 (2007)
18. Kapitanoff, S.H.: Collaborative testing: Cognitive and interpersonal processes related to the enhanced test performance. Active Learning in Higher Education 10 (2009)

Computer Assisted, Formative Assessment and Dispositional Learning Analytics in Learning Mathematics and Statistics

Dirk T. Tempelaar[1], Bart Rienties[2], and Bas Giesbers[3]

[1] School of Business and Economics, Maastricht University, The Netherlands
D.Tempelaar@MaastrichtUniversity.nl
[2] Open University UK, Institute of Educational Technology, Milton Keynes, UK
Bart.Rienties@open.ac.uk
[3] Rotterdam School of Management, Erasmus Universiteit, Rotterdam, The Netherlands
BGiesbers@rsm.nl

Abstract. Learning analytics seeks to enhance the learning process through systematic measurements of learning related data and to provide informative feedback to learners and teachers, so as to support the regulation of the learning. Track data from technology enhanced learning systems constitute the main data source for learning analytics. This empirical contribution provides an application of Buckingham Shum and Deakin Crick's theoretical framework of dispositional learning analytics [1]: an infrastructure that combines learning dispositions data with data extracted from computer assisted, formative assessments. In a large introductory quantitative methods module based on the principles of blended learning, combining face-to-face problem-based learning sessions with e-tutorials, we investigate the predictive power of learning dispositions, outcomes of continuous formative assessments and other system generated data in modeling student performance and their potential to generate informative feedback. Using a dynamic, longitudinal perspective, Computer Assisted Formative Assessments seem to be the best predictor for detecting underperforming students and academic performance, while basic LMS data did not substantially predict learning.

Keywords: blended learning, computer assisted assessment, dispositional learning analytics, e-tutorials, formative assessment, learning dispositions, student profiles.

1 Introduction

Many learning analytics (LA) applications use data generated by learner activities, such as learner participation in discussion forums, wikis or (continuous) computer assisted formative assessments. This user behavior data is frequently supplemented with background data retrieved from learning management systems (LMS) and other student admission systems, as for example accounts of prior education. In their theoretical contribution to LAK2012 [1] (see also the 2013 LASI Workshop [2]), Buckingham Shum and Deakin Crick propose a dispositional LA infrastructure that

M. Kalz and E. Ras (Eds.): CAA 2014, CCIS 439, pp. 67–78, 2014.
© Springer International Publishing Switzerland 2014

combines learning activity generated data with learning dispositions, values and attitudes measured through self-report surveys, which are fed back to students and teachers through visual analytics. However, a combination with intentionally collected data, such as self-report data stemming from student responses to surveys, is the exception rather than the rule in LA ([3], [4], and [5]). In our empirical contribution focusing on a large scale module in introductory mathematics and statistics, we aim to provide a practical application of such an infrastructure based on combining learning and learner data. In collecting learner data, we opted to use a wide range of validated self-report surveys firmly rooted in current educational research, including learning styles, learning motivation and engagement, and learning attitudes. This operationalization of learning dispositions closely resembles the specification of cognitive, metacognitive and motivational learning factors relevant for the internal loop of informative tutoring feedback (see [6], [7] for examples). Other data sources used are more common for LA applications, and constitute both data extracted from a learning management system, as well as system track data extracted from the e-tutorials used for practicing and formative assessments. The prime aim of the analysis is to provide a stepping stone for   predictive modeling, with a focus on the role each of these data sources can play in generating timely, informative feedback. This paper extends our earlier study [8], which found empirical evidence for the role of dispositional data in LA applications.

2   Background

2.1   Computer Assisted Formative Assessment

The classic function of assessment is that of taking an aptitude test. After completion of the learning process, we expect students to demonstrate mastery of the subject. According to test tradition, feedback resulting from such classic assessment is no more than a grade which becomes available only after finishing all learning activities. In recent years, the conception of assessment as a summative function (i.e. assessment of learning) has been broadened toward the conception of assessment as a formative function (i.e. assessment for learning). That is, as a means to provide feedback to both student and teacher about teaching and learning prior to or during the learning process [9, 10]. Examples of formative assessment are diagnostic testing, and test-directed learning approaches that constitutes the basic educational principle of many e-tutorial systems [11]. Because feedback from assessments constitutes a main function for learning, it is crucial that this information is readily available, preferably even directly. At this point digital testing enters the stage: it is unthinkable to get just-in-time feedback from formative assessments without using computers.

2.2   Learning Analytics

A broad goal of LA is to apply the outcomes of analyzing data gathered by monitoring and measuring the learning process, whereby feedback plays a crucial part to assist regulating that same learning process. Several alternative operationalizations are possible to support this. In [12], six objectives are distinguished: predicting learner performance and modelling learners, suggesting relevant learning resources, increasing reflection and awareness, enhancing social learning environments, detecting undesirable learner behaviors, and detecting affects of learners. Although the combination of self-report learner data with learning data extracted from e-tutorial systems allows us to contribute to at least five of these objectives of applying learning analytics (as described in [8]), in this contribution we will focus on the first objective: predictive modeling of performance and learning behavior. The ultimate goal of this predictive modeling endeavor is to investigate which components from a rich set of data sources, best serve the role of generating timely, informative feedback and afford signaling the risk of underperformance.

2.3 Related Work

Previous research by Wolff, Zdrahal, Nikolov, and Pantucek [13] found that a combination of LMS data with data from continuous summative assessments were the best predictor for performance drops amongst 7,701 students. In particular, the number of clicks in a LMS just before the next assessment significantly predicted continuation of studies [13]. As is evident from our own previous research [8], formative assessment data, supplemented with learning disposition data, also had a substantial impact on student performance in a blended course of 1,832 students.

3   Case Study: Mathematics and Statistics

3.1   Internationalization of Higher Education

Our empirical contribution focuses on freshmen students in quantitative methods (mathematics and statistics) course of the Maastricht University School of Business & Economics. The course is the first module for students entering the program. It is directed at a large and diverse group of students, which benefits the research design. The population consists of 1,840 freshmen students, in two cohorts: 2012/2013 and 2013/2014, who in some way participated in learning activities (i.e., have been active in the learning management system BlackBoard). Besides BlackBoard, two different e-tutorial systems for technology-enhanced learning and practicing were utilized: MyStatLab and MyMathLab.

The diversity of the student population mainly lies in its international composition: only 23% received their prior (secondary) education from the Dutch high school system. The largest group, 45% of the freshmen, was educated according to the German Abitur system. The remaining 32% are mainly from central-European and south-European countries. High school systems in Europe differ strongly, most particularly in the teaching of mathematics and statistics. Therefore it is crucial that the first module offered to these students is flexible and allows for individual learning paths.

3.2   Test-Directed E-tutorials

The two e-tutorial systems MyStatLab (MSL) and MyMathLab (MML) are generic digital learning environments for learning statistics and mathematics developed by the publisher Pearson. Although MyLabs can be used as a learning environment in the broad sense of the word (it contains, among others, a digital version of the textbook), it is primarily an environment for test-directed learning and practicing. Each step in the learning process is initiated by submitting a question. Students are encouraged to (try to) answer each question (see Fig. 1 for an example). If they do not master a question (completely), the student can either ask for help to solve the problem step-by-step (Help Me Solve This), or ask for a fully worked example (View an Example). These two functionalities are examples of Knowledge of Result/response (KR) and Knowledge of the Correct Response (KCR) types of feedback; see Narciss [6], [7].

After receiving this type of feedback, a new version of the problem loads (parameter based) to allow the student to demonstrate his/her newly acquired mastery. When a student provides an answer and opts for 'Check Answer', Multiple-Try Feedback (MTF, [6]) is provided, whereby the number of times feedback is provided for the same task depends on the format of the task (only two for a multiple choice type of task as in Fig.1, more for open type of tasks requiring numerical answers).

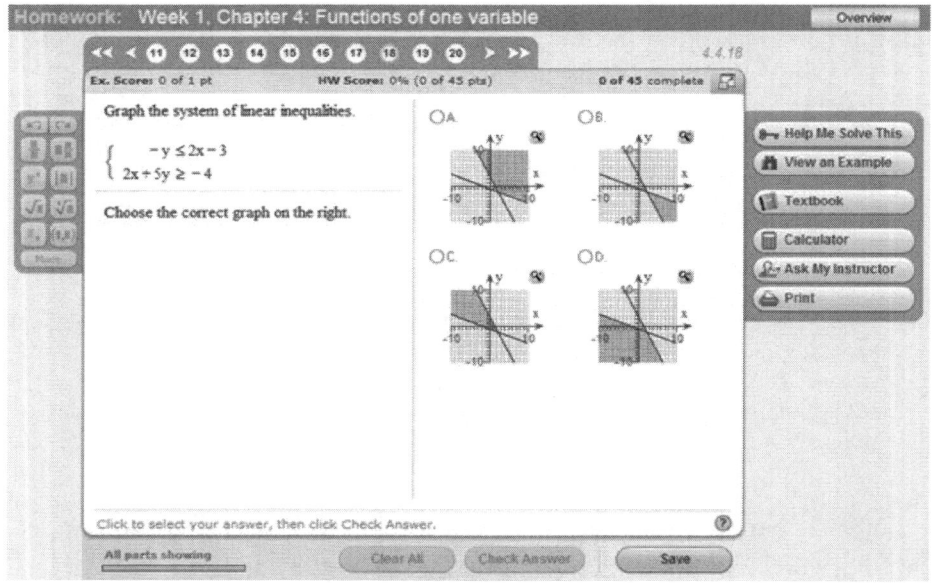

Fig. 1. MyMathLab task and feedback options

In the investigated course, students on average work 35.7 hours in MML and 23.6 hours in MSL, which is 30% to 40% of the available time of 80 hours for learning in both topics. In the present study, we use two different indicators for the intensity of the My-Labs usage: MMLHours and MSLHours indicate the time a student spends practicing in each respective MyLab environment per week; MMLMastery and MSLMastery indicate the average final score achieved for the practice questions in any week.

3.3   Educational Practice

The educational system in which students learn mathematics and statistics is best described as a 'blended' or 'hybrid' system. The main component is 'face-to-face':

problem-based learning (PBL, see [14] for an elaborate overview), in small groups (14 students), coached by a content expert tutor. Participation in these tutor groups is required, as for all courses based on the Maastricht PBL system. The online component of the blend, that is, the use of the two e-tutorials, is optional. The reason for making the online component optional is that this best fits the Maastricht educational model, which is student-centered and places the responsibility for making educational choices primarily with the student. At the same time, due to the diversity in prior knowledge, not all students will benefit equally from using these environments; in particular for those at the high performance end, extensive practicing will not be the most effective allocation of learning time. However, the use of e-tutorials is stimulated by making bonus credits available for good performance in the quizzes, and for achieving good scores in the practicing modes of the MyLab environments. Quizzes are taken every two weeks and consist of items that are drawn from the same item pools applied in the practicing mode. We chose for this particular constellation, since it stimulates students with little prior knowledge to make intensive use of the MyLab platforms. They realize that they may fall behind other students in writing the exam, and therefore need to achieve a good bonus score both to compensate, and to support their learning. The most direct way to do so is to frequently practice in the MML and MSL environments. The bonus is maximized to 20% of what one can score in the exam.

The student-centered characteristic of the instructional model first and foremost requires adequate informative feedback to students so that they are able to monitor their study progress and their topic mastery in absolute and relative sense. The provision of relevant feedback starts on the first day of the course when students take two diagnostic entry tests for mathematics and statistics. Feedback from these entry tests provide the first signals to students of the importance of using the MyLab platforms. Next, the MML and MSL-environments contain a monitoring function: at any time students can see their progress in preparing the next quiz, and can get feedback on the performance in completed quizzes and on their performance in the practice sessions. The same information is also available to the tutors. Although the primary responsibility for directing the learning process lies with the student, the tutor can act complementary to that self-steering, especially in situations where the tutor considers that a more intense use of e-tutorials is desirable, given the position of the student concerned. In this way, the application of LA shapes the instructional situation.

4   The Array of Learning Analytics Data Sources

In order to explore the potential of feedback based on the several components of the learning blend, we investigate the relationship between an array of LA data sources, and academic performance in the Quantitative Methods module. Academic performance consists of the individual scores in both topic components of the final written exam (MathExam and StatsExam), and the overall grade in the module (QMGrade). Both are subject to a weight factor, weighting the final exam with factor 5, and the bonus score from quizzes and homework with factor 1. In designing models covering two class years, performance scores have been standardized by calculating Z-scores in order to compare performance across the two cohorts. Prediction models for these three learning performance measures are based on the following data sources:

- Formative assessment data consisting of:
  - Week0: diagnostics entry tests for mathematics and statistics, with a strong focus on basic algebraic skills, a well-known topic for high school deficiencies.
  - Week1: mastery scores and practice time in MyMathLab and MyStatLab.
  - Week2: mastery scores and practice time in MyMathLab and MyStatLab.
  - Week3: mastery scores and practice time in MyMathLab and MyStatLab, and Quiz1 scores for mathematics and statistics.
  - Week4: mastery score and practice time in MyMathLab and MyStatLab.
  - Week5: mastery scores and practice time in MyMathLab and MyStatLab, and Quiz2 scores for mathematics and statistics.
  - Week6: mastery score and practice time in MyMathLab and MyStatLab.
  - Week7: mastery scores and practice time in MyMathLab and MyStatLab, and Quiz3 scores for mathematics and statistics.
- BlackBoard use intensity data, in terms of number of clicks, again decomposed into weekly figures (BB time on task data was initially included in the study, but appeared to be dominated by click data with regard to predictive power, and was therefore excluded in the final analyses).
- Learning dispositions and demographic data from several concern systems. These data are, in terms of designing longitudinal models, assigned to Week0.

Demographic data were obtained from the regular student administration. An important part of demographic data is prior education. High school educational systems generally distinguish between a basic level of mathematics education preparing for the social sciences, and an advanced level preparing for sciences. An indicator variable is used for mathematics at advanced level (about one third of the students), with basic level of mathematics prior schooling being the reference group. Students with advanced prior schooling are generally better in mathematics, but not in statistics, which corresponds to the fact that in programs at advanced level, the focus is abstract mathematics (calculus) rather than statistics. Other demographic data refer to gender, nationality and age.

Learning style data based on the learning style model of Vermunt [15] constitute the first component of measured learning dispositions (see also: Vermunt & Vermetten, [16]). Vermunt distinguishes four domains or components of learning in his model: cognitive processing strategies, metacognitive regulation strategies, learning conceptions or mental models of learning, and learning orientations. In each domain, five different scales describe different aspects of the learning component. In this study, we applied the two domains of processing and regulation strategies, since these facets of learning styles are most open to interventions based upon learning feedback. In Vermunt's model, three types of learning strategies are distinguished: deep learning, step-wise (or surface) learning, and concrete ways of processing learning topics. In a similar way, three types of regulation strategies are distinguished: self-regulation of learning, external regulation of learning, and lack of regulation. Combining scores on processing and regulation strategies, we can find alternative profiles of learning approaches often seen in students in higher education. For instance, the meaning directed learning approach combines high levels for deep learning, with students critically processing the learning materials, with high levels for self-regulation, both with regard to learning process and learning content. These students are the 'ideal' higher education students: being self-directed, independent learners. The typical learning approach of students with high scores on step-wise learning, who depend a lot on memorization and rehearsing processes, and at the same time score high on external regulation of learning, does carry a lot more risks with regard to academic success. These learning approaches are very often guarantees for success in high school, but start to fail in university. Students with high scores for lack of regulation of any type run the highest risk; drop-out for these profiles is higher than for any other profile.

Recent Anglo-Saxon literature on academic achievement and dropout assigns an increasingly dominant role to the theoretical model of Andrew Martin: the 'Motivation and Engagement Wheel' [17]: see Fig. 2.

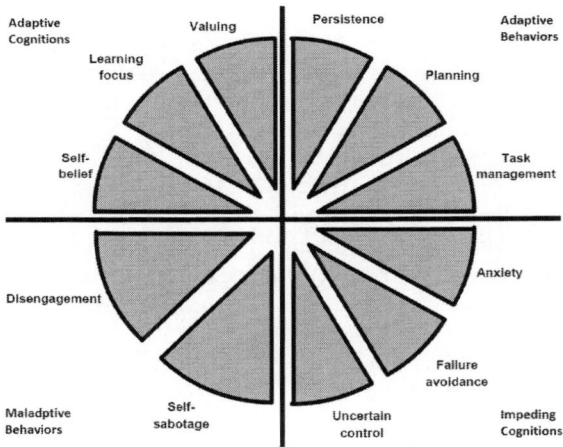

Fig. 2. Motivation and Engagement Wheel (Source: [17])

This model includes both behaviors and thoughts, or cognitions, that play a role in learning. Both are subdivided into adaptive and mal-adaptive or impeding forms. As a result, the four quadrants are: adaptive behavior and adaptive thoughts (the 'boosters'), mal-adaptive behavior (the 'guzzlers') and impeding thoughts (the 'mufflers'). Adaptive thoughts consist of Self-belief, Learning focus, and Value of school, whereas adaptive behaviors consist of Persistence, Planning, and Task management. Maladaptive or impeding thoughts include Anxiety, Failure avoidance, and Uncertain control, and lastly, maladaptive behaviors include Self-sabotage and Disengagement. Further components of learning dispositions are learning attitudes, and intrinsic versus extrinsic motivation to learn. All learning dispositions are administered through self-report surveys. From 1,794 out of 1,840 students (97.5%), complete information was obtained on the various instruments.

Similar to the feedback based on student activity in the two MML and MSL platforms, also learning dispositions data was used to provide feedback during the course. Students were given access to visualizations of their characteristic learning approaches, relative to the profile of the average students. Next to that, all students received individual data on personal dispositions, in order to analyze these data as a required statistical project. The only retrospective part of this study is the investigation of the predictive power of the several data sources with regard to course performance, as discussed in the next section.

5   Predicting Performance

Before turning to longitudinal models predicting performance using week by week data, the first step is to determine the maximum predictive power for each of the data sources, using aggregated data for all weeks. For one category of data, the outcome appears to be simple: BlackBoard track data can predict no more than 1% of variation in the three performance measures. In other words, the (multiple) correlation of BlackBoard user track data and the performance variables is not above 0.1. From a substantial perspective, that excludes the category of BlackBoard data for developing prediction models as being practically insignificant.

With regard to the MyLab data, both overall mastery in MML and MSL correlate strongly with all performance measures (correlations in the range of 0.35 to 0.55), whereas correlations between time in the system and performance measures are weaker, but still substantial (in the range 0.1 to 0.2). Composing regression models that predict performance measures from multiple regressions containing both mastery and time in MyLab systems variables, generates the following prediction equations (in normalized performance measures, using Z-scores, and standardized beta's):

$$ZMathExam = 0.562 * MMLMastery - 0.277 * MMLHours, R = 0.47$$

$$ZStatsExam = 0.506 * MSLMastery - 0.251 * MSLHours, R = 0.40$$

$$ZQMGrade = 0.36 * MMLMastery - 0.196 * MMLHours$$

$$+0.341 * MSLMastery - 0.092 * MSLHours, R = 0.58$$

All prediction equations have substantial multiple correlations, which suggests that feedback based on overall mastery and time for both MyLab systems has good prospects. A remarkable and very consistent feature of all three prediction equations is that the beta of mastery is always positive, and the beta of time in system is always negative, although all bivariate correlations between time in system variables and performance measures are positive. There is however a simple explanation for this sign reversal: mastery and time in system variables are strongly collinear, with a 0.59 correlation for the MML platform, and a .66 correlation for the MSL platform. Practicing longer in the two MyLab systems increases expected performance, since students who practice more, achieve higher mastery levels. In a multiple regression model, one however corrects for mastery level, and now time has a negative impact: for a given mastery level, students who need more time to reach that level, have lower expected performance, which is quite intuitive.

After the potential of building prediction models for performance based on data from the two MyLab systems has been established, the next step is to design these prediction models using incremental data sets of system data. Starting with the Week0 data set, containing data that are available at the very start of the module (in our example: data from the diagnostic entry tests), we extend the data set in weekly steps, arriving at the final set of predictor variables after seven weeks. Thus, the incremental system data contains entry test data, mastery and time in system data of seven consecutive weeks, and MyLab quiz data administered in weeks 3, 5, and 7. Instead of providing regressions for all seven weeks and all three performance measures, Fig. 3 describes the development of the multiple correlation coefficient R in time, that is, over incremental weekly data sets.

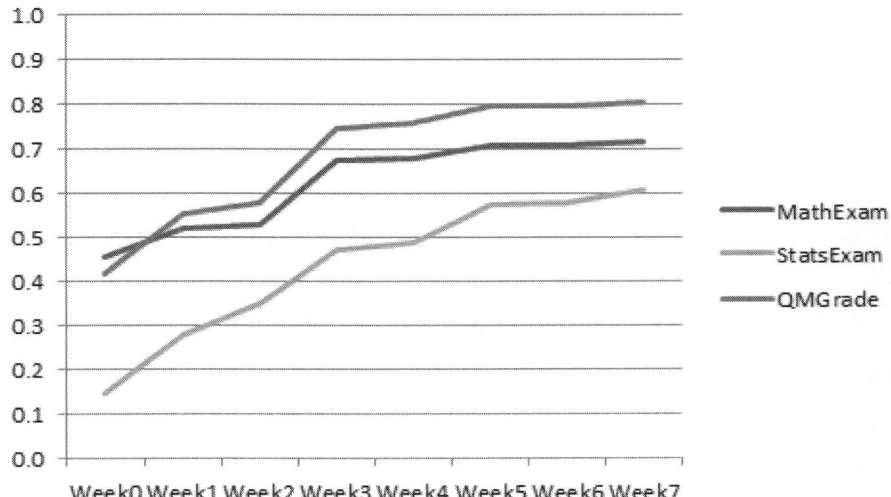

Fig. 3. Longitudinal Performance Predictions based on Formative Assessments: Multiple Correlation R

Since the predictor data sets are incremental, the values of multiple correlation increase over weeks. Those for performance in the mathematics exam, and the overall grade, start at values around 0.45 in Week0, and increase to values between 0.7 and 0.8 in the last week. In contrast, there is less power in predicting performance in statistics, the difference caused by the statistics entry test being less informative for later statistics performance, than the mathematics entry exam is for later mathematics performance. The circumstance that many of the students have not been educated before in statistics is crucial for understanding the entry test being not very informative.

Predictor sets used for the generation of Fig. 3 include only MyLab data, together with entry tests data; no learning dispositions data have been used yet. When we add these data, assuming that these data are available at the start of the course so that they are part of the new Week0 data set, we arrive at Fig. 4 describing the development of the multiple correlation coefficients R over all weeks. The main impact of the availability of learning disposition data is the strong increase in predictive power in the first weeks. From the third week onwards, when data from the first quiz becomes available, the difference in predictive power between models including and those excluding learning dispositions, is minimal. Apparently, collinearity between scores in the first quiz and the set of learning dispositions imply that dispositions have hardly any additional predictive power beyond that of quiz performance; most of their impact is also captured in quiz performance scores.

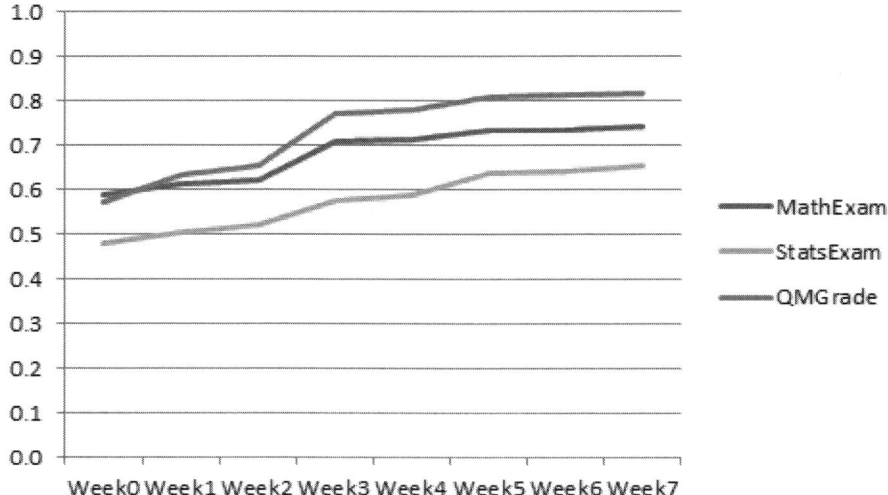

Fig. 4. Longitudinal Performance Predictions based on Formative Assessments and Learning Dispositions: Multiple Correlation R

6   Conclusions

In this empirical study into predictive modeling of student performance, we investigated three different data sources to explore the potential of generating informative feedback using LA: BlackBoard tracking data, students' learning dispositions, and data from systems for formative, computer assisted assessments. The last data source allows further classification into data generated in the practice mode (both mastery and system time data), and data generated by formative assessments (performance data). It appears that the combination of dispositions data and assessment system data dominate the role of BlackBoard track data in predicting student performance, implying that in applications with such rich data available, BlackBoard data have no added value in predicting performance and signaling underperforming students. This seems to confirm initial findings by Macfayden and Dawson [5], who found that simple clicking behavior in a LMS is at best a poor proxy for actual user-behavior of students.

Data extracted from the testing mode of the MyLab systems dominate in a similar respect data generated by the practicing mode of MyLabs, indicating the predictive power of true assessment data, even if it comes from assessments that are primarily formative in nature. However, assessment data is typically delayed data, not available before midterm, or as in our case, the third week of the course. Up to the moment this richest data component becomes available, mastery data and use intensity data generated by the e-tutorial systems are a second best alternative for true assessment data. This links well with Wolff et al. [13], who found that performance on initial assessments during the first parts of an online module were substantial predictors for final exam performance.

A similar conclusion can be drawn with regard to the learning disposition data: up to the moment that assessment data become available, they serve a unique role in predicting student performance and signaling underperformance beyond system track data of the e-tutorials. From the moment that computer assisted, formative assessment data become available, their predictive power is dominated by that of performance in those formative assessments. Dispositions data are not as easily collected as system tracking data from learning management systems or e-tutorial systems. The answer to the question if the effort to collect dispositional data is worthwhile (or not), is therefore strongly dependent on when richer (assessment) data becomes available, and the need for timely signaling of underperformance. If timely feedback is required, the combination of data extracted from e-tutorials, both in practicing and test modes, and learning disposition data suggests being the best mix to serve LA applications.

Acknowledgements. The project reported here has been supported and co-financed by SURF-foundation as part of the Learning Analytics Stimulus program.

References

1. Buckingham Shum, S., Deakin Crick, R.: Learning Dispositions and Transferable Competencies: Pedagogy, Modelling and Learning Analytics. In: Proceedings LAK 2012: 2nd International Conference on Learning Analytics & Knowledge, pp. 92–101. ACM Press, New York (2012)
2. LASI Dispositional Learning Analytics Workshop (2013), http://Learningemergence.net/events/lasi-dla.wkshp
3. Buckingham Shum, S., Ferguson, R.: Social Learning Analytics. Journal of Educational Technology & Society 15(3) (2012)
4. Greller, W., Drachsler, H.: Translating Learning into Numbers: A Generic Framework for Learning Analytics. Journal of Educational Technology & Society 15(3) (2012)
5. Macfadyen, L.P., Dawson, S.: Mining LMS data to develop an "early warning system" for educators: A proof of concept. Computers & Education 54(2), 588–599 (2010)
6. Narciss, S.: Feedback strategies for interactive learning tasks. In: Spector, J.M., Merrill, M.D., van Merrienboer, J.J.G., Driscoll, M.P. (eds.) Handbook of Research on Educational Communications and Technology, 3rd edn., pp. 125–144. Lawrence Erlbaum Associates, Mahaw (2008)
7. Narciss, S., Huth, K.: Fostering achievement and motivation with bug-related tutoring feedback in a computer-based training on written subtraction. Learning and Instruction 16, 310–322 (2006)
8. Tempelaar, D.T., Cuypers, H., Van de Vrie, E.M., Heck, A., Van der Kooij, H.: Formative Assessment and Learning Analytics. In: Proceedings LAK 2013: 3rd International Conference on Learning Analytics & Knowledge, pp. 205–209. ACM Press, New York (2013)

9. Birenbaum, M.: New insights into learning and teaching and their implications for assessment. In: Segers, M., Dochy, F., Cascallar (eds.) Optimizing New Modes of Assessment; in Search of Qualities and Standards, vol. 1, pp. 13–37. Kluwer Academic Publishers, Dordrecht (2003)

10. Wyatt-Smith, C., Klenowski, V., Colbert, P.: Assessment Understood as Enabling. In: Wyatt-Smith, C., Klenowski, V., Colbert, P. (eds.) Designing Assessment for Quality Learning, vol. 1, pp. 1–20. Springer, Netherlands (2014)

11. Shute, V., Kim, Y.: Formative and Stealth Assessment. In: Spector, J.M., Merrill, M.D., Elen, J., Bishop, M.J. (eds.) Handbook of Research on Educational Communications and Technology, 4th edn., pp. 311–321. Springer, New York (2014)

12. Verbert, K., Manouselis, N., Drachsler, H., Duval, E.: Dataset-Driven Research to Support Learning and Knowledge Analytics. Educational Technology & Society 15(3), 133–148 (2012)

13. Wolff, A., Zdrahal, Z., Nikolov, A., Pantucek, M.: Improving retention: predicting at-risk students by analysing clicking behaviour in a virtual learning environment. In: Proceedings LAK 2013: 3rd International Conference on Learning Analytics & Knowledge, pp. 145–149. ACM Press, New York (2013)

14. Loyens, S.M.M., Kirschner, P.A., Paas, F.: Problem-based learning. In: Harris, K.R., Graham, S., Urdan, T., Bus, A.G., Major, S., Swanson, H. (eds.) APA Educational Psychology Handbook: Application to Learning and Teaching, vol. 3, pp. 403–425. American Psychological Association, Washington, D.C (2011)

15. Vermunt, J.D.: Leerstijlen en sturen van leerprocessen in het Hoger Onderwijs. Swets & Zeitlinger, Amsterdam/Lisse (1996)

16. Vermunt, J.D., Vermetten, Y.: Patterns in Student Learning: Relationships between Learning Strategies, Conceptions of Learning, and Learning Orientations. Educational Psychology Review 16, 359–385 (2004)

17. Martin, A.J.: Examining a multidimensional model of student motivation and engagement using a construct validation approach. British Journal of Educational Psychology 77, 413–440 (2007)

Learning Analytics: From Theory to Practice – Data Support for Learning and Teaching

Wolfgang Greller[1], Martin Ebner[2], and Martin Schön[2]

[1] Vienna University of Education, Vienna, Austria
wolfgang.greller@phwien.ac.at
[2] Technical University Graz, Graz, Austria
martin.ebner@tugraz.at

Abstract. Much has been written lately about the potential of Learning Analytics for improving learning and teaching. Nevertheless, most of the contributions to date are concentrating on the abstract theoretical or algorithmic level, or, deal with academic efficiencies like teachers' grading habits. This paper wants to focus on the value that Learning Analytics brings to pedagogic interventions and feedback for reflection. We first analyse what Learning Analytics has to offer in this respect, and, then, present a practical use case of applied Learning Analytics for didactic support in primary school Arithmetic.

Keywords: Learning Analytics, teacher feedback, didactic intervention, primary school, formal education.

1 Introduction

The idea of Learning Analytics has emerged in recent years as an educational way of utilising the enormous amount of learner data produced through activities in electronic systems. Already back in 2006, Retalis et al. (2006) considered interaction analysis a promising way to better understand learner behaviour. However, only the more recent explosion of data and increased utilisation of user data in business and commerce have brought this domain to the full attention of the education sector (Horizon 2011).

Since the Horizon report came out, there has been massive interest and research activity happening in this new domain. Researchers started busily engaging in diverse debates to define and scope Learning Analytics and to contrast it with existing areas of research like educational data mining (EDM). A number of descriptive models and frameworks have been proposed to capture the extent and implications of the research area (cf. Siemens 2011, Elias 2011, Greller & Drachsler 2012, Cooper 2012, Chatti et al. 2012, Friesen 2013).

Because analytics in education are not confined to teaching and learning alone, there were moves to separate the semantics into "unrelated" sister-domains such as Academic Analytics (Siemens 2011). The latter is closely related to business intelligence in that it works more towards efficiency of operations than towards the support for progression in learning (cf. Van Harmelen & Workman 2012). In the same vein, Research Analytics, which relies heavily on bibliometric data and citation indexes,

M. Kalz and E. Ras (Eds.): CAA 2014, CCIS 439, pp. 79–87, 2014.

due to its direct connection to institutional funding mechanisms, can be excluded from the spheres of Learning Analytics in the pedagogic sense.

When scanning the literature on Learning Analytics, we find a heavy slant towards the processing (EDM) side of things with research discussing algorithmic approaches to learner data. Similarly, the institutional data governance and acceptance aspects have played an important part in the evolution of Learning Analytics as a research topic (cf. Graf et al. 2012; Ali et al. 2013). By contrast, the use of analytics as a support tool for teacher interventions is an area with relatively little coverage to date. However, to exploit analytics as an instrument for reflecting current pedagogic practice and for validating didactical patterns, as indicated by Greller & Drachsler (2012), more attention to this aspect is required. In this paper, we want to elaborate on the embedding of analytics approaches into teaching and learning, on how questions can be raised about didactical methods informed by analytics, and where analytics can provide new insights to the preparation of cognitively difficult areas of learning.

This paper is structured in the following way: In Part II, we talk about Learning Analytics and its place in pedagogy. This is then followed in Part III by introducing a practical application of an analytics tool for monitoring the development of children's Maths skills in primary school. Part IV discusses the outcomes of this experiment and the value potential of Learning Analytics. Finally, in Part V, some lessons learnt and conclusions are drawn and prospective research question raised.

2   Pedagogy and Learning Analytics

The relationship between pedagogy and Learning Analytics is understood differently within the community and with respect to everyday practice. Some researchers see Learning Analytics as intrinsically pedagogic in its nature, just by dealing with educational data or with data usable for learning in the widest sense. Feedback systems play an important part in this. Among other examples, Duval (2011) claims that, "a visualisation of eating habits can help to lead a healthier life". In his elaboration it seems, that learning happens by mere visualization of data, though Duval too asks for more orientation towards specific goals. The EDUCAUSE summative report (2012) of a three day online seminar stresses the importance of any analytics program to derive meaningful, actionable insights. We consider the word 'actionable' as being critical for the exploitation of analytics results in teaching and learning.

In our elaborations here we will use a narrower setting of pedagogic application, relating directly to formal education in the classroom. We also follow the model by Greller & Drachsler (2012) who keep pedagogy and data analysis strictly separate, using Learning Analytics as an instrument to reflect upon and to take informed decisions on learning interventions by a human agent. This stands to some extent in contrast with predictive approaches of Learning Analytics, where decisions on follow-up actions can be based directly on the data through automated algorithms.

Greller & Drachsler (ibid.) position Learning Analytics between brackets of pedagogically induced behaviour and the interventions actioned either by a teacher or the learners themselves (Fig.1.). These interventions may lead to changes in pedagogic behaviour (learning activities) that, in turn, (re-)inform the Learning Analytics process for measuring progress against the intended learning outcome (Van Harmelen & Workman, 2012).

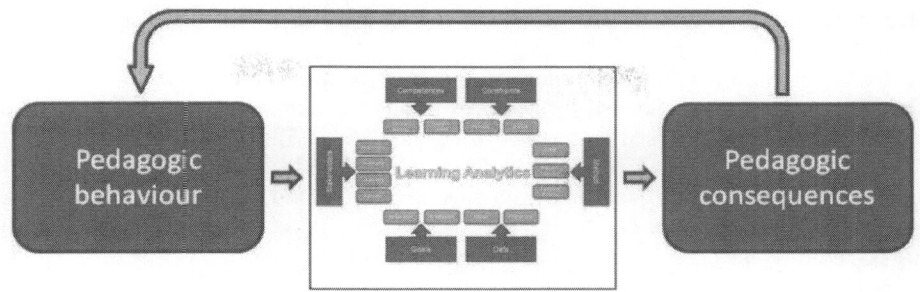

Fig. 1. Learning Analytics embedded in pedagogy (Greller & Drachsler 2012)

One of the strengths of Learning Analytics as a support for teaching and learning is the potential to bring to light insights that would otherwise not be easily visible. Learning Analytics can help backing up "feelings" with data. On the other hand, it may also lead to refuting "general assumptions" about students' behaviour in specific learning actions. On a larger scale, this may lead to rethinking the educational process and pedagogic approach in certain areas of teaching. To illustrate this potential, we will introduce a small application that analyses the performance of primary school children in learning the tables.

3   A Primary School Analytics Application

Graz University of Technology has a long tradition in doing technology enhanced learning (TEL) both in research as well as in academic programmes with a special focus on students and their learning (Ebner et al. 2006). Longitudinal studies pointed out that any student of today now owns an arbitrary amount of different technologies – a Personal Computer, a laptop, a smartphone, maybe also a tablet or an eReader (Ebner et al. 2013; Ebner et al. 2011). In combination with a mobile broadband Internet connection it is save to state that practically everyone has access to information and communication in real time, even while on the move. On the other hand, modern web technologies also allow us to develop innovative information systems that are able to store huge amounts of data. The general idea with respect to education is to enable learners to utilize their personal (mobile) devices to exercise and improve on predefined learning tasks.

Bearing this generic vision in mind, different applications have been developed to gather learner data, interpret and visualise them as they work in these seamless learning environments. Afterwards, a teacher is able to bring the results back to the classroom for reflection and deep learning. In our particular case, three applications have been produced: (1) the *Multiplication Table* (Schön et al. 2012), (2) the *Multi-Math-Coach* (Ebner et al. 2014a), and, (3) the *Addition / Subtraction Trainer* (Ebner et al. 2014b). All of these applications address core maths operations for school children in primary schools. Each application consistently observes the following rules:

1. School children train or play with the application (e.g. web interface or special mobile apps) as often as they want.
2. Each single calculation is stored in a centralised database on a webserver.
3. The entered data is checked for correctness and the current competence level of a child is calculated. Based on this, the next calculation will be chosen.
4. The teacher gets an overview how their class performs as a whole or each child individually. In case of occurring problems, a visualisation prompts the teacher to a pedagogical intervention.
5. To avoid chance successes, each answer has to be entered correctly twice to be accepted as accomplished.

Fig. 2. The Multiplication Trainer (http://mathe.tugraz.at)

Fig.2. shows the main graphic interface of the trainer application that helps pupils learn the 10x10 table. In the middle of it, the current calculation is shown and the answer is expected in the input field during the given time frame (bar running down to time-out). On the left side, an overview of all questions already completed is given. Below the task, a little rabbit should help motivate children doing the next question in a playful manner (the rabbit advances on correct answers towards a carrot). Fig.3. illustrates the teacher's overview: In the first column on the left, the names of the children would appear and following the alignment each single calculation is displayed. Dark green means the particular example has been mastered well by the child, lime green indicates that it is known and red is not known (grey just means that this calculation has not occurred yet). Much more important is the second column from the left called "skill". Here, the application predicts the current learning state in a traffic light metaphor. A yellow or even red box prompts the teacher that a pedagogical intervention is recommended.

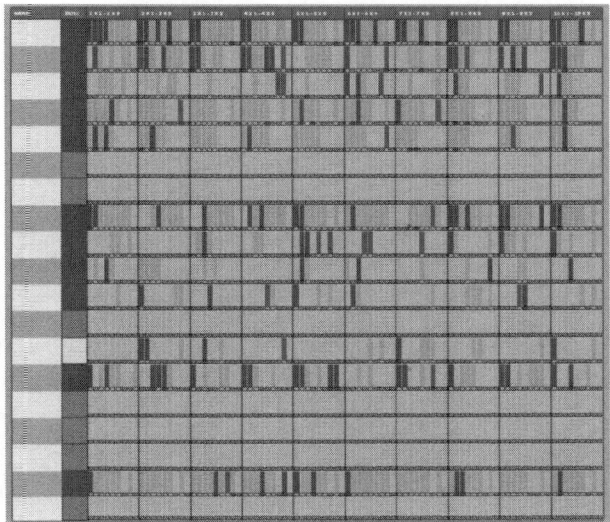

Fig. 3. Teacher's overview

The application, therefore, simultaneously takes a training and assessment perspective. Children can practice the table, but are at the same time measured for correctness and progress. The time taken to answer is also a factor taken into account as an indicator for the level of competence. Although this is a very simplistic case, a number of insights can be deduced from it as we will discuss in the next section.

The analysis of the performance of individual children should, as depicted in the model above (Fig.1.), lead to pedagogic interventions. Rather than waiting for the children learners to complete the table tests, early warning can already alert the teacher to struggling pupils. We will here not express any opinion of what the "correct" intervention would be in each individual child's case, but assume that teachers adopt further interpersonal diagnostics to find out in which way a child is struggling and how to help them. After they have been brought back on track, the cycle of testing can start again.

4   Findings and Discussion

From our test run with about 6,000 pupils at the ages of 7-10, and more than 100 teachers, it clearly emerges that Learning Analytics is more than just collecting, curating and processing data. As indicated in chapter II above, Learning Analytics is about the interpretation of data to actively assist teachers with meaningful and actionable figures or visualisations. In other words, the data itself is not enough to advance learning, because the pedagogical approach must be looked at in its entirety. For this to happen, we find it among other things important that teachers see the performance of each individual learner. Teaching and learning, despite the constraints posed by large cohorts in search for more economic efficiency, from the learner perspective still remains a one-to-one relationship to personalise the pedagogic approach and support the individual in their psychological, mental, and physical development. However, in group situations like a classroom, it is difficult for a teacher to keep an eye on the progression of each child or to surface collective issues that have perhaps not been properly addressed through the chosen delivery method (cf. Drachsler & Greller 2012).

In our little maths application, feedback to the teacher is continuous and formative. The mentioned box indicators are early warning signals should any child begin to struggle with progress on the table. A teacher has the possibility of monitoring the entire class and may intervene when warning signs occur. The timeliness of the feedback to the teacher is perhaps the biggest added value that Learning Analytics brings to teaching practice.

In monitoring the activities of each child in real time, analysing the performance and predicting the likely progression helps the teacher to identify outliers early. Children struggling with certain calculations are timed out by the game. This time-to-response counts towards the prediction algorithm. One interesting finding from the application is the likelihood of success and failure, as well as emerging patterns, which allow approximations of a child's performance. For example, the observation implies that pupils who run into a performance of right-wrong-right-wrong would never come out of this loop switching between correct and incorrect answers for the same given questions (Taraghi et al. 2014). Similarly, when a child answers two consecutive questions wrong, there is a 30% probability that the next two will also be wrong.

A summative analysis across all participants also has interesting things to tell. It highlights where the most difficult items of the multiplication table lie (Fig.4. below). 8*6 as well as 6*8, followed by 7*8, have to be considered as the most difficult questions according to the data evidence. This cumulative knowledge over the entire learner population should be used by teachers to adjust teaching plans and put perhaps more focus on the exercises of difficult areas. In this way, Learning Analytics brings information to light that would otherwise be difficult to spot or to articulate with evidence.

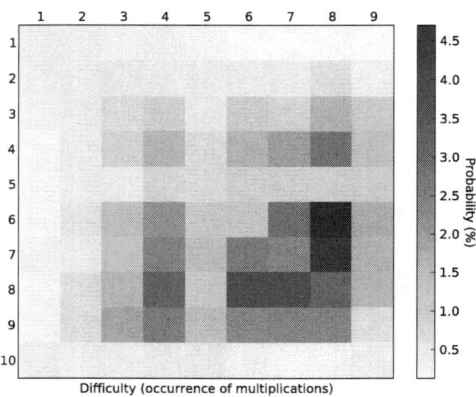

Fig. 4. Heat Map of the most difficult questions

From these findings, we can take a matrix approach to interpreting the data in the application with two main pedagogic intervention paths to follow: The horizontal analysis shows the performance of each child along the posed tasks. Vertically, the summative group analysis can be performed with views on the individual posited tasks and the relative cognitive challenge they pose to the learners. While the horizontal axis may lead to personalised intervention and support, the vertical axis provides food for curriculum adjustments to cover more challenging areas with greater teaching efforts. The predictive warning signals of possible difficulties a child experiences provides added support for timely focussing teacher attention where it is needed.

5   Conclusions and Future Research Questions

One of the results of our tests is that Learning Analytics must be easy. The practical experiments pointed out clearly: – teachers have no time to interpret data in detail, due to the fact that in the classroom they have to observe and react to many different events at once. This has already been pointed out as a risk in previous works (Van Harmelen & Workman 2012). In our case, traffic light signalling was chosen to quickly provide the appropriate hint. It goes without saying that the prediction algorithm running in the background must be carefully tested and tuned, and has to be adapted if necessary.

From the learner perspective, Learning Analytics helps the individualisation of the learning process: The strength of interpreting data of a single learner is that we exactly know about their learning problems. Therefore, pedagogic help can be provided in a very personal way. On an ethical note, though, we have to concede that Learning Analytics is about data, and one of the major concerns of this emerging field is how the collected data is protected against abuse. First studies on this topic point out that teachers as well as researchers have to address this topic with great sensitivity (Kay, 2012). However, it is our opinion that in a protected classroom environment (whether a physical or virtual environment), it is absolutely essential for the holistic pedagogic development of a child that teachers have direct access to personal information relating to their pupils learning.

As a matter for future research, we consider our trial limited in the way of covering a well-defined and limited space of maths education. Confirmation of Learning Analytics support for pedagogic interventions from more complex and abstract areas would be highly relevant for unleashing the fuller potential of Learning Analytics. Among other aspects, the psychometric conditions of children, who come at different levels of preparedness could be studied against the mastery of the table questions. Repeat runs with the same pupils could potentially highlight the changing conditions of the test parameters and difficulty level (cf. Item Response Theory, Thomsen 2009).

Furthermore, there have been some attempts to "socialise" Learning Analytics (e.g. Buckingham-Shum & Ferguson 2012) and to apply it to open education spaces like learning networks and MOOCs (Fournier 2011). Free analytics tools like SNAPP provide first interesting results, but, at present, they still remain rather specialist tools that are hard to grasp for teachers and are difficult to build into reflection and learning design of everyday teaching. However, this is an interesting space to watch not only with respect to supporting open learning with Learning Analytics, but also to bring social aspects of analytics into the classroom. In future studies, we, therefore, aim to look into experiments with social character such as group work or social network analysis (SNA).

References

1. Ali, L., Asadi, M., Gašević, D., Jovanović, J., Hatala, M.: Factors influencing beliefs for adoption of a learning analytics tool: An empirical study. Computers and Education 62, 130–148 (2013)
2. Buckingham-Shum, S., Ferguson, R.: Social Learning Analytics. Journal of Educational Technology & Society (JETS) 15(3), 3–26 (2012)
3. Chatti, M.A., Dyckhoff, A.L., Schroeder, U., Thüs, H.: A reference model for learning analytics. International Journal of Technology Enhanced Learning (2012)
4. Cooper, A.: A Framework of Characteristics for Analytics. CETIS Analytics Series 1(7) (2012)
5. Drachsler, H., Greller, W.: The pulse of learning analytics - understandings and expectations from the stakeholders. In: Buckingham Shum, S., Gasevic, D., Ferguson, R. (eds.) Proceedings of the 2nd International Conference on Learning Analytics and Knowledge, LAK 2012, pp. 120–129. ACM, New York (2012)
6. Duval, E.: Attention Please! Learning Analytics for Visualization and Recommendation. In: Proceedings of LAK 2011: 1st International Conference on Learning Analytics and Knowledge 2011 (2011)
7. Ebner, M., Scerbakov, N., Maurer, H.: New Features for eLearning in Higher Education for Civil Engineering. Journal of Universal Science and Technology of Learning 1(1), 93–106 (2006)
8. Ebner, M., Nagler, W., Schön, M.: "Architecture Students Hate Twitter and Love Dropbox" or Does the Field of Study Correlates with Web 2.0 Behavior? In: Proceedings of World Conference on Educational Multimedia, Hypermedia and Telecommunications, pp. 43–53. AACE, Chesapeake (2013)
9. Ebner, M., Nagler, W., Schön, M.: The Facebook Generation Boon or Bane for E-Learning at Universities? In: World Conference on Educational Multimedia, Hypermedia and Telecommunications, pp. S.3549–S.3557 (2011)
10. Ebner, M., Schön, M., Taraghi, B., Steyrer, M.: Teachers Little Helper: Multi-Math-Coach. IADIS International Journal on WWW/Internet 11(3), 1 (2014a)
11. Ebner, M., Schön, M., Neuhold, B.: Learning Analytics in basic math education – first results from the field. eLearning Papers 36, 24-27 (2014b)
12. EDUCAUSE Analytics Sprint 24-26 July 2012 (2012), http://www.educause.edu/library/resources/analytics-3-day-sprint-summary
13. Elias, T.: Learning Analytics: Definitions, Processes and Potential. (2011), http://learninganalytics.net/LearningAnalyticsDefinitionsProcessesPotential.pdf
14. Fournier, H., Kop, R., Sitlia, H.: The Value of Learning Analytics to Networked Learning on a Personal Learning Environment. NRC Publications Archive (2011), http://nparc.cisti-icist.nrc-cnrc.gc.ca/npsi/ctrl?action=rtdoc&an=18150452
15. Friesen, N.: Learning Analytics: Readiness and Rewards. Canadian Journal of Learning and Technology (CJLT) 39(4) (2013), http://www.cjlt.ca/index.php/cjlt/article/view/774/379

16. Graf, S., Ives, C., Lockyer, L., Hobson, P., Clow, D.: Building a data governance model for learning analytics. In: Proceedings of the 2nd International Conference on Learning Analytics and Knowledge - LAK 2012 (2012)
17. Greller, W., Drachsler, H.: Translating Learning into Numbers: A Generic Framework for Learning Analytics. Educational Technology & Society 15(3), 42–57 (2012)
18. Horizon Report, New Media Consortium (2011),
    http://wp.nmc.org/horizon2011/sections/learning-analytics/
19. Kay, D., with inputs from Korn, N., Oppenheim, C.: CETIS Analytics Series. Legal, Risk and Ethical Aspects of Analytics in Higher Education 1(16) (2012),
    http://publications.cetis.ac.uk/2012/500
20. Retalis, S., Papasalouros, A., Psaromiligkos, Y., Siscos, S., Kargidis, T.: Towards Networked Learning Analytics – A concept and a tool. Networked Learning (2006),
    http://www.lancaster.ac.uk/fss/organisations/netlc/past/nlc2006/abstracts/pdfs/P41%20Retalis.pdf
21. Schön, M., Ebner, M., Kothmeier, G.: It's Just About Learning the Multiplication Table. In: Shum, S.B., Gasevic, D., Ferguson, R. (eds.) Proceedings of the 2nd International Conference on Learning Analytics and Knowledge (LAK 2012), pp. 73–81. ACM, New York (2012)
22. Siemens, G.: Learning Analytics: A foundation for informed change in higher education. In: Educause Conference Presentation (2011), http://www.slideshare.net/gsiemens/learning-analytics-educause
23. Taraghi, B., Ebner, M., Saranti, A., Schön, M.: On Using Markov Chain to Evidence the Learning Structures and Difficulty Levels of One Digit Multiplication. In: Proceedings of the 4th International Conference on Learning Analytics and Knowledge, LAK 2014 (accepted, in print, 2014)
24. Thomsen, N.A.: Ability Estimation with Item Response Theory. Assessment Systems Corporation, St. Paul (2009), http://www.assess.com/docs/Thompson_2009_-_Ability_estimation_with_IRT.pdf
25. Van Harmelen, M., Workman, D.: Analytics for Learning and Teaching. CETIS Analytics Series 1(3) (2012)

Using Confidence as Feedback in Multi-sized Learning Environments

Thomas L. Hench

Delaware County Community College, Media, Pennsylvania, USA
thench@dccc.edu

Abstract. This paper describes the use of existing confidence and performance data to provide feedback by first demonstrating the data's fit to a simple linear model. The paper continues by showing how the model's use as a benchmark provides feedback to allow current or future students to infer either the difficulty or the degree of under or over confidence associated with a specific question. Next, the paper introduces Confidence/Performance Indicators as graphical representations of this feedback and concludes with an evaluation of s trial use in an online setting. Findings support the efficacy of using of the Indicators to provide feedback to encourage students in multi-sized learning environments to reflect upon and rethink their choices, with future work focusing on the effectiveness of Indicator use on performance.

Keywords: confidence, feedback, multi-sized learning environments.

1   Introduction

Confidence provides a means to assess the metacognitive knowledge students have about their performance – in essence, do students know what they know and what they don't know. Darwin Hunt [1], one of the early researchers in the role of confidence, stated that the importance of having this knowledge is critical, for being misinformed is "much worse than being uninformed". Traditionally, one-dimensional assessment (performance only) supplies very little information about what students know and what they don't know. However, the addition of confidence as a second dimension provides important additional information in assessing students' knowledge of their performance [2] while also promoting a potentially deeper level of reflection and self-regulation. Work by Bruno [3], another early investigator, to measure knowledge quality led to the development of a two-dimensional assessment process which attempts to measure both correctness and confidence by a single quantity. Employed with success in training situations, this methodology, however, involves extensive calculations to implement which limits its potential use in middle to large scale learning situations containing hundreds or thousands of students.

Another approach is the confidence (or certainty) based marking (CBM) scheme developed by Gardner-Medwin and Gahan [4] which assumes a linear relationship between the confidence (here referred to as certainty) and the mark expected by the students as shown by the left-hand figure in Figure 1.

M. Kalz and E. Ras (Eds.): CAA 2014, CCIS 439, pp. 88–99, 2014.

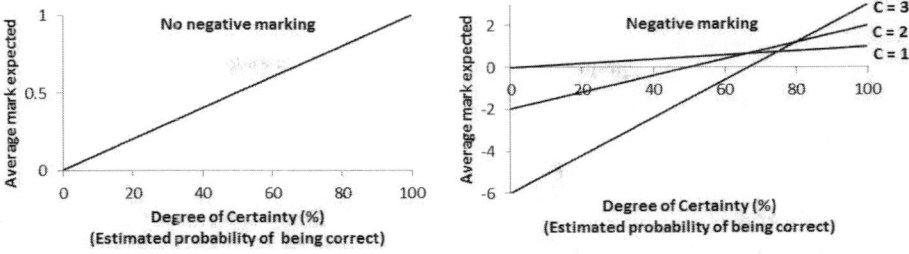

Fig. 1. Confidence-based marking schemes

Building upon this assumed relationship, Gardner-Medwin and Gahan proposed the use of a negative marking scheme (right-hand figure), where students are penalized for under or over estimating confidence and rewarded for reflection and deeper thought before answering. In this scheme, students receive points of 3, 2, or 1 for correct responses and 0, -2, or -6 for incorrect responses, depending on their estimated probability (confidence) of being correct. In essence, the scheme uses confidence as a motivating factor. While results [5] obtained from the use of CBM, primarily in medical school education, yielded positive results in terms of improved performance, the method does not focus specifically on obtaining quantifiable confidence levels. Other research into incorporating confidence into grading utilized methods such as a Problem Solving Inventory [6]   and the calculation of a "confidence score" [7] as ways to achieve what Paul [8] calls "scoring systems which encourage honesty" and thus reliable measures of confidence. Additionally, recent research describes the use of the difference between confidence and accuracy as part of a "bias score" component of a mark [9] and as a measure of a "metacognitive gap" [10]. An important part of these approaches [6, 7, 9, 10] is their use of a quantifiable measure of confidence as a second dimension of assessment in multi-sized (i.e. small, medium, or large) learning environments. However, the use of confidence as this additional dimension requires knowing the relationship, if any, between confidence and performance. If confidence has no correlation with performance, then its use in assessment becomes unclear. Thus, the research question addressed in this paper is as follows – "What relationship, if any, exists between confidence and performance?" The answer to this question determines whether or not the use of confidence as a second dimension of assessment along with performance is possible.

2   Method

The experimental data gathered to investigate the research question comes from student responses in the author's online Astronomy course over a period of six semesters (September 2010 to December 2013) using the commercially available SurveyMonkey© software linked to the course syllabus. As part of the coursework, each new group of students answered the same baseline set of fifty six multiple choice questions each semester and then indicated either a low, medium, or high confidence level in their answers. Class size varied from 30 to 50 students per semester with the total number of responses per baseline question ranging from N = 170 to 288. Figure 2 shows the overall confidence level distribution and performance for a typical question presented each semester over the period of the study.

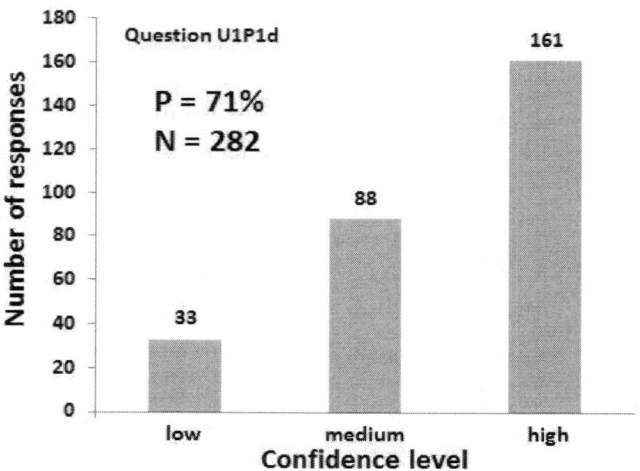

Fig. 2. Survey software output

In addition, Bloom's revised taxonomy [11] permitted critical thinking levels to be assigned to each question. As shown in Figure 3, questions designated as Level I require factual and conceptual knowledge resulting from remembering and understanding to complete, whereas Level II questions need procedural knowledge obtained through the processes of applying and analyzing.

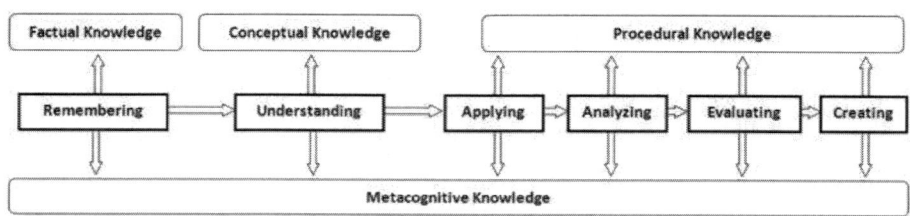

Fig. 3. Bloom's revised taxonomy

The determination of a quantifiable confidence level from student responses employed a physical analogy. The left-hand side of Figure 4 illustrates a confidence level distribution similar to that shown in Figure 2 and displayed as a bar chart with the magnitude of the total low, medium, and high confidence level responses are indicated by ℓ, m, and h.

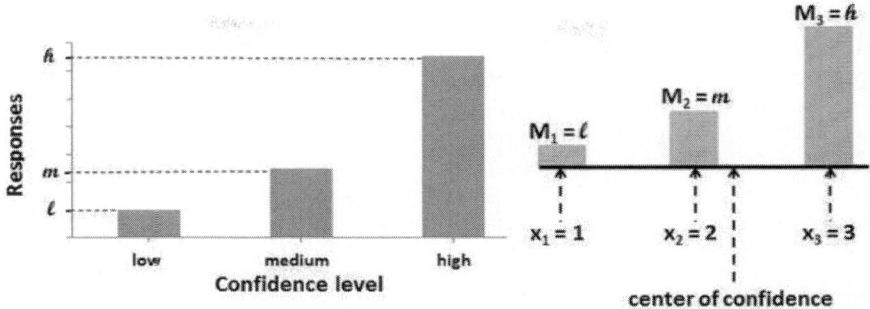

Fig. 4. Bar chart of typical confidence and center of confidence

As noted in the figure, the distribution of the confidence level responses provides an approximate description of the overall level for this particular question, in this case between medium and high. The right-hand side of Figure 4 illustrates another way of viewing this same information. Here the confidence magnitudes (ℓ, m, and h) correspond to masses M_1, M_2, and M_3 distributed at distances along a horizontal axis of $x_1 = 1$ (low confidence), $x_2 = 2$ (medium confidence), and $x_3 = 3$ (high confidence), with the center of mass of this system given by the familiar expression

$$\text{center of mass} = \Sigma M_i x_i / \Sigma M_i. \tag{1}$$

Substituting confidence magnitudes for masses and confidence levels for distances yields an analogous quantity called the center of confidence denoted algebraically as C, or

$$C = (\ell + 2m + 3h)/(\ell + m + h). \tag{2}$$

Applying equation (2) to the data shown in Figure 2 yields a center of confidence value of 2.45, in agreement with a visual estimate of the center of mass of an analogous physical system. Closer inspection of equation (2) reveals this result also corresponds to the expression used to determine the weighted average of the confidence magnitudes shown in the bar graph. Therefore, in addition to providing a visual representation, the center of confidence also provides the confidence level expected for a particular question. Stated in another way, each question has associated with it a center of confidence specific to that question. This result suggests an interpretation of the meaning of confidence based not upon the response given by an individual student after answering a specific question but to the expected response to that specific question before it is answered. It is this latter interpretation which is used as the meaning of confidence in this paper.

Before investigating the relationship between the confidence associated with a question (as represented by the center of confidence) and the performance on that question, the meaning of the latter needs further clarification. For each question, P represents the percentage of students who answered a particular question correctly as indicated in Figure 2. Conversely, this percentage also represents the expected or probable performance associated with that specific question. Thus, similarly to the treatment of confidence, each question has associated with it an expected or probable performance. Consequently, the meaning of performance here becomes the expected or probable outcome for a specific question rather than the outcome resulting from the answer given by an individual student to a specific question. This paper employs the probabilistic interpretation for the meaning of performance with the quantity P now denoted as the performance probability and expressed as a percentage. In view of the previous discussion, the research question is restated as "What relationship, if any, exists between the center of confidence C and performance probability P?"

3   Results

Gardner-Medwin and Gahan's assumed linear "no negative marking" case shown in Figure 1 suggests a possible model for the relationship between C and P. Specifically, as the confidence level of increases the probability of answering correctly increases in direct proportion. The model as adapted here assumes that if all students answer a question correctly ($P = 100\%$), they all would response at the highest confidence level thus yielding a center of confidence of $C = 3$. Similarly, if all students answer incorrectly ($P = 0\%$), they do so at the lowest center of confidence level giving a center of confidence of $C = 1$. For the case of $P = 50\%$, half of the students answer correctly and select the highest confidence level and the other half answers incorrectly and choses the lowest confidence level, thereby yielding a center of confidence of $C = 2$. A plot of these points results in the modeled performance probability P_m as a function of the center of confidence C (the dashed line and equation in Figure 5).

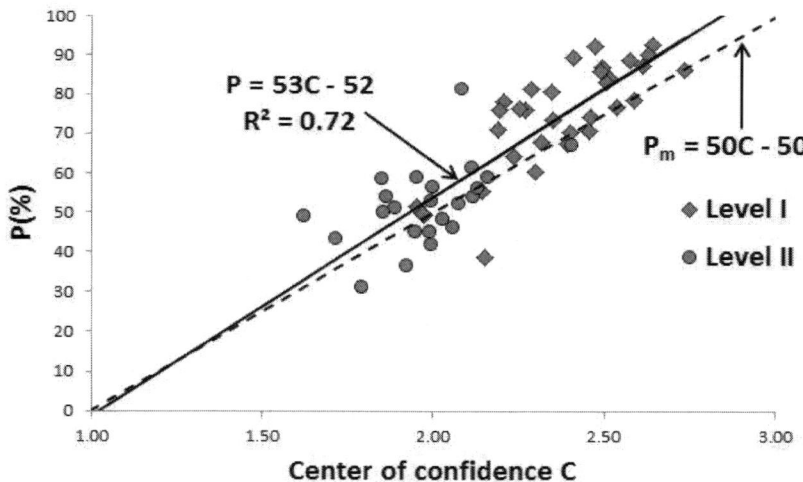

Fig. 5. Performance probability versus center of confidence for all responses

Also included in the figure are the experimental values of **P** and **C** as determined from the data for each baseline question, the accompanying linear regression line (solid line) and best fit equation to these points, the R-squared value, and the question critical thinking level for each question. Included in this plot is the point (71, 2.45) corresponding to the question referenced in Figure 2.

On first inspection, the data appears to be a reasonable fit to the model. To test the validity of the linearity of the model, the four assumptions shown in Table 1 regarding the use of a linear regression to describe the relationship need further examination. The violation of any of these assumptions as indicated by the validity tests calls into question the use of a linear model.

Table 1. Assumptions and validity tests for linear regressions

Assumption	Validity Test
Linearity – the independent and dependent variables are linearly related to one another	No discernible pattern in the distribution of points about a horizontal line in a standardized residual versus predicted value plot
Homoscedasticity - the variance of values of the dependent variable from the regression line is constant	Approximately constant spread of points about a horizontal line in a standardized residual versus predicted value plot
Independence – the random errors associated with the dependent variable are unrelated to one another	Durbin-Watson statistic of ~ 2.0 with an acceptable range of 1.75 to 2.25
Normality – the residual errors associated with the dependent variable are randomly distributed	Presence of a diagonal line resulting from normal probability plot

Figure 6 shows, on the left, the plot of the standard residual versus predicted performance probability P obtained by an Excel analysis of the data. The apparent linear relationship from Figure 5 and the discernment of no pattern associated with the points in Figure 6 both support the validity of the linearity assumption. In addition, the spread of points above and below the zero line is approximately equal therefore supporting the homoscedasticity of the data. (Possible outliers seen in Figure 6 will be addressed later in the paper). A value for the Durbin-Watson statistic of 1.93, calculated using Excel, supports the independence assumption and Figure 6 shows the diagonal line obtained from the normal probability plot, again obtained via Excel, again lending support of the normality assumption.

Furthermore, in a normal distribution, 63% of the total residual points fall within plus and minus one standard deviation and 95% between plus and minus two standard deviations. These conditions are also met by the data in Figure 6.

In summary, the validation of the four assumptions stated in Table 1 supports the use of linear relationship to model the behavior between the experimentally determined centers of confidence and the performance probabilities and, as such, provides an answer to the research question posed in the paper.

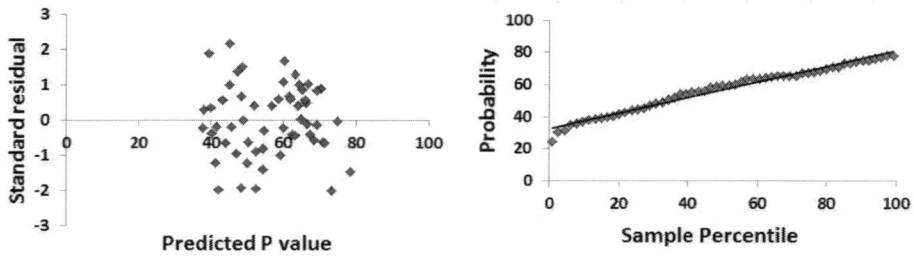

Fig. 6. Standard residual/predicted P plot and normal probability plot

4   Discussion

The closeness of agreement between the experimental line and the model line shown in Figure 5 suggests the use of the latter as a benchmark for comparing and interpreting the experimentally determined values of **C** and **P**. To examine this possibility, Figure 7 shows the previously plotted data with only the model line shown.

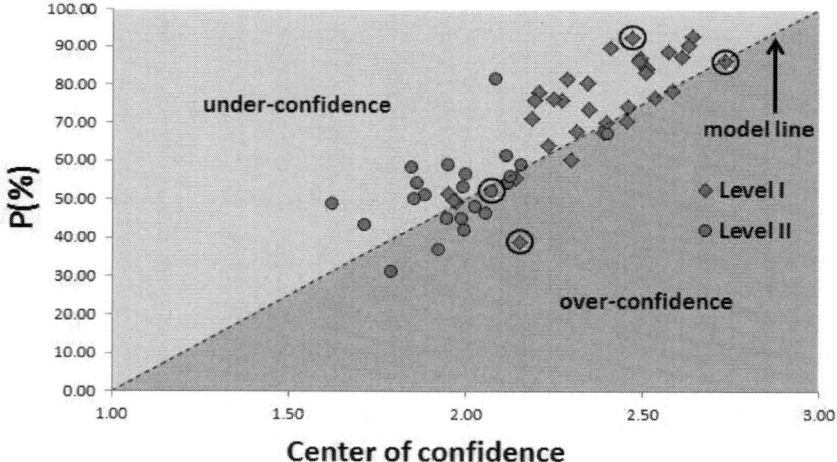

Fig. 7. Confidence regions

Specifically, points lying in the region either above or below the model line indicate situations of under or over confidence For example, the encircled point in the lower center of Figure 7 corresponds to a center of confidence **C** of 2.2 and an actual performance probability **P** of 39%. At this confidence level, the model predicts an expected performance probability of 60%. Thus, this question has associated with it an overestimation of the confidence in performance. For the point in the upper right of the figure given by **C** = 2.5 and **P** = 92%, the model predicts a performance probability of 75%. For this question, an under confidence in performance for that question is expected. For the two other encircled points lying on or close to the model line,

$C = 2.1$, $P = 52\%$ and $C = 2.7$ $P = 86\%$, the expected performance probabilities are 55% and 85% respectively. In these two cases, the performance predicted by the centers of confidence is in close agreement with the experimental performance probability. In this case, each question is considered calibrated, the difference between these two calibrated questions possibly attributable to the degree of difficulty of one question compared to the other. Thus, the use of the model line as a benchmark for comparing actual centers of confidence and performance probabilities allows for the identification of relative problem difficulty and the degree of under or over confidence associated with a question. Furthermore, the concept of miscalibration [12] offers an explanation for the variation in confidence seen in the Figure 7 by describing how judgment errors result in over confidence on difficult problems and under confidence on less difficult ones. The predominance of Level I questions in the under confidence region and the over confidence associated with some Level II questions supports this explanation.

While this interpretation does not presume the absence of errors in the data which may account for some of the differences shown, it nevertheless offers an alternative explanation for deviations from the model. Indeed, points lying at large distances from the model line possibly result from content or structure differences in questions, with outliers (under and over confidence points) indicating issues as to how the questions were phrased and resulting in a possible misinterpretation of the question and subsequent misplaced confidence. In any case, the deviation from the benchmark model line reveals differences in questions, whether intended or not.

The Confidence/Performance Indicators shown in Figure 8 graphically represent the information previously discussed for the four examples taken from Figure 7. Importantly, the indicators allow for both confidence and performance to be combined in a straightforward manner. In each indicator, the benchmark performance probability predicted by the model for a given center of confidence (top circle) is shown by the position of the arrow on the performance scale. The lower circle indicates the actual performance probability as found from the data.

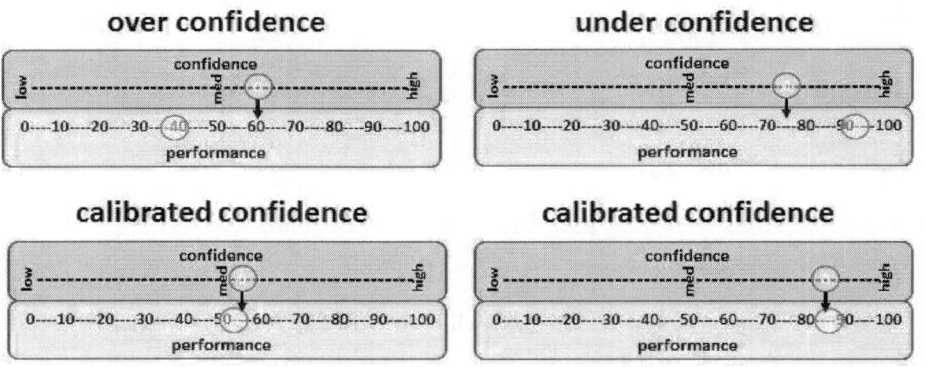

Fig. 8. Confidence/Performance Indicators

When included as part of a question, the indicators provide information which allows students to gauge the relative difficulty of a question as well as checking for any degree of under or over confidence associated with the question. In this sense, the Confidence/Performance Indicators provide a mechanism to deliver feedback by addressing what Glasson [13] notes as "what has been done well in relation to the success criteria", "what still needs to be done in order to achieve the success criteria", and "advice on how to achieve that improvement". Specifically, the use Confidence/Performance Indicators suggests a means to encourage reflection and rethinking on the part of the student without using negative grading.

The author conducted a trial of the indicators to determine the efficacy to encourage rethinking and reflection on the part of students. Specifically, the indicators, embedded into nineteen of the fifty six baseline questions over the course of eight weeks provided students in an online Introduction to Astronomy class with the option of referring to them as part of the determining an answer. Prior to this, all students completed a tutorial on the concept of the indicators and their use in identifying the relative difficulty of questions and cases of under or over confidence. After answering the questions, students then completed a survey to determine the number who had or had not chosen to use the indicators, their reasons for using or not using them, and their level of helpfulness for those who had used the indicators. The two areas previously mentioned, question difficulty and under/over confidence, and two additional questions regarding rethinking and reflection and the overall helpfulness comprised the four survey questions given to those students who chose to use the indicators. Table 2 shows these questions, along with the rating scale employed. In addition, two open ended questions asked the students to comment about why they did or did not use the indicators. As only those who used the indicators responded to the survey, a forced-choice format provided the possible responses to survey questions. Research [14,15] which suggests that people who answer forced-choice questions spend more time and invoke deeper processing when answering supports this choice.

Table 2. Survey questions for students using the Confidence/Performance Indicators

Scale → Survey questions ↓	very unhelpful 1	unhelpful 2	helpful 3	very helpful 4
Question Difficulty	How would you rate the Confidence/Performance Indicators in helping you judge the difficulty of the questions?			
Under/Over Confidence	How would you rate the Confidence/Performance Indicators in alerting you to under or over confidence issues with the questions?			
Reflect/Rethink	How would you rate the Confidence/Performance Indicators in making you rethink or reflect on your answers?			
Overall	Overall, how would you rate the Confidence/Performance Indicators in helping you to answer the follow-up questions?			

Of the 47 students answering the nineteen baseline questions containing the indicators, 87% (41) indicated that they referred to the Confidence/Performance Indicator when answering and thus completed the survey questions. Figure 9 shows the distribution of responses to the four survey questions and Table 3 provides an analysis of the three most common areas mentioned in the open-ended questions answered by all students. (Note: Cases of greater than 100% result from rounding errors.)

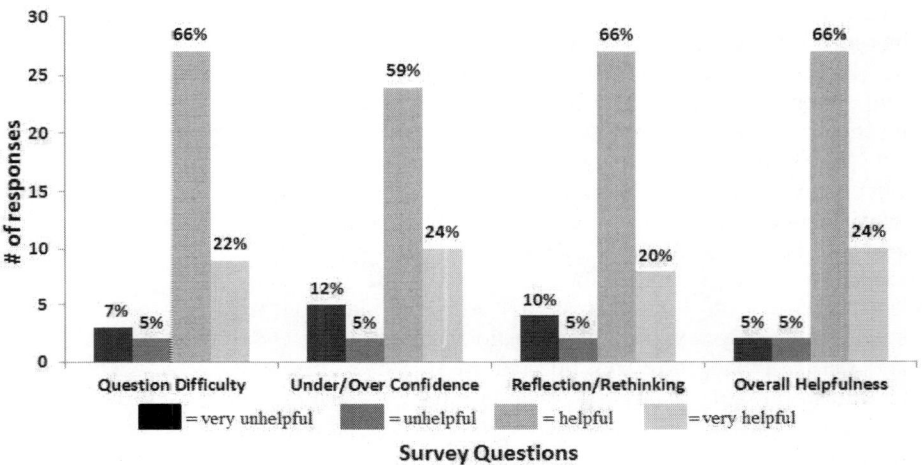

Fig. 9. Survey results of feedback areas

Table 3. Open-ended survey questions and response areas

Students using the indicators: "In the space below, enter any comments (pro or con) about the use of the Confidence/Performance Indicators in answering the follow-up question."
 	
Three most common response areas:
  1) Rethink, review, recheck, or reflect: 10 occurrences
  2) Comparisons: 6 occurrences
  3) Usability issues: 5 occurrences

Students not using the indicators: "Briefly list below the reason(s) why you did not use the Confidence/Performance Indicators when answering the follow-up questions."
 	
Three most common response areas:
  1) Already possess sufficient confidence in answer = 4 occurrences
  2) Negative effect on answers (lower confidence) = 2 occurrences
  3) No real reason = 2 occurrences

As illustrated in Figure 9, the majority of students (equal to or greater than 83%) selected with either helpful or very helpful responses when responding to the questions shown in Table 2. Additionally, analysis of the open-ended questions indicates that students felt the indicators encouraged rethinking and comparison, a result consistent with the survey results. A sample of comments regarding the use of the indicators include "definitely helps me rethink and recheck my answer", "make you think before answering questions", "offer a view of how other students are looking at problems and the level of difficulty", "helped me gauge how accurate my questions were and gave me more confidence for each answer I submitted", and "they let me know that the reason I was taking so long to answer was that it was a more difficult question." Important comments regarding the usability of the indicators such as "a better understanding on how to use the indicator, when answering questions will be helpful" and "Only con is it takes some getting used to but once you understand it its useful" suggest that those students finding the indicators unhelpful or very unhelpful need better preparation. Indeed, one student's comment that "I can't see how past students answers can help me, because they could be wrong or right" suggests a lack of understanding of what information the indicators provide.

Comments from those students not using the indicators such as "I wanted to see how much I really new about the questions without using the performance indicators" and "I am not really sure why I do not use them, I just do not" again suggest incomplete knowledge of indicators' function and their use at providing feedback.

In view of the survey results and open-ended responses, the results of the trial use of the Indicators support their efficacy as a feedback mechanism to encourage rethinking and reflection. To address the usability concerns identified in Table 3, the Confidence/Performance Indicator tutorial requires a revision to include more examples and situations of their application with students. Furthermore, the Indicators will be employed in all baseline questions in an online section of ninety to one hundred students. Having demonstrated here their ability to foster rethinking and reflection, the author plans to pursue further research to determine the effectiveness of the use of Confidence/Performance Indicators on student performance.

In summary, using existing data of student responses to a set of fifty-six baseline questions gathered over a period of six consecutive semesters, analysis showed that the calculated centers of confidence and corresponding performance probabilities followed a linear model. This model, in turn, provided a benchmark for interpreting the experimental data which resulted in feedback regarding question difficulty and the degree of under or over confidence associated with a question. The introduction, demonstration, and subsequent positive evaluation of Confidence/Performance Indicators as a graphical means of displaying feedback suggests their continued use as an effective method of providing this feedback to encourage rethinking and reflection on the part of students. More specifically, once created and implemented the indicators require no interaction with an instructor and function in small, medium, or large learning situations. Furthermore, generating the data necessary to establish the indicators requires only the addition of low, medium, or high confidence response options as part of formative or summative assessments with data collection and analysis performed electronically. Thus, as a feedback mechanism, Confidence/Performance Indicators provide a quantifiable second dimension to assessment which is adaptable to multi-sized learning environments.

References

1. Hunt, D.: The concept of knowledge and how to measure it. Journal of Intellectual Capital 4(1), 100–113 (2003)
2. Adams, T., Ewen, G.: The Importance of Confidence in Improving Educational Outcomes. In: Proceedings of the 25th Annual Conference on Distance Teaching & Learning, Board of Regents of the University of Wisconsin System (2009)
3. Bruno, J.: Using Testing to Provide Feedback to Support Instruction: A Reexamination of the Role of Assessment in Educational Organizations. In: Leclercq, D., Bruno, J. (eds.) Item Banking: Interactive Testing and Self-Assessment. NATO ASI Series Computer and Systems Sciences, vol. F112, pp. 190–209. Springer, Heidelberg (1993)
4. Gardner-Medwin, A., Gahan, M.: Formative and Summative Confidence-Based Assessment. In: Proc. 7th International Computer-Aided Assessment Conference, Loughborough, UK, pp. 147–155 (July 2003)
5. Schoendorfer, N., Emmett, D.: Use of certainty-based marking in a second-year medical student cohort: a pilot study. In: Advances in Medical Education and Practice, vol. 3, pp. 139–143. Dove Medical Press Ltd. (2012)
6. Larson, D., Scott, D., Neville, M., Knodel, B.: Measuring Student's Confidence with Problem Solving in the Engineering Design Classroom. In: Proceedings of the Annual Conference American Society for Engineering Education, Seattle, Washington, June 28-July 1 (1998)
7. Petr, D.: Measuring (and Enhancing?) Student Confidence with Confidence Scores. In: Proceedings of the 30th ASEE/IEEE Frontiers in Education Conference, Kansas City, MO, October 18-21 (2000)
8. Paul, J.: Improving educational assessment by incorporating confidence measurement, analysis of self - awareness, and performance evaluation: The computer-based alternative assessment (CBAA) Project (2007), http://www.jodypaul.com/ASSESS/
9. Michailova, J., Katter, J.: Thoughts on quantifying overconfidence in economic experiments, MPRA Paper No. 53112, Helmut-Schmidt University & York University (2013)
10. Hench, T.: Assessing Metacognition Via An Online Survey Tool. In: Proceedings of the 10th International Conference on Computer-Based Learning in Science, Barcelona, Spain, June 26-June 29 (2012)
11. Krathwohl, D.: A Revision of Bloom's Taxonomy: An Overview. Theory Into Practice 41(4) (2002), Copyright C) 2002 College of Education, The Ohio State University, Autumn
12. Klayman, J., Soll, J., Gonzalez-Vallejo, C., Barlas, S.: Overconfidence: It Depends on How, What, and Whom You Ask. Organizational Behavior and Human Decision Processes 79(3), 216–247 (1999)
13. Glasson, Y.: Improving Student Achievement: A Practical Guide to Assessment for Learning. Education Services Australia 78 (2008)
14. Rasinski, K., Mingay, D., Bradburn, N.: Do respondents really mark All That Apply on self-administered questions. Public Opinion Quarterly 58(3), 400–408 (1994)
15. Smyth, J., Dillman, D., Christian, L., Stern, M.: Comparing Check-All and Forced-Choice Question Formats in Web Surveys. Public Opinion Quarterly 70(1), 66–77 (2006)

A Review of Static Analysis Approaches for Programming Exercises

Michael Striewe and Michael Goedicke

University of Duisburg-Essen, Germany
{michael.striewe,michael.goedicke}uni-due.de

Abstract. Static source code analysis is a common feature in automated grading and tutoring systems for programming exercises. Different approaches and tools are used in this area, each with individual benefits and drawbacks, which have direct influence on the quality of assessment feedback. In this paper, different principal approaches and different tools for static analysis are presented, evaluated and compared regarding their usefulness in learning scenarios. The goal is to draw a connection between the technical outcomes of source code analysis and the didactical benefits that can be gained from it for programming education and feedback generation.

1 Introduction

Automated grading and assessment tools for programming exercises are in use in many ways in higher education. Surveys from 2005 [3] and 2010 [16] list a significant amount of different systems and numbers have grown since then. One of the most common features of systems for automated grading of programming exercises is static analysis of source code. The range includes checks for syntactical correctness of source code up to checks for structural similarities between a student's solution and a sample solution [32]. Different approaches are used and different tools and techniques are integrated into these systems. For each decision for a tool or technique individual positive and negative effects on the quality of feedback given by the system can be assumed. However, reviews and comparisons of program analysis tools usually focus on bug finding quality in the context of industrial applications by running some kinds of benchmark contests (e.g. [24]) or analyzing case studies (e.g. [1]). Thus it is the goal of this paper to compare and evaluate different principal approaches to static code analysis specifically in the context of automated grading and assessment. Special attention is paid to the connections between technical outcomes of source code analysis and the didactical benefits that can be gained from it for programming education and feedback generation.

This paper focuses on techniques applicable in automated grading and assessment systems that are running as a server application, allowing on-line submission of exercise solutions. We are not concerned with analysis and feedback mechanisms integrated into special IDEs as learning environments. To ensure a

M. Kalz and E. Ras (Eds.): CAA 2014, CCIS 439, pp. 100–113, 2014.

reasonable limited scope, this paper also focuses on approaches and tools useful in the context of object-oriented programming with Java. Results may be partially valid for other object-oriented programming languages than Java. Similarly, some results may be partially valid for static analysis for other programming paradigms.

Static analysis capabilities of tools for automated grading and assessment have also been reviewed in the context of structural similarity analysis [22]. This type of analysis intends to give hints on the systematic extension of incomplete solutions as also considered in this paper. Another large branch of static analysis in learning scenarios is the use of metrics (e.g. [20]). Research and application in this area is more focused on an overall quality measure for solutions than in detailed feedback for single mistakes and will not be considered in this paper.

This contribution is organized as follows: Section 2 gives an overview on the special requirements of static analysis of source code in the context of automated grading and assessment. It also gives an overview on prominent systems for automated grading and tutoring. Section 3 discusses differences between approaches, such as differences between analysis of source code and byte code. These comparisons are made as independently from actual tools as possible. Section 4 discusses features of several tools which are known to be used in current automated grading and tutoring system. Section 5 concludes the paper.

2 Static Analysis in Automated Grading and Tutoring

The goal of automated grading and tutoring tools in learning scenarios is twofold: First, automated tutoring is intended to enable students to develop correct solutions for exercises without intensive assistance by a human teacher. Thus it focuses on giving useful hints on incorrect and incomplete solutions that go beyond plain messages like "error in line X". Second, automated grading is intended to assist teachers in the tedious task of grading large numbers of assignments, especially if formative assessments are conducted several times in a course. In this scenario it focuses on giving adequate marks for solutions, which especially includes distinctions between major and minor errors. The common ground for both scenarios is to generate meaningful feedback automatically, based on a thorough analysis of source code submitted by students.

```
int x,y,z = 0;
// << some code here >>
if (x + y < y + z);
{
  x = y - z;
}
```

Listing 1.1. A piece of Java source code which is syntactically correct, but contains a completely useless if-statement

The most basic way of giving feedback to a solution of a programming exercise are reports on syntactical errors as generated by a compiler. For many students, writing syntactically correct code is the first obstacle in learning programming [9] and thus compiler messages are the first automated feedback they see. As this type of feedback can be generated locally on the student's own computer it is of minor importance for on-line submission systems. Anyway, compiler messages as feedback on programming errors are not specific to learning scenarios. Instead, more specific requirements for automated feedback can be derived from learning scenarios:

- Static analysis can check for source code which is syntactically correct but shows misunderstood concepts. A typical example for Java is shown in Listing 1.1. Even an experienced teacher may need some time to realize that this `if`-statement is useless because of the extra semicolon at the end of its line. Mistakes like this can be detected by static analysis and reported in conjunction with a short explanation of the related concepts. The same applies for violated coding conventions. Similar to compiler messages, detecting this kind of mistakes is not necessarily specific to learning scenarios, as these mistakes can in general also be made by experienced programmers. However, we can state as a requirement, that static analysis in learning scenarios needs to check for more than syntactical errors. As a second requirement we can also state that static analysis in learning scenarios must be able to give feedback to parts of the program that have no relevant functionality.
- Static analysis can check for source code which is correct in general terms, but not allowed in the context of a certain exercise or execution environment. For example, an exercise may ask students to implement a linked list on their own. Obviously, the use of `java.util.LinkedList` should not be allowed in this case. In contrast to the requirement discussed above, this is no general coding convention, but specific to a particular exercise. Other exercises may allow to use this existing implementation. Thus static analysis in learning scenarios needs to be easily configurable for each specific exercise.
- Similar to the requirement discussed above, there may be code structures that are required in any correct solution of an exercise. For example, an exercise may ask students to solve a problem by implementing a recursive algorithm. In this case, any solution that does not involve recursion is wrong in terms of the task description, even if the running program produces the correct output. Hence static analysis in learning scenarios must be able to report not only the presence of undesired code structures, but also the absence of desired code structures.
- In tutoring scenarios students may expect to be not only informed about the existence of a mistake, but to get hints on how to correct this mistake and improve their solution. This is especially true for solutions that are correct in syntax and functionality, but do not completely fulfill the requirements for the given exercise. In these cases, students may expect to get a hint on the next step to be taken. Thus the most sophisticated requirement for static analysis is to give feedback on how to systematically extend an incomplete piece of source code to reach a given goal.

Note that there is at least one more requirement in automated grading and assessment systems which involves source code analysis: Checks for plagiarism. We leave this (and similar requirements) out of the scope of this paper, since the required analysis is of different nature than the others discussed in this paper. Checks for plagiarism in general include comparisons between many solutions created by students instead of analysis of a single solution or a comparison between one student's solution and a sample solution. For a study on plagiarism detection tools in automated grading systems refer e.g. to [13].

Not only requirements in the context of automated grading and tutoring can be characterized, but also typical properties of solutions submitted by students. In most cases, automated tools are used in the context of introductory courses, where large numbers of solutions have to be graded. Exercises in these courses are of moderate complexity, so solutions do not consist of more than a few Java classes and a few methods in each of these classes. Enhanced concepts like Aspect Oriented Programming or reflection are typically not among the topics of these courses, so there is no need to care about these in static analysis. Solutions are often created based on code templates or at least prescribed method signatures, so assumptions about existing names for methods and perhaps variables can be used as an entry point for static analysis. As already mentioned above, checking the existence of such prescribed structures is an explicit requirement in grading and tutoring.

Table 1. Static code analysis capabilities of some automated grading and tutoring systems

Name	Source Code Analysis	Byte Code Analysis
ASB	yes (CheckStyle)	yes (FindBugs)
CourseMarker	yes	no
Duesie	yes (PMD)	no
EASy	no	yes (FindBugs)
ELP	yes	no
JACK	yes	no
Marmoset	no	yes (FindBugs)
Praktomat	yes (CheckStyle)	no
Web-CAT	yes (CheckStyle/PMD)	yes

From the literature the following automated grading and tutoring systems for Java could be reported (in alphabetical order): ASAP [10], ASB [21], BOSS [17], CourseMarker [14], Duesie [15], EASy [12], eduComponents [4], ELP [31], GATE [28], JACK [29], Marmoset [27], Mooshak [19], Online Judge [6], Praktomat [33], Web-CAT [26], xLx [25]. Table 1 gives a more detailed overview on those tools that involve more static code analysis capabilities than plain compiler checks. The use of other external tools than CheckStyle [7], FindBugs [11], and PMD [23] could not be found in the literature. All three tools are open source and non-commercial projects. CourseMarker and ELP employ software metrics for static analysis. ELP uses a XML representation of the abstract syntax tree for this purpose and offers also comparison of syntax trees for students' solutions and sample solutions [32]. JACK uses a graph transformation engine [18] and the graph query language GReQL [5] for analysis of abstract syntax graphs, which are abstract syntax trees enriched by additional elements. We will elaborate more on this later on.

All systems listed above understand static code analysis in automated grading primarily as applying rule based checks. All tools named above do also handle code analysis as rule based or query based inspection, respectively. Consequently, Section 3 and Section 4 of this paper focus on rule based checks as well.

3   Comparing Approaches

This section compares technical approaches used in the tools and systems identified above. Comparison is focused on the general benefits and drawbacks of a specific technique, ignoring limitations or extensions raising from a specific implementation of that technique.

3.1   Source Code vs. Byte Code Analysis

As already suggested by the layout of Table 1 it is important to know whether static code analysis is carried out on source code or byte code. For programming languages other than Java, which are not considered in this paper, byte code may be replaced by machine code. While source code is directly written by students, byte code is generated from the source code by a compiler. Thus the first question to answer is whether byte code can be generated in any case. Since we restricted ourselves to on-line submission systems and assumed students to be able to compile source code on their own, we can also assume that submitted solutions do not contain compiler errors. Thus byte code of a complete solution can be generated and byte code analysis tools have no disadvantage in comparison to source code analysis tools regarding this aspect.

Regarding checking capabilities beyond syntactical checks both source code and byte code analysis are able to report more than syntactical errors. For example, inheritance structures, number of method parameters or types of fields are visible both in source code and in byte code.

Regarding feedback on irrelevant code statements it is important to know that a compiler may be able to remove unnecessary statements for code optimization. While this is beneficial for several reasons in productive environments, it may be a drawback in learning scenarios: Static analysis on byte code is not necessarily able to report unnecessary statements, if these are removed by the compiler. If the compiler gives a notice about removed statements, these messages can of course be used as feedback messages to students. Source code analysis can give feedback on unnecessary statements without general limitations.

Regarding configurability with respect to individual exercises it can be observed that exercise specific hooks like names for classes, methods, or fields are available both in source code and in byte code. Technically there is no major difference in analyzing e.g. the parse tree of source code or its related byte code. So if a flexible and configurable way of defining checks exist, it can be used for both formats.

Regarding feedback on missing statements the desired granularity has to be taken into account. For example, any kind of loop statement is represented by goto-statements in byte code. If a task description requires to use a loop, but there is no goto-statement in the byte code, this can be reported as a mistake. However, if the task description requires to use a specific type of loop, it cannot reliably be derived from an existing goto-statement, whether this specific type of loop has been used. Although all loop constructs in Java result in typical byte code patterns, analysis of these patterns is not trivial in all cases. In source code analysis, this problem does not exist, since every statement can be recognized from the source code directly.

Regarding hints on systematic extension of incomplete solutions the same concerns as above have to be applied. By comparison of a student's solution and a sample solution a missing loop can be determined both in source code or in byte code. In this case the system can suggest to think about loops. However, if both solutions contain a loop, only source code analysis is able to give more specific hints on completing a certain type of loop, e.g. by detecting a missing termination condition in a for-statement.

In summary, byte code analysis does not fulfill all requirements for learning scenarios, while source code analysis seems to do so with respect to all aspects.

3.2 Trees vs. Graphs

As mentioned towards the end of Section 2, there are approaches using an abstract syntax tree, while other approaches use an abstract syntax graph. An abstract syntax graph is basically an abstract syntax tree, which is enriched by additional arcs, e.g. for connecting method call nodes to the respective method declaration or accesses to fields to the respective field declaration [30]. See Figure 1 for an illustrating example. Solid arcs belong to the abstract syntax tree, while dashed arcs extend this tree to an abstract syntax graph. The information used for insertion of this arcs is computed in a post-processing step after parsing by resolving names and scopes. Hence it has to be noticed that the difference between graphs and trees is mainly a difference of data formats. In fact, syntax graphs are generated from syntax trees, so any information available in the graph is also available in the tree. However, it can be considered to make a difference whether this information is available explicitly or implicitly.

The capabilities of checking for more than syntactical errors are not affected by the choice of data format. The same is true for capabilities in reporting missing elements of a solution, because in both cases basically the same structures have to be searched. Configurability with respect to individual exercises is also not affected by the choice of data format.

Irrelevant pieces of code can possibly be found more easily in syntax graphs, e.g. unused methods can be detected by searching method declaration nodes without incoming arcs from respective method call nodes. Hints on systematic

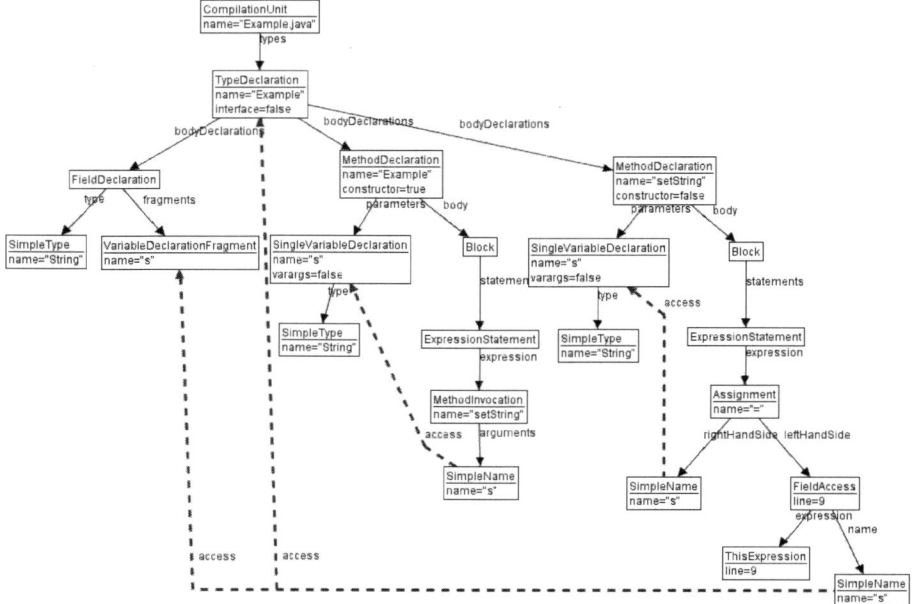

Fig. 1. Example showing an abstract syntax graph for a simple Java class with a constructor and a method. The solid arcs form the underlying abstract syntax tree.

extension of incomplete solutions can have benefits from this fact, because this way hints on missing connections between parts of a solution can easily be given. So generating abstract syntax graphs from abstract syntax trees before starting an analysis seems to be a valuable preprocessing step, which makes some operations easier. However, it does not add functional benefits in the learning scenario. Another aspect is discussed in Section 4.2 later in this paper.

3.3 Single File vs. Multi File Analysis

From the tools discussed in this paper, CheckStyle limits itself to checking only single source files, while all other tools allow to analyze multiple files. Since automated grading is often used in courses with several hundred students, analysis time is a limited resource. Time can possibly be saved by performing analysis in parallel, which is easier if only single files have to be handled. Thus it is a reasonable question whether multi file analysis is necessary because of other requirements of the learning scenario.

The goal of checking for more than syntactical errors is not affected by this question, since other mistakes can also be found in single files. In fact, many solutions of simple programming exercises do not consist of more than one source file at all and static program analysis is not blocked this way.

Finding irrelevant code statements is much harder when single file analysis is applied. For example a method may appear unused in a single file because it is not called by the class defined in this file, but at the same time it can be called from another class defined in a separate file. To handle this issue, storing results from each file analysis and reviewing this intermediate results would be necessary. The same applies for the search for missing elements, if the task description does not state a specific class where the element has to be located. If no intermediate results are stored, some properties of a solution cannot be assessed. Consequently, configurability for individual exercises can considered to be decreased with single file analysis in this case.

Giving hints on systematic extensions of an incomplete solution based on the comparison to a sample solution is not affected by single or multi file analysis. The total number of features compared may be reduced because of the reasons given above, but each feature found in a single file of the sample solution and missing in the student's solution can be used for directing feedback.

4   Comparing Tool Features

In addition to general benefits and drawbacks of analysis approaches, tool specific issues have to be taken into account when integrating static checks into automated grading and tutoring systems. This integration covers both technical and organizational aspects: Technically, solution data has to be passed from the systems to analysis tools and analysis results have to be passed back to the systems. Regarding organization, tools have to be configured for individual exercises and results have to be interpreted with respect to marking schemes. All these aspects are investigated in this section based on the five tools named already above (Section 2): CheckStyle, PMD, FindBugs, GReQL, and graph transformations. For the latter, graph transformation rules written in AGG [2] are taken into account. Other tools for graph transformations exist, but to the best of the authors knowledge they are not used for static code analysis in automated grading and tutoring systems.

From these five tools, the first three are dedicated code analysis tools and do thus provide features specific for this domain. GReQL and graph transformations are general approaches for handling graphs, which can be used for checking syntax graphs. However, they do not provide any features specific to static source analysis natively and hence they require additional programming effort before they can be used in automated grading and tutoring systems.

Quality of analysis results in terms of false positives or false negatives is not considered in this paper, because they do not only depend on general capabilities of tools and approaches, but on the quality of individual checking rules. Writing precise rules surely requires a good and powerful tool, but also experience and domain knowledge. Thus it is beyond the scope of this paper dealing with approaches and tools from a technical point of view.

4.1   Tool Integration

In general, two different ways exist to integrate an external tool into an existing system: Integrating the external tool as a library and using its API or assuming

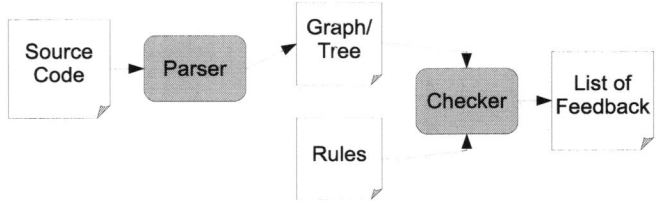

Fig. 2. Analysis process in case of tool integration via an API

it as an existing separate installation and starting it from the command line as a separate process. Further integration with respect to LMS is not considered here, as this has to be done on the level of automated assessment tools as a whole and not on the level of specific checking facilities.

CheckStyle, PMD, and FindBugs can be used via the command line as well as via an API. GReQL as a query language can be executed via a library named JGraLab, thus only API integration is possible. AGG does not offer possibilities for being used via the command line, so it has to be integrated as library, too. Figure 2 illustrates the general process of analysis in cases where the analysis tool is connected via an API.

Regarding feedback quality for static analysis, these differences do not matter. Once the integration is done, no further technical changes have to be applied when the system is used. Since all tools offer API integration, no relevant limitations regarding command line options or possible run time environments for installation of these tools have to be obeyed.

Another aspect of integration is the aspect of semantics of checking rules and results of checks. In CheckStyle, PMD and FindBugs it is clearly defined how rules are applied and which results are returned when a rule matches or is violated. Operations for executing specific checks and obtaining the results are offered directly via the API or via command line options and result files of a specified format, respectively. Different to that, the integration of GReQL and AGG into automated grading and tutoring tools is completely left to the developer. The APIs just offer general methods for executing queries or transformation rules, respectively. If a single check in terms of static program analysis is broken down into several queries or transformation rules, the correct execution of the checking process has to be handled by the developer of the tool integration. The same applies for the interpretation of analysis results. In particular, GReQL and AGG can be integrated in the following way:

– **AGG:** In AGG, rules applied during analysis can be realized by graph transformation rules which introduce additional nodes (e.g. error markers) into the abstract syntax graph. Since these markers can be reused and removed by other rules, this allows for chaining AGG rules to represent more complex analysis rules. If all rules have been applied, the remaining error markers are collected and a list of feedback can be assembled from the error messages contained in each marker.

- **GReQL:** In GReQL, queries on graph structures can be written (somewhat similar to SQL) that report tuples of nodes that match the query. Hence analysis rules can be expressed through a graph query and an expected result, which may be an empty set if the query looks for undesired code structures. If the actual result of the query does not match the expected result, a feedback message is added to the list of feedback, which is returned at the end of the process after all queries have been executed.

On the one hand, this requires much more effort in integration than with dedicated analysis tools. On the other hand, this allows for more freedom in defining complex input and interpreting results.

In summary, these results are not surprising. The more general a tool is, the more effort is necessary to perform specialized tasks. However, since learning scenarios may require very specialized and even exercise specific checks which are not among the standard checks offered by dedicated program analysis tools, the higher effort in tool integration can save effort in productive use.

4.2 Writing Checks and Feedback Rules

One of the requirements as listed in Section 2 is configurability for individual exercises. Thus it is an important question how easy and flexible checking rules can be written for specific tools. Since exercise specific feedback can only be given if exercise specific checks are created, this is a core criterion. As discussed at the beginning of this paper, this focus on feedback is a key difference between industrial use of static analysis tools and use of these tools in e-assessment.

In CheckStyle and PMD, checking rules are implemented using the visitor pattern which traverses the syntax tree. Both tools come with a large predefined set of standard checks, which can be switched on and off as needed. Writing own checks is possible by defining own operations for the visitor and integrating the new implementation to the existing installation via a configuration file. As an alternative, PMD also offers the possibility to define checks as XPath queries on the syntax tree. These additional queries are also integrated by adding them to the configuration. See Listing 1.2 for an example of an XPath query looking for a broken `if`-statement as shown in Listing 1.1. FindBugs offers also a predefined set of checks, but no simple facility to add own checks by implementing new operations. Customizing FindBugs for individual exercises is thus not possible.

As more general approaches, GReQL and AGG offer native support for defining own rules and queries. In fact, GReQL as a query language does not offer anything else than executing queries on graphs in a specified language and reporting results as tuples of nodes as described above. See Listing 1.3 for an example for a GReQL query looking for a broken `if`-statement as shown in Listing 1.1. The rule looks somewhat more complex than the one for PMD, but this is no general observation. In fact, some of the rules built-in to PMD are implemented directly in Java, because an XPath query for them would be too complex [8]. GReQL allows to implement additional functions that can be used in queries to realize complex checks, which allows to shorten queries as well.

```
//IfStatement[@Else='false']/Statement[EmptyStatement]
```

Listing 1.2. XPath query for PMD searching for an `if`-statement that is broken because of an extra semicolon following the condition

```
from x : V{IfStatement}
with not isEmpty(x -->{IfStatementThenStatement}&{EmptyStatement}) and
    isEmpty(x -->{IfStatementElseStatement}&{Statement})
report x end
```

Listing 1.3. GReQL query searching for an `if`-statement that is broken because of an extra semicolon following the condition. See listing 1.2 for the equivalent XPath query for PMD.

AGG even offers a graphical interface for defining graph transformation rules, so no explicit knowledge on graph traversals or query languages is needed. However, as a graph transformation engine, AGG is somewhat oversized for pure matching of graph patterns. Writing code checks as graph transformation rules is hardly intuitive and requires deep understanding of the way, the graph transformation engine is integrated into the grading and tutoring system.

Tools which require to write and compile program code and to reconfigure an existing installation for adding new checks can be considered not appropriate or at least not convenient for learning scenarios with the need for exercise specific checks. The same applies for tools which do not allow any easy extension at all. Query languages like GReQL or XPath are much more appropriate in this scenario, as long as the queries can be passed to the tool individually as needed. Graphical editors may make writing rules easier, but currently no editors specialized on checking rules for static program analysis in learning scenarios exist.

It can be noticed that the differences between syntax trees and syntax graphs as discussed in Section 3.2 are also important for the ease of writing checks. Finding recursive methods can easily be expressed in a graph pattern by two nodes for method declaration and method call, connected by a path from the declaration to the call and an additional access arc from the call to the declaration. Finding the same situation on a syntax tree would require at least string comparison for method names. In addition, finding indirect recursion where `methodA` calls `methodB` and this calls `methodA` again requires additional effort for storing and comparing partial results. In this case, preparing a syntax graph serves as a preprocessing step which performs exactly this additional operations once, so they need not be defined again for every check.

4.3 Weighting Checks

An important issue in automated grading is the design of a marking scheme. Often it is desirable to distinguish between smaller and greater mistakes and to give grades depending on which checking rules have been violated.

CheckStyle, PMD and FindBugs allow weighting by using severity levels for rules. This allows for simple marking schemes where solutions with mistakes of low severity get better grades than solutions with mistakes of higher severity. Constructing more fine grained marking schemes requires additional effort and additional input, providing weights for each checking rule. The data formats used to specify rules in the external tools are not capable of handling these additional information directly.

Graph transformations and GReQL as general approaches for finding patterns in graphs do not offer any native support for weights. As already discussed above, a specific data format for defining rules has to be written anyway, so it is no major additional effort to extend this data format to handle weights.

In summary, dedicated program analysis tools which use severity levels or similar facilities allow to construct simple marking schemes. More general approaches require additional effort even for simple schemes. However, if fine grained schemes with individual weights for every rule are desired, additional effort is necessary in any case.

5   Conclusions

In this paper, several approaches and tools for static source code analysis in automated grading and tutoring tools have been reviewed and compared. It can be stated that it is necessary in learning scenarios to use tools that are able to handle multiple source files. Preprocessing steps, which extend syntax trees to syntax graphs with additional information turned out to be helpful for more flexible and exercise specific configuration of checking tools. Consequently, some of the tools discussed in this paper can be considered insufficient to use the full power of static analysis for feedback generation in e-assessment systems.

Every approach investigated in this paper can be integrated into automated grading and tutoring systems with no major technical obstacles, but additional effort is needed to map fine grained marking schemes to checking rules. Additional effort is unavoidable if general approaches like GReQL or graph transformations should be used, but these approaches do also offer more flexibility towards the integration of customized and exercise specific checks. Consequently, it can be considered acceptable to spent time on this integration work in order to obtain better results and more detailed feedback opportunities.

From these results, a mixture of PMD, GReQL and AGG seems to be the best goal for future development work: It should result in graphical editing of checking rules for multiple source code files based on syntax graphs, focused on static source code analysis and capable of handling fine grained marking schemes. None of the tools discussed in this paper has already reached this level of quality.

References

1. Static Analysis Tool Exposition (SATE 2009) Workshop, Co-located with 11th semiannual Software Assurance Forum, Arlington, VA (2009)
2. AGG website, http://tfs.cs.tu-berlin.de/agg/

3. Ala-Mutka, K.M.: A Survey of Automated Assessment Approaches for Programming Assignments. Computer Science Education 15(2), 83–102 (2005)
4. Amelung, M., Forbrig, P., Rösner, D.: Towards generic and flexible web services for e-assessment. In: ITiCSE 2008: Proceedings of the 13th Annual Conference on Innovation and Technology in Computer Science Education, pp. 219–224. ACM, New York (2008)
5. Bildhauer, D., Ebert, J.: Querying Software Abstraction Graphs. In: Working Session on Query Technologies and Applications for Program Comprehension (QTAPC 2008), Collocated with ICPC 2008 (2008)
6. Cheang, B., Kurnia, A., Lim, A., Oon, W.-C.: On automated grading of programming assignments in an academic institution. Comput. Educ. 41(2), 121–131 (2003)
7. CheckStyle Project, http://checkstyle.sourceforge.net
8. Copeland, T.: PMD applied. Centennial Books (2005)
9. Denny, P., Luxton-Reilly, A., Tempero, E.D., Hendrickx, J.: Understanding the syntax barrier for novices. In: Rößling, G., Naps, T.L., Spannagel, C. (eds.) Proceedings of the 16th Annual SIGCSE Conference on Innovation and Technology in Computer Science Education, ITiCSE 2011, Darmstadt, Germany, June 27-29, pp. 208–212. ACM (2011)
10. Douce, C., Livingstone, D., Orwell, J., Grindle, S., Cobb, J.: A technical perspective on ASAP - automated systems for assessment of programming. In: Proceedings of the 9th CAA Conference, Loughborough University (2005)
11. FindBugs Project, http://findbugs.sourceforge.net/
12. Gruttmann, S.J.: Formatives E-Assessment in der Hochschullehre. MV-Wissenschaft (2009)
13. Hage, J., Rademaker, P., van Vugt, N.: A comparison of plagiarism detection tools. Technical report, Department of Information and Computing Sciences, Utrecht University (2010)
14. Higgins, C., Hegazy, T., Symeonidis, P., Tsintsifas, A.: The CourseMarker CBA System: Improvements over Ceilidh. Education and Information Technologies 8(3), 287–304 (2003)
15. Hoffmann, A., Quast, A., Wismüller, R.: Online-Übungssystem für die Programmierausbildung zur Einführung in die Informatik. In: Seehusen, S., Lucke, U., Fischer, S. (eds.) DeLFI 2008, 6. e-Learning Fachtagung Informatik. LNI, vol. 132, pp. 173–184. GI (2008)
16. Ihantola, P., Ahoniemi, T., Karavirta, V., Seppälä, O.: Review of recent systems for automatic assessment of programming assignments. In: Proceedings of the 10th Koli Calling International Conference on Computing Education Research, Koli Calling 2010, pp. 86–93. ACM, New York (2010)
17. Joy, M., Griffiths, N., Boyatt, R.: The BOSS Online Submission and Assessment System. Journal on Educational Resources in Computing (JERIC) 5(3) (2005)
18. Köllmann, C., Goedicke, M.: A Specification Language for Static Analysis of Student Exercises. In: Proceedings of the International Conference on Automated Software Engineering (2008)
19. Leal, J.P., Silva, F.: Mooshak: a Web-based multi-site programming contest system. Software–Practice & Experience 33(6), 567–581 (2003)
20. Mengel, S.A., Yerramilli, V.: A case study of the static analysis of the quality of novice student programs. In: The Proceedings of the Thirtieth SIGCSE Technical Symposium on Computer Science Education, SIGCSE 1999, pp. 78–82. ACM, New York (1999)

21. Morth, T., Cechsle, R., Schloß, H., Schwinn, M.: Automatische Bewertung studentischer Software. In: Workshop "Rechnerunterstütztes Selbststudium in der Informati", Universität Siegen, 17 (September 2007)
22. Naude, K.A.: Assessing Program Code through Static Structural Similarity. Master's Thesis, Faculty of Science, Nelson Mandela Metropolitan University (2007)
23. PMD Project, http://pmd.sourceforge.net/
24. Rutar, N., Almazan, C.B., Foster, J.S.: A Comparison of Bug Finding Tools for Java. In: Proceedings of the 15th International Symposium on Software Reliability Engineering, pp. 245–256. IEEE Computer Society, Washington, DC (2004)
25. Schwieren, J., Vossen, G., Westerkamp, P.: Using Software Testing Techniques for Efficient Handling of Programming Exercises in an e-Learning Platform. The Electronic Journal of e-Learning 4(1), 87–94 (2006)
26. Shah, A.: Web-CAT: A Web-based Center for Automated Testing. Master's thesis, Virginia Polytechnic Institute and State University (2003)
27. Spacco, J., Hovemeyer, D., Pugh, W., Emad, F., Hollingsworth, J.K., Padua-Perez, N.: Experiences with Marmoset: Designing and using an advanced submission and testing system for programming courses. SIGCSE Bull. 38(3), 13–17 (2006)
28. Strickroth, S., Olivier, H., Pinkwart, N.: Das GATE-System: Qualitätssteigerung durch Selbsttests für Studenten bei der Onlineabgabe von Übungsaufgaben? In: DeLFI 2011 - Die 9. e-Learning Fachtagung Informatik der Gesellschaft für Informatik e.V. LNI, vol. 188, pp. 115–126. GI (2011)
29. Striewe, M., Balz, M., Goedicke, M.: A Flexible and Modular Software Architecture for Computer Aided Assessments and Automated Marking. In: Proceedings of the First International Conference on Computer Supported Education (CSEDU), Lisboa, Portugal, March 23-26, vol. 2, pp. 54–61. INSTICC (2009)
30. Striewe, M., Balz, M., Goedicke, M.: Enabling Graph Transformations on Program Code. In: Proceedings of the 4th International Workshop on Graph Based Tools, Enschede, The Netherlands (2010)
31. Truong, N., Bancroft, P., Roe, P.: A Web Based Environment for Learning to Program. In: Proceedings of the 26th Annual Conference of ACSC, pp. 255–264 (2003)
32. Truong, N., Roe, P., Bancroft, P.: Static Analysis of Students' Java Programs. In: Lister, R., Young, A.L. (eds.) Sixth Australasian Computing Education Conference (ACE 2004), Dunedin, New Zealand, pp. 317–325 (2004)
33. Zeller, A.: Making Students Read and Review Code. In: Proceedings of the 5th ACM SIGCSE/SIGCUE Annual Conference on Innovation and Technology in Computer Science Education (ITiCSE 2000), Helsinki, Finland, pp. 89–92 (2000)

High Speed High Stakes Scoring Rule

Assessing the Performance of a New Scoring Rule for Digital Assessment

Sharon Klinkenberg

University of Amsterdam, Faculty of Social and Behavioural Sciences,
Department of Psychology, Weesperplein 4
1018 XA Amsterdam, The Netherlands
s.klinkenberg@uva.nl

Abstract. In this paper we will present the results of a three year subsidized research project investigating the performance of a new scoring rule for digital assessment. The scoring rule incorporates response time and accuracy in an adaptive environment. The project aimed to assess the validity and reliability of the ability estimations generated with the new scoring rule. It was also assessed whether the scoring rule was vulnerable for individual differences. Results show a strong validity and reliability in several studies within different domains: e.g. math, statistics and chess. We found no individual differences in the performance of the HSHS scoring rule for risk taking behavior and performance anxiety, nor did we find any performance differences for gender.

Keywords: "computer adaptive testing", "speed accuracy trade-off", "scoring rule", "digital assessment", validity, reliability, CAT, DIF.

1   Introduction

This paper covers the results of the project: "New scoring rule for digital assessment" performed for SURF, the national collaborative organization for ICT in Dutch higher education and research. The project was part of a nationwide tender called "Testing and Test-Driven Learning". The program stimulated institutions to cooperate in digital testing. It aimed to generate a positive impact of digital testing in terms of study success, lecturer workloads and test quality (SURF[1]). In the following sections we will describe the speed accuracy trade-off, guessing behavior in testing and how the high speed high stakes (HSHS) scoring rule could offer a solution for digital assessment.

1.1   Speed Accuracy Trade-Off

One of the two classic problems in assessment is the trade-off between speed and accuracy (Wickelgren, 1977). The problem concerns for example the comparison of

---

[1] http://www.surf.nl/en/themes/learning-and-testing/
digital-testing/testing-and-test-driven-learning-
programme/index.html

M. Kalz and E. Ras (Eds.): CAA 2014, CCIS 439, pp. 114–126, 2014.
© Springer International Publishing Switzerland 2014

two respondents, of whom one answered more items correct and the other responded faster. The question is how speed should be balanced against accuracy. Much research has been done on this subject. Not only in the assessment domain but also within experimental psychology and psychonomics. The developed solutions within experimental psychology are based on mathematical decision models (Bogacz et al., 2006). One of the best known examples is the Ratcliff diffusion model for dichotomous decisions where a respondent decides when the evidence transcends a certain threshold (Ratcliff, 1978). This model describes the relationship between speed and accuracy very well (Ratcliff & Rouder, 1998), but is hard to apply in the context of testing and examination. The estimation of the model parameters of the diffusion model requires many observations of behavior within one person on identical items (Vandekerckhove & Ruerlincks, 2007). Within psychometrics, Van der Linden (2007) recently proposed a hierarchical model where speed and accuracy are modelled separately. Item and person parameter within this model are merged on a higher level. This approach is applicable to digital testing.

Both approaches share that the trade-off between speed and accuracy is left to the respondent and is modeled afterwards. Individual differences in chosen strategies will affect ability scores. It is conceivable that sequential answering of items will result in different results than selective answering, e.g. first answering easier items. Strategy choice can be reduced by imposing a scoring rule. The effectiveness of such a rule depends on the understanding of the rule by the participant.

1.2   Guessing Behavior

The second classical problem consists of guessing behavior of respondents. Due to costs and psychometric problems with the scoring of open ended questions, multiple choice questions are still very popular, but they have their constraints. Simply stated, chance plays an important role in the test results, especially for respondents who score just below or above the caesura. To reduce the role of chance, test constructors must either increase the amount of items or the amount of answer options, which results in overly complex or long assessments. Some respondents may be better at guessing, excluding irrelevant alternatives or distributing the available time for all items in a test. This differentiation poses a threat to the unidimensionality of the test. Many solutions have been proposed in the history of psychometrics (Lord, 1974).

The most frequently used scoring rule that we know is the sum correct rule, which sums the amount of correctly answered items. The result of this rule is that every wrong and non answer has a negative effect on the final score. Students who are aware of this will benefit by always giving an answer, while students who are not will lose points when leaving an item unanswered. The probability of a correct answer is indeed $1/M$, where M is the number of answer options. A scoring rule that corrects for the number of answer options is the following. Suppose we have an item with M answer options. Respondents can choose to answer or skip an item. For skipping respondents gain no points, for answering correct respondents gain one point and for an incorrect answer they lose c points. Now there is a penalty for incorrect responses. When the penalty c is larger than $1/(M-1)$ it is unwise to make a random guess. Suppose there are M=4 answer options and the penalty c=1, then the expected value for a blind guess is negative $-1/2$. If c is equal to $1/(M-1)$, this scoring rule is known as correction for guessing (Holzinger, 1924; Thurstone, 1919; Lord, 1975). If respondents do not have a clue of the wright answer, then the expected value for guessing or skipping is equal. This scoring rule has been for many years implemented in important assessments in the US (Budescu and Bar-Hillel, 1993). The success of this rule has been debated. Burton (2005) and Lord (1975) are mostly positive but Budesco and Bar-Hillel (1993) have expressed concerns. The choice for c=1/(M-1) is a bit strange for when subjects blindly guess it does not matter if they guess or skip the item, but if they possess just a bit of (partial) knowledge, it is always better to guess. All in all it is always better to guess, though not all respondents understand this. The majority of honest students will skip all items that they are not sure of, resulting in systematic score reduction. This of course can be solved by choosing c>1/(M-1), but even then the drawback proposed by Budesco and Bar-Hillel remains that knowing how to use this rule implies an added skill in with respondents can systematically differ.

1.3   High Speed High Stakes

The scoring rules described in the previous section only provide a solution for guessing, but not for the speed accuracy trade-off problem. Van der Maas and Wagenmakers (2005) proposed a solution for the second problem. Their scoring rule consists of a per item time limit d, in their study on chess ability measuring 30 seconds. The accuracy (acc) was scored 0 for incorrect and 1 for correct answers. The score per item was equal to the remaining time multiplied by the accuracy: acc(d-RT). A wrong answer will result in no points while a fast correct response will yield more than a slow correct response. Using this scoring rule, Van der Maas and Wagenmakers (2005) managed to increase the validity of their test. Maris and Van der Maas (2010) proposed an important improvement to this rule. The described rule has the disadvantage that it can, as the earlier rules, provoke risk taking behavior. If the respondent recognizes that an item is too difficult, it is better to guess immediately, since a score higher than zero is then still probable. Maris and Van der Maas therefore propose to make the rule symmetric by transforming accuracy to -1 (incorrect) and 1 (correct). The same formula (d-RT) multiplied by acc*2-1 now makes fast guessing extremely risky. A fast wrong answer will result in a very negative score (fig. 1).

The high speed high stakes scoring rule thereby offers a solution for guessing as well as the speed accuracy problem. Given that the certainty about an answer increases with time (an assumption in almost all decision theories), there is an optimal moment for actually responding. Interestingly, Maris and Van der Maas (2005) have proven, providing that the scoring rule is a sufficient statistic for measuring ability, that the model for the probability for answering correctly is identical to the most frequently used model in assessment, namely the two parameter logistic model (Van der Linden & Hamleton, 1997). The discrimination parameter is shown to be equal to the time limit d for the item. This elegant result offers many opportunities for, among others, adaptive testing with reaction times. Maris & van der Maas (2011) have to this end derived all relevant conditional probability distributions.

It is still relevant that respondents understand the rule. Through digital assessment this rule can easily be visualized. Figure 2 shows an implementation of this rule in the Math Garden. Respondents see their remaining time decreasing with the amount of available coins. The result of their response is shown by increasing or decreasing the total amount of coins, hereby shortening the feedback loop.

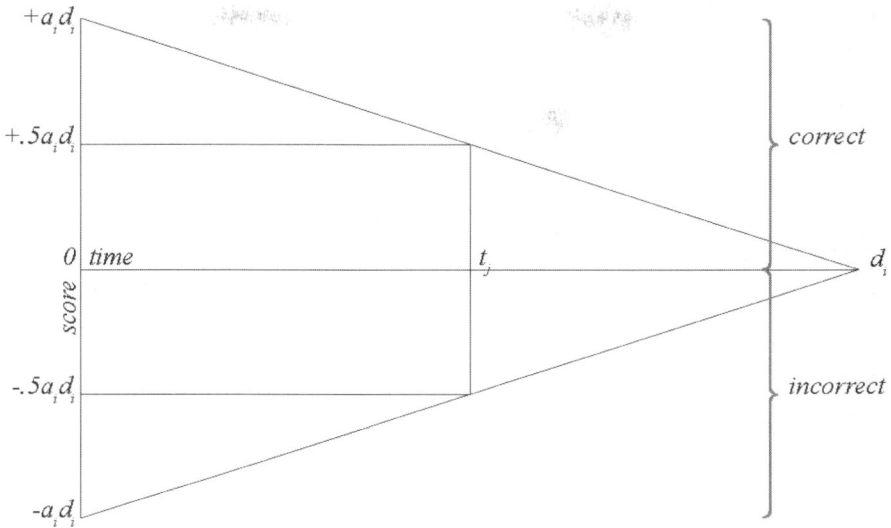

Fig. 1. High speed high stakes scoring rule, where d is the time limit and a is a scaling factor

Fig. 2. Math garden multiplication game

In the following section we will concisely present the main results of the carried out research. We will attempt to answer the following research questions.

1. Does the use of the HSHS scoring rule result in an increased reliability and validity?
2. Are respondents able to find an optimal balance between speed and accuracy?
3. Are there individual differences in this ability?
4. Do these differences relate to background variables as experience, gender and ability?
5. Do respondents need to learn how to use the scoring rule or can it be applied easily?
6. Does the use of the scoring rule result in more accurate ability estimations in adaptive testing with easy items?

To answer these questions data has been analyzed from the Math Garden, from data gathered at the CORUS chess event 2008 and results from the "statistiekfabriek". A short description of these three sources is in order here. In 2007 the department of psychological methods from the University of Amsterdam initiated the development of the Math Garden, a computer adaptive practice and tracking system for math in which the HSHS scoring rule was implemented. Currently Math Garden is commercialized by Oefenweb and about 1100 schools in the Netherlands are subscribed to the service. The responses, about half a million per day, form the basis for the Math Garden data set. Parallel to this development at the CORUS chess tournament of 2008, a chess test was administered where the same scoring rule was used. National and international chess players ranging from novices to grand masters participated in this event. Their responses form the chess test data set. Within SURF's nationwide tender "Testing and Test-Driven Learning" another project ran in which a statistics version of the Math Garden was being developed, called "Statistiekfabriek". The results of that project form the basis for the statistics data set.

In the following section a brief overview of the main results from the different data sources will be presented. We have chosen not to include the result section as the theoretical introductions due to the resumptive nature of this paper. The descriptions can be found in the original works, though some are only available in Dutch.

2   Results

2.1   Validity

To get an indication of the convergent validity the HSHS scores had to be compared with an external measure. For the Math Garden data, scores could be compared to the national Dutch norm reverenced CITO scores. The chess players from that data set all had national or international chess ratings that could be used for comparison. Finally the "Statistiekfabriek" scores could be compared to different partial exams in statistics. Convergent validity criteria where thus available for all three data sets.

The correlations with the external measure proved significant for all three sources. For the Math Garden and the chess data sets, these where particularly high. Figure 3 shows the scatterplots for the Math Garden where the domains addition, subtraction, multiplication and division where correlated with the CITO scores (Klinkenberg, 2011). The correlations ranged from .78 to .84 all with p<.05. Regression lines are also plotted for each grade.

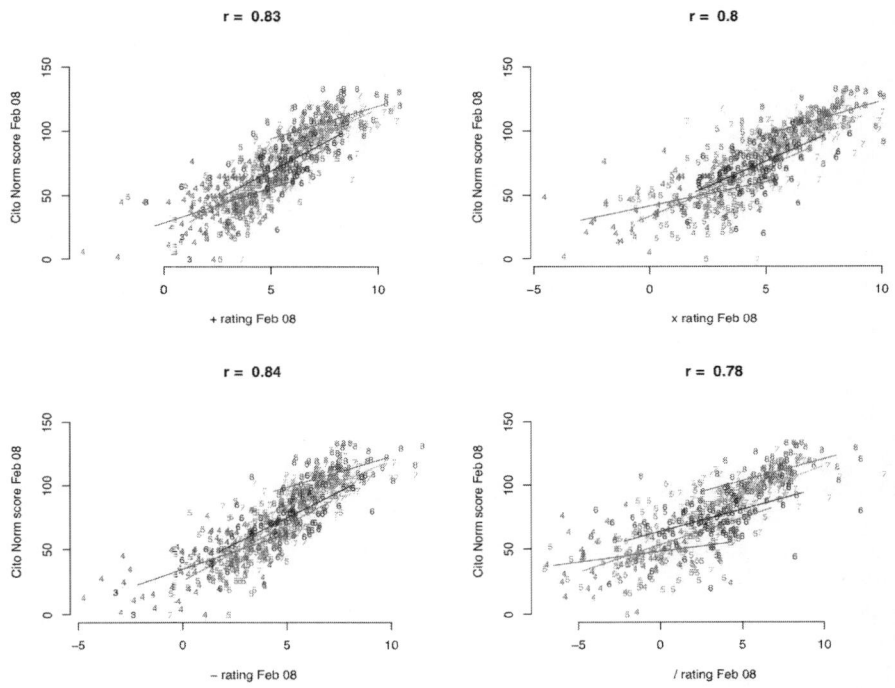

Fig. 3. Correlations of HSHS rating with CITO scores

The chess scores also showed, with regard to the known Elo ratings, high correlations (Table 1). It is striking that the correlation between the HSHS sum score is higher than the sum correct score with the FIDE rating but not with the tournament performance rating (TPR). Evidently ratings based on an adaptive procedure perform considerably better (Klinkenberg & Van der Maas, 2013).

Table 1. Correlations of test performance and with known chess ratings (FIDE) and tournament performance ratings (TPF). All p's < .05.

Response time	Method	FIDE	TPR
Excluded	Som score	0.575	0.547
Included	HSHS test rating	0.808	0.777
	HSHS som score	0.617	0.525

The correlations between the statistics exams and the HSHS sum scores and the sum correct rule also indicate a better performance. The sum correct score correlated r=.39 while the HSHS sum score correlated r=.48 though these differences were not significant (Özen et. al., 2012).

A different way of looking at validity is to assess if ability increases over time. It could be expected that children in higher grades in the Math Garden would perform better at math. This has been analyzed with the math data (Klinkenberg, 2011). It was tested whether children in higher grades performed better on the four domains. Figure 4 shows the increase of rating for ascending grades.

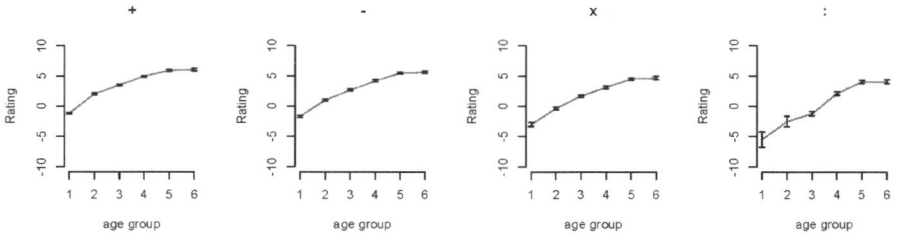

Fig. 4. Rating per domain per group

We see a clear increase in ability across ascending grades except for the last grade. This can be explained by the fact that in Dutch education no new knowledge is taught in the final grade.

Everything indicates that the HSHS score gives a valid indication of ability. In most cases the rule performs better than the sum correct, especially while testing adaptively.

2.2   Reliability

The reliability of the HSHS test scores r=.60 did not significantly differ from the reliability of the sum correct scores r=.57 in "statistiekfabriek" (Özen et. al., 2012). Here non adaptive tests where administered using both rules. Determining the reliability in an adaptive dynamic test is somewhat more challenging. Given the adaptive method, normal procedures do not apply. To still get an indication of reliability in the Math Garden, parallel test where used for the domain addition and multiplication. For these domains n+m and nxm could be paralleled with m+n and mxn, resulting in correlations of r=.74 for addition and r=.71 for multiplication (p<.05) (Klinkenberg, 2011).

A different approach is to look at test retest reliability. The difficulty of items at point x should than be equal to that at point x+y. This would indicate stability of item difficulty over time and therefore a reliable measurement tool. The dotted line in figure 5 shows that after two months, item ratings are stable and do not fluctuate much in the following months (Klinkenberg, 2011). These results show that both the HSHS test scores as the adaptive HSHS test rating are reliable indicators of ability.

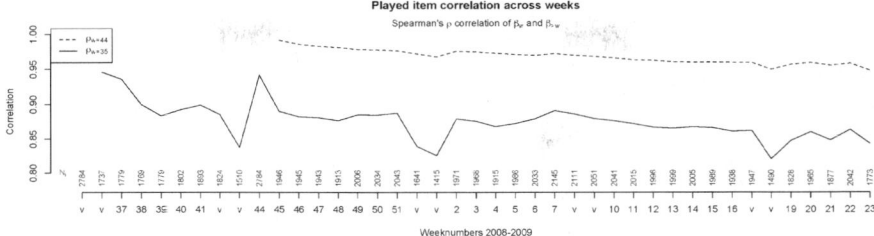

Fig. 5. Stability of items ratings for initial ratings (solid line) and established ratings after 2 months (dotted line). The x-axis displays week numbers (v = vacation). Correlations are computed over active (played) items in each week (N_i = amount of administered items).

2.3   Optimal SAT

To determine the optimal balance between speed and accuracy given the HSHS scoring rule, we plotted the frequency distribution of correct and incorrect answers at response time intervals. Figure 6 superimposes the scoring rule on these distributions. Given the HSHS scoring rule one would expect, if the rule is understood correctly, that respondents would not guess quickly, but would respond as quickly as possible once they found the answer. The expected frequency distribution would in that case be skewed to the right. The expected distribution for incorrect answers is harder to predict. One would at least expect few fast responses but the frequency of slower responses could increase.

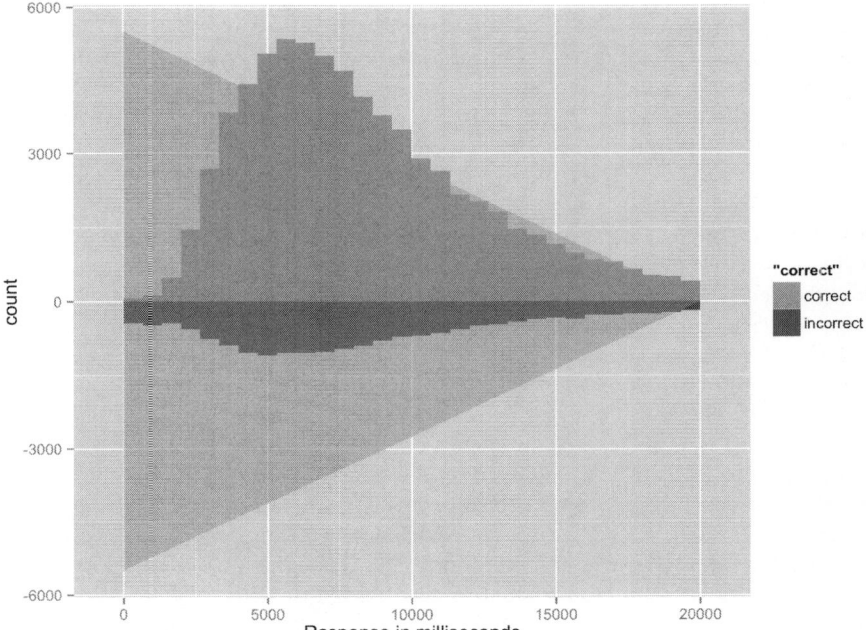

Fig. 6. Frequency distributions of correct and incorrect responses with the HSHS scoring rule superimposed

Figure 6 shows both distributions based on 100,000 responses of 65,000 unique players in the Math Garden. The distribution of correct answers looks as expected. Very fast correct responses are rare, given that respondents need a few seconds to read the question. For incorrect responses we see no massive guessing and a rather flat distribution. It is notable that in the first two seconds there is a relatively high frequency of incorrect answers. We presume this could be accounted for by a small group of risk takers. Further analysis would have to shed more light on this.

2.4   Individual Differences

With the introduction of response times in the assessment the question immediately rises if respondents could feel pressured and therefore perform worse than without a time constrain. The susceptibility for this could be a determining factor in the ability estimation and therefore diminishing the effect of the HSHS scoring rule.

"Statistiekfabriek" results (Barkhof et. al., 2013) suggests no relation between positive or negative performance anxiety and ability. Ability correlated r=.09, p=.142 with negative and r=.01, p=.85 with positive performance anxiety. The latter is noteworthy because positive performance anxiety was expected to enhance ability.

There was also no relation between risk orientation and the mean deviation with the expected score. Based on the available information of the item difficulty and the ability of respondents generated by to the computer adaptive algorithm, the expected score could be inferred. It was expected that risk takers would deviate more from this expected score and that their variation would be larger than non risk takers. Neither showed in the data. The mean deviation correlated r=.01, p=.125 and the dispersion of the deviation correlated r=.02, p=.404 with risk orientation.

Risk orientation also did neither relate to response time nor to accuracy. The correlations were r=-.06, and r=.03 respectively (p>.05). Differences in the amount of risk orientation did not manifest in the speed of responding or the amount of correct answers. Nor was there a difference in ability between males and females.

In "statistiekfabriek" (Özen et. al., 2012) the effect of risk taking behavior was examined to assess if the items showed differential item functioning (DIF). Students were asked to indicate if they saw themselves as risk takers or not. Subsequently, it was investigated if items performed different for these groups. Only one out of twenty items showed DIF when the HSHS scoring rule was applied, in comparison to six out of twenty when applying the sum correct rule.

The above analyses imply that the HSHS scoring rule in these samples does not work differently for respondents with varying amounts of sensitivity to performance anxiety. Nor did the items perform different for risk takers and non risk takers.

In Jansen et. al. (2013) we were not able to show, while using the adaptive assessment procedure in the Math Garden with the HSHS scoring rule, that the perceived math anxiety decreased with ascending levels of administered item difficulty. Also the perceived math competence was not higher with easier items. Math performance did increase as the difficulty of administered items was lower. As mediation analysis showed, this appeared to be mediated by the amount of items played. Administering easy items increased the playing frequency which in turn resulted in higher math performance. In all situations there was no effect of grade nor where there any differences between boys and girls.

2.5   Learning the Rule

Both in the Math Garden as in the "Statistiekfabriek" respondents were able to apply the HSHS scoring rule immediately. The short feedback loop ensures that respondents directly see what the result of their response is. Figure 2 showed how this was implemented in the Math Garden. In the "Statistiekfabriek" the available time is visualized by a countdown indicator and the total earned points is displayed as a numeric indicator (fig. 7).

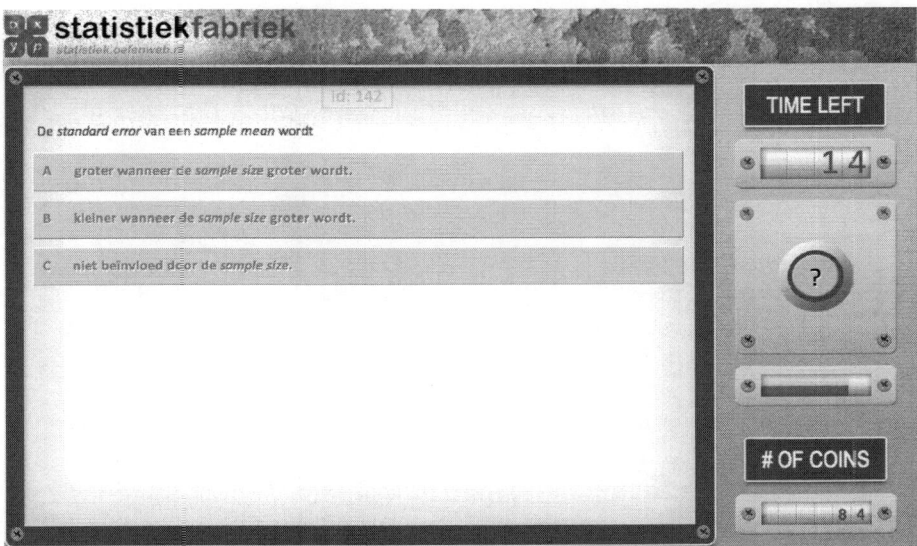

Fig. 7. "Statistiekfabriek" descriptive statistics game. Remaining time is displayed in the upper right, total earned coins in the lower right corner.

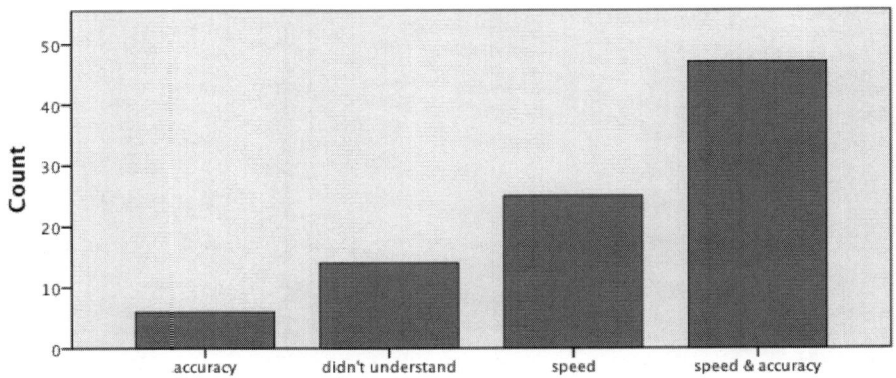

Fig. 8. HSHS scoring rule assessment

Students were asked to indicate what they thought would result in the highest possible points per question. Most realized that speed and accuracy played the primary role but figure 8 also shows that a portion thought only speed was important and some did not have a clue while only a few thought only accuracy was involved.

With the exception of one person, a limited amount of guessing took place while performing a statistics trial exam. Of the 20 items in the trial exam using the HSHS scoring rule the frequency distribution was skewed to the right, indicating that most students guessed less than eight items out of twenty. It appeared, however, that the appreciation of the HSHS scoring rule varied widely. Figure 9 shows these verdicts on a Likert scale ranging from 1, strongly negative, to 7, strongly positive. Semi high stakes testing using the HSHS scoring rule appear to result in some mixed verdicts.

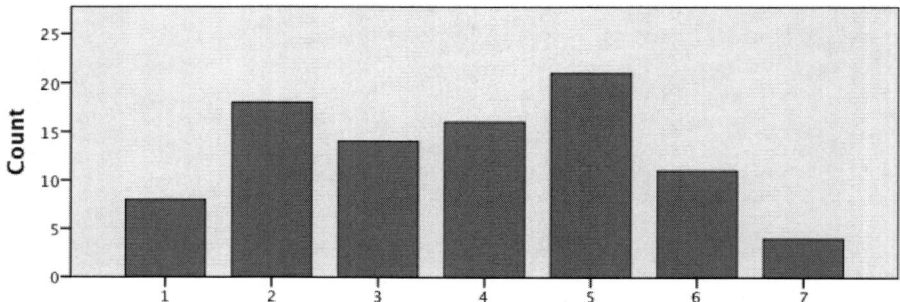

Fig. 9. Positive vs negative verdict about the HSHS scoring rule

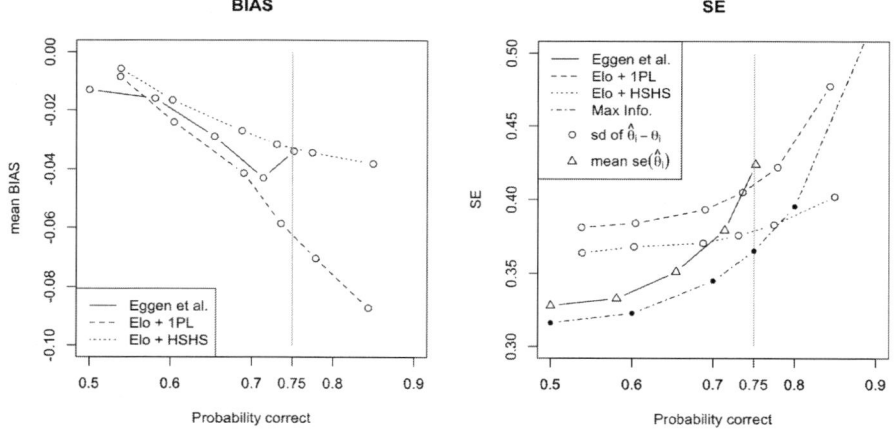

Fig. 10. Bias and standard error for different computer adaptive methods at different values of the expected probability correct

2.6   Ability Estimation

To assess if the use of the HSHS scoring rule in an adaptive setting results in accurate estimations of ability while administering easy items, it is necessary to perform some simulations. Figure 10 displays the simulations performed by Klinkenberg (2011). The left graph shows the mean deviation from the simulated 'real' ability for a weighted maximum likelihood method (Eggen et. al., 2006), an Elo procedure based only on accuracy (Elo + 1PL), and an Elo procedure based on the HSHS scoring rule

(Elo + HSHS). The x-axis shows the item difficulty from hard (left) to easy (right). The graph on the right shows the standard error of these deviations for the same three procedures supplemented by the maximum information possible in a maximum likelihood setting. With easy items, the HSHS procedure exhibits the least amount of bias and the standard error is lower than when only accuracy is involved. The HSHS scoring rule is potentially better at estimating ability while administering easy items.

3   Conclusion

Applying the HSHS scoring rule to both a non-adaptive and an adaptive setting yields valid and reliable estimations of ability. Though the reliability does not seem to be better than other scoring rules, the validity is shown to be higher than when only accuracy is used, especially in an adaptive setting. In particular when administering easy items, the adaptive HSHS scoring rule performs better. Risk taking disposition does not seem to influence the performance of the HSHS scoring rule in terms of ability estimation, though respondents do indicate a wide range of positive and negative feelings towards the rule. While the frequency distributions of response times for correct and incorrect answers show that respondents comply with the aim of the scoring rule, a considerable amount of students also reported a wrong interpretation of the rule. Either the intuitive behavior does not coincide with the perceived rule or the "statistiekfabriek" implementation fundamentally differed from the Math Garden. This is partly the case as the "statistiekfabriek" incorporated a semi high stakes environment by applying the rule in a trial exam. Experiencing the rule for weeks on end in the Math Garden would result in a more elaborate understanding of the rule than applying is once in a trial exam. This would argue for getting students to familiarize with the rule before applying it in high stake assessments.

We are encouraged by the research findings in the ability of the HSHS scoring rule to produce valid and reliable estimations of ability, though we remain mindful of individual differences and of the perceived attitude towards the rule in high stakes testing. We are, nonetheless, confident these attitudes are less of an issue in low stakes testing. The HSHS scoring rule promises to bridge the gap between speed and accuracy and we think we are on track with this approach.

References

1. Barkhof, J., Bekker, T., Bersma, M., Groenendijk, E., Maza, S.: Oefening Baart Kunst (unpublished research report). University of Amsterdam, Netherlands (2013)
2. Bogacz, R., Brown, E., Moehlis, J., Holmes, P., Cohen, J.C.: The Physics of Optimal Decision Making: A Formal Analysis of Models of Performance in Two-Alternative Forced-Choice Tasks. Psychological Review 113(4), 700–765 (2006)
3. Budescu, D., Bar-Hillel, M.: To Guess or Not to Guess: A Decision-Theoretic View of Formula Scoring. Journal of Educational Measurement 30(4), 277–291 (1993)
4. Burton, R.F.: Multiple-choice and true/false tests: myths and misapprehensions. Assessment & Evaluation in Higher Education 30(1), 65–72 (2005)
5. Eggen, T.J.H.M., Verschoor, A.J.: Optimal Testing with Easy or Difficult Items in Computerized Adaptive Testing. Applied Psychological Measurement 30(5), 379–393 (2006)

6. Holzinger, K.J.: On Scoring Multiple Response Tests. Journal of Educational Measurement 15, 445–447 (1924)
7. Jansen, B.R.J., Louwerse, J., Straatemeier, M., Van der Ven, S.H.G., Klinkenberg, S., Van der Maas, H.L.J.: The influence of practicing maths with a computer-adaptive program on math anxiety, perceived math competence, and math performance. Learning and Individual Differences 24, 190–197 (2013)
8. Klinkenberg, S., Straatemeier, M., Van der Maas, H.L.J.: Computer adaptive practice of maths ability using a new item response model for on the fly ability and difficulty estimation. Comput. Educ. 57(2), 1813–1824 (2011)
9. Klinkenberg, S., Van der Maas, H.L.J.: A dynamic paired comparison based computer adaptive testing method. Unpublished manuscript (2013)
10. Lord, F.M.: Formula Scoring and Number-right Scoring. Journal of Educational Measurement 12(1), 7–11 (1975)
11. Maris, G., Van der Maas, H.L.J.: Speed-accuracy response models: scoring rules based on response time and accuracy. Psychometrika 77(4), 615–633 (2012)
12. Özen, S., Pronk, A., Sanchez Maceiras, S., Stel, N., Van Wersch, T.: De Invloed van de HSHS scoreregel op het Meten van Werkelijke Vaardigheid (Unpublished research report). University of Amsterdam, Netherlands (2012)
13. Ratcliff, R.: A theory of memory retrieval. Psychological Review 85(2), 59–108 (1978)
14. Ratcliff, R., Rouder, J.N.: Modeling Response Times for Two-Choice Decisions. Psychological Science 9(5), 347–356 (1998)
15. Thurstone, L.L.: A method for scoring tests. Psychological Bulletin 16, 235–240 (1919)
16. van der Linden, W.J.: A hierarchical framework for modeling speed and accuracy on test items. Psychometrika 72, 287–308 (2007)
17. Van der Linden, W.J., Hambleton, R.K. (eds.): Handbook of modern item response theory. Springer, New York (1997)
18. Van der Maas, H.L.J., Wagenmakers, E.J.: The Amsterdam Chess Test: a psychometric analysis of chess expertise. American Journal of Psychology 118, 29–60 (2005)
19. Vandekerckhove, J., Tuerlinckx, F.: Fitting the Ratcliff diffusion model to experimental data. Psychonomic Bulletin & Review 14, 1011–1026 (2007)
20. Wickelgren, W.A.: Speed-accuracy tradeoff and information processing dynamics. Acta Psychologica 41, 67–85 (1977)

Do Work Placement Tests Challenge Student Trainees to Learn?

Jelly Zuidersma and Elvira Coffetti

Netwerk ZON, Haren, The Netherlands
{j.zuidersma,e.coffetti}@netwerkzon.nl

Abstract. The study described in this article shows that embedding formative work placement tests in the student's learning process facilitates the student's development while on the work placement. This study measured the development of the student's learning process by determining the extent to which students gained an understanding of their current and desired levels of knowledge, felt challenged to learn, and more deeply explored the specialism of their work placement department. The exchange of knowledge between the student trainee and the work supervisor was measured. The E-Flow Nursing project was used as a case study. In this project, it was agreed that students were to include their test results in their personal activity plans, in line with recommendations from previous research into formative testing in general, which had revealed that formative testing can lead to positive developments in the learning process provided that it is embedded in the learning process.

Keywords: Digital formative work placement tests, Learning process, Nursing students.

1 Introduction

In the fields of education and science, the importance of digital testing at the student trainee's work place is being recognised more and more. Digital testing provides both student and lecturer with insight into academic performance. Provided a digital test is psychometrically sound, it can be an effective tool for increasing the level of knowledge of student trainees. However, it needs to be combined with a number of additional measures [6].

Digital testing has not been entirely without criticism. For example, the results of the 'Building Bridges' project revealed that the expectations raised by the test were too rarely met by student trainee nurses at the higher professional education level. The test alone is not enough if the digital test is to help optimise work placement supervision [6]. Both the trainee nurses and the work supervisors report that the test is still not sufficiently well regarded as a more effective means of preparing for the work placement. The results show that additional steps are required if the digital test is to benefit the structure of the student's learning process as well as the work placement supervision performed by the work supervisor [6]. It is expected that student trainees

M. Kalz and E. Ras (Eds.): CAA 2014, CCIS 439, pp. 127–137, 2014.

will be better able to address gaps in their knowledge (and draw up appropriate action plans for addressing these gaps) if the test results are included in their Personal Development Plans (PDP), Personal Action Plans (PAP) or Work Placement Plans, and if they discuss these results with their work supervisors and fellow students [6].

Another important point is that the digital work placement test must be only one of a number of interventions in the learning process, and not a stand-alone element. The learning pathway must be designed so that not only does it get the best out of the student, but also has educational benefits for the work supervisors [6]. The E-Flow Nursing project, the case study in this article, elaborates on the expectations arising from the above studies and has embedded the intervention, namely the digital formative work placement test, more deeply in the student trainee's overall supervisory process.

2   Theoretical Framework

Tests are usually divided into two different categories: summative and formative. The aim of summative testing is to assess academic performance, whereas the aim of formative testing is to gain an insight into the learning process and to make adjustments where necessary [5]. Cilliers et al. [2] claim that carrying out formative tests enhances the learning process. It has become clear that formative knowledge testing has a positive effect on the student's learning outcome, on condition the answers provided to students are accompanied by feedback [1], [3].

According to Black & William [1], a formative test is an effective and valid tool for boosting students' learning outcomes, provided students receive feedback on their answers. It is important that students gain an understanding of their own shortcomings. According to Dousma, Horsten and Brants [3], the greatest advantage offered by a formative test is that it allows students to adapt their learning at an earlier stage. The formative test is advantageous for the learning process if students receive feedback on their answers.

The study carried out by Dijksterhuis et al. [4] shows that feedback, the credibility of feedback and a supporting learning environment with work supervisors are key factors for active student involvement in doing formative tests. A study by Rotterdam University of Applied Sciences [7] demonstrates that students and work supervisors view formative tests as an excellent way to prepare for the work placement. Where formative work placement tests are used, it is important to deploy subsequent interventions to ensure that students and supervisors actually work on the test.

Samuels and Uil [8] studied the knowledge level of student trainee nurses. A key finding of their study was that student trainee nurses have insufficient knowledge to begin their work placements responsibly. Four hospitals therefore decided to improve student trainees' grasp of theory prior to the work placement, and to introduce a work placement test. This work placement test improves students' basic knowledge. Moreover, the test provides greater clarity with regard to the work placement department's expectations. The evaluations reveal that taking work placement tests motivates students to prepare better for their work placements [8].

According to the above studies, in order for formative tests done during work placements to positively impact a student's development, they must form part of the student's learning process as well as the work supervisor's supervisory process. 'Positive development' is understood as referring to 'students' insight into their current and desired levels of knowledge in the work placement department', whereas 'a positive effect on the learning process during the work placement' refers to being challenged and motivated to learn, as well as undertaking 'in-depth study of the specialism in the work placement department'. In terms of the supervisory process, 'development' can be defined as 'contributing to the exchange of knowledge between student trainees and work supervisors'. The research questions we therefore aim to answer in this article are the following:

- To what extent does a formative test contribute to students' insight into their current and desired levels of knowledge?
- To what extent does a formative test have a positive effect on the students' learning process?
- To what extent does a formative test have a positive effect on the in-depth study of the specialism?
- To what extent does a formative test contribute to the exchange of knowledge between student trainees and work supervisors?

3   Digital Work Placement Tests within the E-Flow Nursing Project

The case study used in this study was the E-Flow Nursing project. The objectives of the E-Flow Nursing project are to develop a consistent, workplace-independent, digital test for 3rd and 4th-year senior secondary vocational education (MBO) nursing students, 1st and 2nd-year higher professional education (HBO) nursing students (without an MBO qualification in nursing) and 3rd and 4th-year higher professional education (HBO) nursing students (with an MBO qualification in nursing). The tests focus on both knowledge and attitude development as well as students' insight into their future professional careers as nurses in general hospitals (AGZ), care for the disabled (GHZ), psychiatry (GGZ) and care for the elderly (OZ).

The E-Flow Nursing project employed an approach whereby nurses from a work placement department prepare tests with specific questions about their department. These are the nurses who also supervise the student trainees. The *Leerstation Zorg* digital test bank is used during this process. This test bank contains more than 13,000 practice-based questions about various healthcare specialisms. This number is continuously updated and supplemented with new test items. The questions address knowledge, attitude and insight.

3.1   The Initial Test

Doing the test forms part of the student's preparations for the work placement. The rule 'No E-Flow, No PAP' was introduced for this purpose. The test level is equivalent to the knowledge level of a nurse with two years' work experience. By doing the tests, the students gain an understanding of what to expect in the work placement department in terms of subject areas. After answering each question the student sees a 'knowledge flash': a brief explanation of the question and the correct answer. The most recent source of the information concerned is also referenced.

3.2   Insight into Results

The student and the supervisor do the test on the work placement department prior to the work placement, and are the only ones who have access to their own results. Students include their result in their PAP or Work Placement Plan. The student and supervisor discuss the result during their introductory meeting in the work placement department. This encourages students and their supervisors to discuss the desired level of knowledge for the trainee, as appropriate to his or her phase in the learning process. They jointly discuss which learning objectives the student trainee is going to work on during the work placement period. The student may work on achieving these objectives through catch-up tests, by studying the relevant professional literature or by discussing the objectives with the supervisor (Table 1, section C).

3.3   Catch-Up Tests

Catch-up tests are short tests centred around repetition: the student chooses a number of subjects that he or she wants to practise. The student then does short tests, consisting of ten questions per subject. These tests assess basic knowledge of the subjects selected. If the student's score is too low, he or she is automatically presented with a new test on the same subject. The standard is determined on the basis of the average test score. The level of difficulty of the second test equals that of the first. Through a process of repetition, the student practises and reduces his or her knowledge gaps in this subject.

3.4   Final Test

At the end of the work placement, the students and their supervisors have the option of doing the initial test again in order to compare the results and give both student and supervisor an idea of how the student's knowledge has developed over the course of the work placement. When discussing the test results during the final work placement interview, the student and supervisor could agree to new learning objectives to be pursued as the student continues his or her study programme or during a possible follow-up work placement.

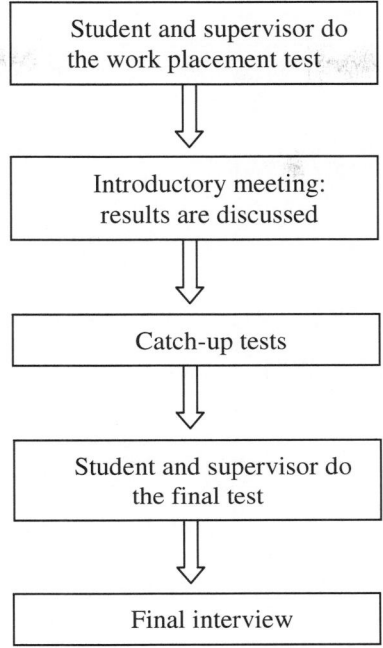

Fig. 1. E-Flow Nursing digital work placement test

4   Research Method

A quantitative study was carried out. In the period 4 January 2013 to 13 March 2014, written questionnaires were conducted among the students and supervisors following completion of the formative test as part of the work placement. The data was collected from MBO and HBO Nursing programme students at a Regional Training Centre or higher professional education institution in the Groningen, Drenthe and Noord-Overijssel region. These were 3rd and 4th-year MBO nursing students and 2nd, 3rd and 4th-year HBO nursing students. Questionnaires were also conducted among the work supervisors who supervised these students during their work placements. These supervisors were employed at a healthcare institution in the Groningen, Drenthe and Noord-Overijssel region, and worked in one of the following sectors: general hospitals (AGZ), care for the disabled (GHZ), psychiatry (GGZ) and care for the elderly (OZ).

The measuring tool used was a written questionnaire. This questionnaire was conducted previously during the 'Building Bridges' project (Rotterdam University of Applied Sciences, 2011). Two types of questionnaire were used: one for students and one for supervisors. All items were measured on a scale of 1 (= strongly disagree) to 5 (= strongly agree). To determine the extent to which the formative test influences the variables, the items were merged into three sub-scales for students. Table 1 shows sub-scales A, B and C for students.

Table 1. Scales and items (students)

Scales: insight into the current and desired levels of knowledge, positive effect on the learning process, in-depth study of the specialism

A. Insight into the current and desired levels of knowledge

Doing the work placement test ..
has made me aware of my current level of knowledge of the specialism
has made me aware of the desired level of knowledge of the specialism
has made it clear to me what I need to know in order to understand syndromes and their treatment
has made it clear to me what I need to know in order to account for my actions
has made it clear to me what I need to know in order to provide the patient/client with the right information
has made me aware of what I need to know in order to contribute to the exchange of knowledge with colleagues
means that I can focus during my work placement on increasing my level of knowledge within this specialism
has made me acquire more knowledge about this specialism
means that I can ask my work supervisor for specific help in acquiring knowledge

B. Positive effect on the learning process

Doing the work placement test has ...
had a positive effect on my learning process
had a positive effect on my work placement
challenged me to learn
motivated me more for my work placement within this specialism
motivated me to study the specialism in greater depth

C. In-depth study of the specialism

I prepared for the work placement test by studying theory
Having done the work placement test, I will now gather information specifically to fill the gaps in my knowledge
Having done the work placement test, I will now study the specialism in greater depth by talking to my work supervisor about the specialism
Having done the work placement test, I will now study the specialism in greater depth through reading relevant literature
I will prepare myself better for the final test
Because I will gain experience within the specialism during my work placement, I expect to obtain a higher score in the final test than in the first work placement test
Having done the work placement test, I studied the specialism in greater depth by talking to fellow students about the specialism

To measure the extent to which students gain greater insight into their current and desired levels of knowledge, nine items were merged into sub-scale A. Current and desired level of knowledge. Cronbach's alpha > 0.79 allows us to assume that these items can be merged into a single sub-scale. It included items such as "Doing the work placement test has made me aware of my current level of knowledge of the specialism", "Doing the work placement test has made me aware of the desired level of knowledge of the specialism" and "Doing the work placement test has made it clear to me what I need to know in order to understand syndromes and their treatment".

To measure the extent to which the learning process was positively affected, five items were merged into sub-scale B. Positive effect on the learning process. Cronbach's alpha > 0.94 allows us to assume that these items can be merged into a single sub-scale. It included items such as "Doing the work placement test has had a positive effect on my learning process", "Doing the work placement test has had a positive effect on my work placement" and "Doing the work placement test has challenged me to learn".

In-depth study of the specialism was measured using eight items (sub-scale C). Cronbach's alpha > 0.90 allows us to assume that these items can be merged into a single sub-scale. It included items such as "Having done the work placement test, I will now study the specialism in greater depth by talking to my work supervisor about the specialism" and "Having done the work placement test, I will now study the specialism in greater depth through reading relevant literature".

To determine the extent to which knowledge is exchanged as part of the supervisory process, items from the questionnaire for supervisors were merged into the two sub-scales D and E. See Table 2. To measure the extent to which knowledge is exchanged between supervisor and student as a result of the test, five items were merged into sub-scale D. Knowledge exchange. Cronbach's alpha > 0.80 allows us to assume that these five items can be merged into a single sub-scale. It included items such as "The work placement test helped me to exchange knowledge with the student" and "The work placement test has helped me to supervise the student's knowledge development more effectively".

To measure the supervisors' views as to whether the formative test has a positive effect on the learning process, ten items were merged into sub-scale E. Positive effect on the learning process. Cronbach's alpha > 0.81 allows us to assume that these ten items can be merged. The sub-scale included items such as "I feel that doing a work placement test is part of proper preparation for the work placement", "I feel that the questions in the work placement test are relevant to my specialism", "I expect that doing the work placement test will challenge the student to learn".

Table 2. Scales and items (supervisors)

Scales: knowledge exchange and positive effect on the learning process

D. Knowledge exchange

I expect that doing the work placement test will ensure that the student is able to ask me for specific help in acquiring knowledge
The work placement test has helped me to exchange knowledge with the student
The work placement test has helped me to supervise the student's knowledge development more effectively

Table 2. (*continued*)

Scales: knowledge exchange and positive effect on the learning process

Doing the work placement test myself has helped me to exchange knowledge with the student

Doing the work placement test myself has helped me to supervise the student's knowledge development more effectively

E. Positive effect on the learning process

I feel that doing the work placement test is informative for a student within my specialism

I feel that the work placement test accurately reflects the content of the specialism

I feel that a work placement test should be compulsory for every work placement

I feel that doing a work placement test is part of good preparation for the work placement

I feel that the questions in the work placement test are relevant to my specialism

I expect that doing the work placement test will challenge the student to learn

I expect that doing the work placement test will motivate the student

I expect that doing the work placement test will have a positive effect on the student's learning outcomes

I feel that the work placement test encourages the student to study the specialism in more depth

I feel that the work placement test motivates the student for a work placement within this specialism

5   Results

The questionnaire was completed by the students and supervisors who did the tests in E-flow Nursing. The test was done by a total of 1102 students, of whom 559 also completed the questionnaire. This is a response rate of 50.70%. Questionnaires were also completed by the students' supervisors. The test was done by a total of 333 supervisors, of whom 148 completed the questionnaire. This is a response rate of 44.4%.

The results in Table 3 show that students indicate that the formative test provided them with greater insight into the current and desired levels of knowledge (average score of 3.53 on a scale of 1 to 5). They also indicate that the formative test had a positive effect on the learning process (average score of 3.4 on a scale of 1-5). Finally, students indicate that doing the test enabled them to specialise more in the specialism (average score of 2.96 on a scale of 1-5).

To measure the link between insight into current and desired levels of knowledge, the positive effect on the learning process and the in-depth study of the specialism, a correlation coefficient (Pearson R) was used to test whether a linear relationship exists between the three scales. The Pearson R correlations in Table 3 show that there is a significant positive relationship between these three variables. A particularly strong relationship exists between 'Learning Process' and 'In-depth Study of the Specialism', with a correlation of 0.83. This demonstrates that, in addition to the formative test having a positive effect on the three elements, the three elements are also connected.

Table 3. N, averages, standard deviations, range, missing values and correlations between scales A, B and C

	N	M	SD	Range	Missing values	Insight into the current and desired levels of knowledge	Learning process	In-depth study of specialism
Insight into the current and desired level of knowledge	549	3.53	0.59	1-5	10	1	0.57**	0.49**
Learning process	543	3.40	1.12	1-5	16	0.57**	1	0.83**
In-depth study of specialism	550	2.96	1.05	1-5	9	0.49**	0.83**	1

** = $p < 0.01$ (2-sided)

The work supervisors indicate that the formative test led to a greater exchange of knowledge with the students (average score of 3.68 on a scale of 1-5). Work supervisors also indicate that the formative test has a positive effect on the learning process (average score of 3.84 on a scale of 1-5).

To measure the link between knowledge exchange and positive effect on the learning process, a correlation coefficient (Pearson R) was used to test whether a linear relationship exists between the two scales. The Pearson R correlations in Table 4 show that there is a significant positive relationship between these two variables, with a correlation of 0.54. It can be deduced from this analysis that a connection exists between the exchange of knowledge between work supervisors and students and a positive effect on the learning process.

Table 4. N, averages, standard deviations, range, missing values and correlations between scales D and E

	N	M	SD	Range	Missing values	Exchange of knowledge	Positive effect on the learning process
Exchange of knowledge	144	3.68	0.90	1-5	4	1	0.54**
Positive effect on the learning process	145	3.84	0.63	1-5	3	0.54**	1

** = $p < 0.01$ (2-sided)

6   Conclusion and Discussion

The study described in this article examined the embedding of a formative work placement test in the learning process of MBO and HBO Nursing students, based on expectations from previous research. The case study for this research is the E-Flow Nursing project. In this project, a digital work placement test was deployed as an intervention as part of the learning process. A key rule was 'No E-Flow, No PAP/Work Placement Plan'. The aim was for students to incorporate the results of the knowledge test into their learning objectives and activities during the work placement, and to discuss them with their work supervisor. The measurement tool employed, the questionnaire, was used previously in a similar project, in which the formative test did not form part of the learning process but was instead a stand-alone element. It was expected that since the formative test was now embedded in the learning process, it would indeed lead to development in the learning process, namely the acquisition of greater insight into the current and desired levels of knowledge, a positive effect on the learning process and more in-depth study of the specialism in the work placement department. It was furthermore expected that knowledge would be exchanged between the student and the work supervisor.

The results confirmed these expectations, with both students and work supervisors giving positive assessments. Students indicate that they have greater insight into the current and desired levels of knowledge, that the test has a positive effect on the learning process and that they have started studying their respective specialisms in greater depth. The supervisors indicate that more knowledge is exchanged and that the test has a positive effect on the students' learning process. There is also evidence of a significant positive relationship between the three scales 'insight into the current and desired levels of knowledge', 'positive effect on the learning process' and 'in-depth study of the specialism'.   The strongest relation exists between 'in-depth study of the specialism' and 'positive effect on the learning process' in the case of students. The study demonstrates that students believe that doing the formative tests has resulted in studying their respective specialisms in greater depth and that they consequently experienced the tests as having a positive effect on their learning process. The students also experience this effect on their insight into the current and desired levels of knowledge, though less strongly.

7   Scientific Contribution

This study has contributed to scientific research by confirming that embedding the formative knowledge test in the learning process results in enhanced development, more insight on the part of the student into his or her starting situation (the current and desired levels of knowledge), greater motivation by the student to study the respective specialism in more depth, and a positive effect on the learning process.

This study also has methodological limitations, however. This study used a questionnaire to measure how the student and supervisor experienced development in the learning process. Consequently, the study measured the development as experienced and not the progress in that development. There may be some degree of distortion due to a tendency by respondents to give socially desirable responses.

The average test scores were not analysed for this study since the objective of the intervention, formative testing, is to provide students with insight into the learning process, and adapt it where necessary. The assessment of academic performance is an objective of summary testing, which was not the intervention investigated. Furthermore, the results of the catch-up tests were not analysed since the students were not obliged to take these tests. The students were free to decide how they worked on filling their knowledge gaps through, for example, reading the professional literature or engaging in discussions with their supervisors. Although students indicated, for example, that they went about collecting more information, the study did not verify how the students went about collecting this additional information. More in-depth research into the activities that students undertake would be interesting as it would provide insight into student behaviour and action when it comes to actual learning.

For these reasons it was decided that in order to answer the research questions formulated for this study - the extent to which a formative questions contributes to insight, the learning process, deepening of knowledge and knowledge exchange - the study should measure how students and supervisors perceived the items.

The students and supervisors were analysed as two research groups. The supervisors were asked to give their opinion about the use of formative testing in general, and not in respect of individual students. Since the supervisors often supervised three to four students, it was not possible to link the results of supervisors to the results of the students. In the event of a follow-up study, this would be an interesting link to monitor, in combination with the activities undertaken by the students and the feedback provided by the supervisors.

Finally, a follow-up study would yield valuable information if it measured whether the use of formative tests combined with supervisor feedback and student learning activities resulted in better study results (summative testing). This would require a longitudinal study linking test results, study results, and student and supervisor perceptions.

References

1. Black, P., Wiliam, D.: Assessment and classroom learning. Assessment in Education 5(1), 7–74 (1998)
2. Cilliers, F.J., Schuwirth, L.W.T., Herman, N., Adendorff, H.J., van der Vleuten, C.P.M.: A Model of the Pre-assessment Learning Effects of Summative Assessment in Medical Education. Advances in Health Sciences Education 17(1), 39–53 (2012)
3. Dousma, T., Horsten, A., Brants, J.: Tentamineren. Wolters-Noordhoff, Groningen (1997)
4. Dijksterhuis, M.G., Voorhuis, M., Teunissen, P.W., Schuwirth, L.W., ten Cate, O.T., Braat, D.D., Scheele, F.: Assessment of competence and progressive independence in postgraduate clinical training. Med. Educ. 43(12), 1156–1165 (2013)
5. Kennisnet: Formatieve versus summatieve toetsing. Kennisnet (2013), http://toetswijzer.kennisnet.nl/ (retrieved March 14, 2014)
6. Ossevoort, E., Streumer, J.: Brug(gen) tussen onderwijs en zorg? Onderwijs & Gezondheidszorg 37(3), 20–23 (2013)
7. Ossevoort, E., Streumer, J.: Bruggen bouwen tussen onderwijs en zorg. Onderzoek naar de resultaten van, verwachtingen over en ervaringen met de digitale toetsbank van Leerstation Zorg. Kenniskring Beroepsonderwijs, Hogeschool Rotterdam (2011)
8. Samuels, A., Uil, M.: Voorbereiding van stagiaires op de praktijk: Kennis Over-Bruggen, 11/12, pp. 40–42 (2008)

Digital Script Concordance Test for Clinical Reasoning

The Development of a Dutch Digital Script Concordance Test for Clinical Reasoning for Nursing Specialists

Christof Peeters[1], Wil de Groot-Bolluijt[2],
Robbert Gobbens[2], and Marcel van Brunschot[3]

[1] Fontys Hogeschool, Eindhoven, The Netherlands
c.peeters@fontys.nl
[2] Hogeschool Rotterdam, Rotterdam, The Netherlands
wil@grootbolwerk.nl
GobRJ@hr.nl
[3] Stichting Leerstation Zorg, Houten, The Netherlands
m.v.brunschot@leerstationzorg.nl

Abstract. The Master of Advanced Nursing Practice (MANP) programme in the Netherlands is the professional training for the nursing specialist. The field of MANP is in flux; taking independent medical action and prescribing medication are among the principle aspects of this. Consequently clinical reasoning is an important part of the curriculum and makes great demands on the level of medical and nursing knowledge. At the moment the clinical reasoning capabilities of students are tested by means of two methods (assessment, case-history papers) that are frequently very labor-intensive for the teachers in regard to both developing questions and evaluation. The case-history papers also have a low inter-assessor validity, which is undesirable. The digital test is not suitable for this method of examination. In addition, the field of work is not involved in either the development of the questions or their validation.

Three Universities of Applied Sciences (Rotterdam, Fontys, Zuyd), along with the Learning Station Care Foundation initiated this project. The question was whether there was a suitable type of question to assess digitally the clinical reasoning capabilities of the trainee nursing specialist. The aim was greater possibilities for the teacher and trainee nursing specialist to support learning and to establish and pursue the desired level of knowledge. Based on a literature study it was jointly decided that the question type Script Concordance Test (SCT) could be used for this. The SCT type is in English and has been in use for 15-20 years. The starting point is the generic knowledge of the MANP trainee (medical and nursing) that is necessary for clinical reasoning. As the MANP programme is practice oriented it has the added value that in constructing SCT questions experts (medical and nursing specialists) working in the field have an essential role in validating the questions. Accordingly, this project will investigate whether there are digital test systems that can support this process and improve the quality of the tests.

In this project the SCT question type is digitalized, and digital tests have been developed for the complex practice of clinical reasoning for the MANP programme. The SCT question type has been included in the system of the

M. Kalz and E. Ras (Eds.): CAA 2014, CCIS 439, pp. 138–144, 2014.

Learning Station Care Foundation especially for this project. The conclusion is that the digital training and testing with the SCT type offers new possibilities for education and retraining. It must be noted that construction of the question type is labor-intensive and recruiting experts for the validation process is time-consuming. An expected result of the project is that the question type supports the learning process of clinical reasoning and teachers are enthusiastic about the various possibilities. The SCT question type can make an important contribution to the development and maintenance of clinical reasoning skills in (trainee) nursing specialists.

1   Introduction

Teachers of the Master of Advanced Nursing Practice (MANP) programme must meet the challenge of training students with a nursing background   in professional actions in the medical and nursing domain at master's level, and in a relatively short time. Clinical reasoning is an essential part of this and one in which makes high demands in quality. What is unique about the MANP programme is that medical and nursing reasoning are used together. In what are called the Dublin Descriptors the differences between doctor, master, and bachelor are set out.

Clinical reasoning has always been aimed at establishing a medical diagnosis of a health problem and its treatment. In this, clinical reasoning is linked to the establishment and treatment of the concomitant nursing care questions and needs. It is an extremely complex process that consists chiefly of collecting cues, interpreting these, and, with the patient, using them by setting up a plan and/or intervention and then evaluating this. The process of clinical reasoning is not easy to teach. It demands from the student a solid basis of knowledge and insight. During the process of differential diagnostic thought what is relevant is separated from the irrelevant in the data collected, then interpreted and examined for possible mutual relations that put the nursing specialist in the position of being able by means of deduction or clustering to form a logical differential diagnosis. A casual comment by a patient, for example, can throw a whole new light on the likelihood of possible hypotheses, examination or treatment contemplated.

The test methods for clinical reasoning are often very labor-intensive, both in the development and the evaluation. Students are usually given case-history papers with concrete questions by which they pursue the diagnostic process.

In order to digitally test clinical reasoning capabilities for the MANP programme the "knowledge test bank" of the Learning Station Care Foundation (www.leerstationzorg.nl) was used as a basis. Learning Station Care is already used by care institutions and all Bachelor Nursing programmes in the Netherlands, and in this present project is also adapted for the MANP programmes. Learning Station Care offers an integrated "Learning Management System" and a databank. Thanks to this, there is a unique combination of more than 13,000 test items, including the possibility of question construction with a media bank, test structure, test distribution, examination, and question maintenance. Learning Station Care has been developed from the viewpoint of learning value.

2   Theoretical Framework (Relation to State-of-the-Art)

It is expected of the (trainee) nursing specialists that they are able reason clinically to make an integral medical and nursing diagnosis of a patient with a health problem. To do this they should have the competencies to draw up a complete anamnesis, to carry out a technically competent physical examination, and to write a report in an interdisciplinary manner in the patient's case file. Even more important is the ability to make a logical differential diagnosis based on the patient's complaint. In order to do this it is essential to differentiate which data from the anamnesis, physical examination, and other examinations are relevant for the diagnostic process and why. This is followed by the interpretation based on deduction and/or clustering of the data collected. In other words, the (trainee) nursing specialists are capable of making the right decisions in the diagnostic process by means of clinical reasoning. For this a thorough knowledge of anatomy, physiology, patho-physiology and epidemiology is necessary. Clinical reasoning is based on nursing classifications such as NANDA, NIC, and NOC. In the reasoning process trainee nursing specialists are expected to integrate the wishes and values of patients and the scientific evidence, as well as their own knowledge, following the principles of Evidence-Based Practice.

At the start of the project a choice was made from the most suitable digital question types. From a thorough literature study the Script Concordance Test (SCT) type seemed to offer good possibilities for the MANP programme. The SCT question type can make an important contribution to the development and maintenance of clinical reasoning skills in (trainee) nursing specialists. Literature indicated that testing clinical reasoning with the help of SCT items is very real possibility, as long as the test also checks the underlying facts, concepts, and connections in a more classical manner.

The SCT question consists of three parts, the first of which is the clinical sketch. This is a real clinical situation in which a patient comes with a complaint, as it would happen in daily practice. In the second part (the scenario), in relation to the sketch a potential diagnostic hypothesis, examination, or treatment option is described. In the third part new information is provided in the form of a new symptom or the results of further examination. The participant should answer the question of the degree to which this new data impacts or has effect on the hypothesis, examination, or treatment option described in part two. The candidate can answer on a 5 point Likert scale ranging from unlikely to extremely likely. Below each sketch there are various scenarios that, according to the literature, emphasize the importance of complete mutual independence. In fact, based on the on-going experience and insights of the construction group an important adaption has been made: the independence of the data in the various sketches is found to be confusing and not in accordance with the practice. In the functional design this has been adapted, whereby a variant of the original SCT type has been created.

The construction of the SCT question is based on the differentiation in scoring rules. An important part of the development of an SCT question is that practice trainers in clinical practice have a part to play in the validation of the questions in (specific) practice. The recruitment of experts for the panels strengthens the involvement of those in the field of practice in the programme, both nursing specialists (alumni) and medical specialists are asked to participate.

From the literature research it appears that the differential possibilities in the score of the SCT question type lead to higher Rit values, and thereby contribute to the greater reliability of a test. It is argued that in clinical practice answers are not always 100% right or wrong. The use of scoring rules with weighted answers is closer to the clinical practice. With such a scoring rule the score that a student can make reflects the degree to which there is agreement between the student's answer and that of the reference panel of experts. The development of the Functional Design (FD) of the Script Concordance Test (SCT) question type is based on the open access article[1]: Script Concordance Tests: Guidelines for Construction (2008) http://www.biomed central.com/1472-6947/8/18. The SCT question type was specially developed for this project in the system of the Learning Station Care Foundation.

3   Research Questions

This project involves three questions:

1. Is there a suitable question type that can test digitally the clinical reasoning competence of the (trainee) nursing specialist, and at the same time meets the demands of the educational institution and professional practice?
2. What is the degree of user satisfaction of the (trainee) nursing specialist and the teachers in respect of the question type and the digital testing?

4   Objectives

In this project the SCT question type has been digitalized, and for the MANP programme digital tests have been developed for the complexity of clinical reasoning in practice. The point of departure for the content of the questions is the generic knowledge of the MANP programme (medical and nursing) that is necessary for clinical reasoning. With the help of focus groups insights were obtained into the effects and experiences of (trainee) nursing specialists and teachers after the use of the digital tests with the SCT question type that had been developed.

5   Method

5.1   Literature Study

At the start of the project a choice was made of the most suitable digital question types. This choice was based on the literature study of the SURF project "Digital testing of clinical reasoning in medical programmes." From this literature study, it appears that the SCT type offers good possibilities for the testing of (aspects of)

---

[1] © 2008 Fournier et al; licensee BioMed Central Ltd.

This is an Open Access article distributed under the terms of the Creative Commons Attribution License (http://creativecommons.org/licenses/by/2.0), which permits unrestricted use, distribution, and reproduction in any medium, provided the original work is properly cited.

clinical reasoning for the MANP programme. At the same time, the adaptability of the question type in relation to the aims of the programme was taken into consideration. The quality and the digital use of the question type were of primary importance.

5.2   SCT Question Type

For this project a workgroup was set up to consider the SCT question type, and in which the three colleges involved were represented by at least one teacher. The workgroup first had to become thoroughly familiar with the question type by constructing SCT questions themselves and then in plenary session to evaluate and discuss these. It was decided to develop questions for the specialisms of cardiology, neurology, pulmonology, gastroenterology, endocrinology and psychiatry. This was done by a number of experts who set questions in their own area of expertise. After formulation, the questions were evaluated by an editorial board on their content, language, and structure. After this, the questions were laid before a panel of experts who were asked to validate them. The validation process was done digitally, making use of internet. The three colleges made use of their networks of medical and nursing practice teachers in order to involve experts in the field and set up panels for each discipline.

5.3   Effects and Experiences of (Trainee) Nursing Specialists

In two separate focus groups of around ten volunteer alumni and trainee nursing specialists from the three Universities of Applied Sciences (Rotterdam, Fontys, Zuyd) the participants will be interviewed on their effects and experiences in the digital testing of clinical reasoning capabilities with the help of the SCT question type.

Through these focus groups we also expect to gain input on the level of difficulty of the SCT questions. The meeting of these focus groups will be held during the annual symposium of the Fontys Hogescholen MANP. Respondents could sign up for this meeting. The time frame was set to 45 minutes. Two weeks before the meeting each respondent received a trial version of some SCT questions. They were asked to answer the questions and document their first experiences with the aid of a survey. The technique that is used in this survey is the tree model (Evers, 2007). This model consists of predetermined main and sub themes. The tree model is a structured interview in which the research topic forms the stem and the sub themes the branches. Both the main and the sub themes are translated into several main questions. In the model all the themes are emphasized equally. By using this model the interview has width and depth.

During the focus group meeting there will be a discussion leader and an observer. The observer will guard the timeframe and register the interactions and events that take place. Special attention will be payed to personal dominants and group formation and the effect this has on the participants. The meeting will also be recorded with a voice recorder. After the meeting the voice recording will be analyzed. To support the dialogue participants have access to a white board/flip-over.

The meeting will start with the main question. The discussion leader is going to lead the discussion and ensure that all sub themes are discussed. Within 5 days the results of the meeting will be analyzed. After the meeting the discussion leader and the observer will individually evaluate the focus group meeting. After the individual evaluation the discussion leader and the observer will discuss the results.

5.4   Experiences of Teachers

Considering the small number of teachers (N=5) involved in this project, qualitative methods have been chosen – focus group interviews. All teachers from the three institutions who were members of the SCT workgroup will participate in the focus group.

By doing so the experiences with developing SCT questions can be mapped out. This will also offer an insight into the stimulating and restricting factors in the developing process of questions up and to the validation by experts.

6   (Expected) Results

6.1   Literature

The SCT question type gives the future professional direct insight into the fact that there is not always a single correct answer (reaction of the panels of experts), and also the insight into the choices that are made from limited data in order to arrive step by step at a good treatment plan. Digital training and testing with the SCT type will offer new possibilities for education and retraining in the field of clinical reasoning. Considering the complexity of clinical reasoning, there is great need for a good and applicable method of learning, and on the basis of this project both the formulation of the questions and doing the tests was seen as a powerful learning instrument by teachers.

6.2   Project

The SCT type is ready for use in the MANP programmes, and as soon as sufficient questions are produced and validated it can be used independently of teachers and the test results directly reproduced. At the moment 40 questions (patient sketches), each with six scenarios, have been formulated in this project. The SCT questions have been constructed by teachers and doctors from the courses involved. Each question was validated by a panel of about 20 experts. Considering the total of developed items, for the present the test items will be used only as diagnostic learning tools (formative) and not used in examination (summative). In the coming period the tests will be expanded by alumni and we would like to present the result of this at the conference.

6.3   Effects and Experience

The expectation is that the results of the focus groups will indicate that the SCT-questions can make an important contribution to the development of the clinical reasoning skills of MANP students and that teachers will be enthusiastic about the digital possibilities.

6.4   Limitations

An important drawback of the question type is that the formulation and editing process take a great deal of time. This is also true for the recruitment of experts used for the validation. Since the number participants was limited and the time scale of the project was short, it is impossible to establish unambiguous qualitative and quantitative results.

True effects will be visible only once the implementation is complete and, thanks to the digital intervention, a new situation has come into being. That means that a cycle of a number of academic years will be needed to examine whether the learning process of clinical reasoning has really improved.

6.5   Experience of the Process

Nevertheless, above all, on the basis of the experience gained in the project it can be stated that the joint development of tests with various institutions contributes to the quality and clarity of the tests. For the results of this project the emphasis is on the contribution to the learning process, the enthusiasm and satisfaction of the teachers, and the usefulness of the digital testing.

References

1. de Vries, T.P.G.M., Henning, R.H., Hogerzeil, H.V., Fresle, D.A. (1994). Guide to good prescribing. A practical manual. World Health Organization, Geneva. WHO/DAP/94.11, http://apps.who.int/medicinedocs/pdf/whozip23e/whozip23e.pdf (geraadpleegd op 19 juni 2010)
2. Schwartz, A., Elstein, A.S.: Clinical reasoning in medicine. In: Higgs, J., Jones, M.A., Loftus, S., Christensen, N. (eds.) Clinical Reasoning in the Health Professions, 3rd edn., pp. 223–234. Elsevier Butterworth-Heinemann, Oxford (2008)
3. Dublin Descriptoren (2004), http://www.nvao.net/page/downloads/Dublin_Descriptoren.pdf
4. Grundmeijer, H.G.L.M., Reenders, K.: Het geneeskundig proces: klinisch redeneren van klacht naar therapie (3e herz. ed.). Elsevier gezondheidszorg, Maarssen (2009)
5. North American Nursing Diagnosis Association (NANDA), NANDA-I nursing diagnoses: definitions & classification. NANDA International, Philadelphia (2009-2011)
6. Bulechek, G.M., Butcher, H.K., Dochterman, J.M.: Nursing Interventions Classification (NIC), 5th edn. Mosby Elsevier, St. Louis (2008)
7. Moorhead, S., Johnson, M., Maas, M.L., Swanson, E.: Nursing outcomes classification (NOC), 4th edn. Mosby, St. Louis (2008)
8. Johnson, M., Bulechek, G.M., Butcher, H.K., McCloskey, D.J.C., Maas, M.L., Moorhead, S., et al.: NANDA, NOC, and NIC linkages: nursing diagnoses, outcomes, & interventions, 2nd edn. Mosby Elsevier, St. Louis (2006)
9. Offringa, M., et al.: Klinisch handelen gebaseerd op bewijsmateriaal. Bohn Stafleu van Loghum (2010)
10. Evers, J.: Kwalitatief interviewen: kunst én kunde. Uitgeverij Lemma, Den Haag (2007)
11. Humbert, A.J., et al.: Assessment of clinical reasoning: A Script Concordance test designed for pre-clinical medical students. Medical Teacher 33(6), 472–477 (2011)
12. Charlin, B., van der Vleuten, C.: Standardized Assessment of Reasoning in Contexts of Uncertainty: The Script Concordance Approach; Eval Health Prof 2004; 27; 304 (2004)

Practical Implementation of Innovative Image Testing

Corinne Tipker-Vos[1], Kim de Crom[1], Anouk van der Gijp[2], Cécile Ravesloot[2],
M. van der Schaaf[3], Christian Mol[2], Mario Maas[1],
Jan van Schaik[2], and Koen Vincken[2]

[1] Academic Medical Center, Amsterdam, The Netherlands
[2] University Medical Center Utrecht, Utrecht, The Netherlands
[3] Utrecht University, Utrecht, The Netherlands

Abstract. The testing of image interpretation skills within the profession of Radiology (often paper- pencil) lags behind practice. To increase the authenticity of assessment of image interpretation skills, the Dutch national progress test for medical specialists in training to become radiologists, is digitized using the program VQuest. This programme makes it possible to administer a test with 2D and 3D images, in which images can be viewed and processed as they can in practice. During implementation, the entire assessment cycle from test design to assessment analysis and evaluation has been run through twice. Excluding some small improvements, both trainee specialist and organizational members were satisfied with the digitized assessment. Amongst other things, the trainee specialist feel that this application of digital testing is more consistent with the situation in practice than the conventional testing method.

Keywords: Radiology, test, VQuest, images, assessment cycle, test design item construction, test administration, preconditions.

1   Background

The current state of the art in radiology allows for the viewing and interpretation of both two-dimensional (2D) and multidimensional (3D) images. However, the testing of image interpretation skills lags behind practice and is still based on written work. The now completed SURF 'Testing visualised' project investigated the quality of digital testing with 2D and 3D images. The 'Digital testing using images, an additional dimension' project, also subsidised by SURF, builds on this work and will implement digital testing with 2D and 3D images in the national test for medical specialists in training to become radiologists (progress test, VGT).

The national progress test (VGT) was introduced within the radiology specialist study programme in 2003. It is designed to monitor, and to encourage via feedback, the development of image interpretation skills and radiological knowledge by doctors during their five-year specialist training period. A formative written test, the progress test is administered simultaneously to all trainee specialists in radiology in the Netherlands every six months.

M. Kalz and E. Ras (Eds.): CAA 2014, CCIS 439, pp. 145–148, 2014.

As the testing process lags behind practice, new methods of assessing image interpretation skills are needed, such as digital testing using 3D image questions and digital processing options for 2D image questions. A unique programme that allows this type of assessment and that can be applied within various disciplines is the VQuest programme [1]. The VQuest programme makes it possible to administer a test with 2D and 3D images, in which the images can be viewed and processed as they can in practice. In order to integrate testing with digital 2D and 3D image questions into the national progress test on a large scale, an adequate ICT infrastructure, the right test design with the right types of questions and an effective feedback system are required. The aim of this project is therefore to implement innovative image testing in practice.

2   Method and Results

The final digital test has been developed on the basis of the assessment cycle in combination with the preconditions. The assessment cycle [2] is made up of the following four stages:

1. Test design
2. Item construction
3. Test administration
4. Assessment, analysis and evaluation

2.1   Test Design

Before the questions can be drafted, the first step is to produce a test matrix that corresponds to the formulated learning objectives in the educational context. This matrix provides an overview of the topics and skills that need to be covered in the test (the 'content' of the test). In the progress test matrix, the learning objectives for each sub-area are described in the HORA (radiology training review committee) training plan. Examinees can be tested on the syndromes listed here using text questions or using image questions.

2.2   Item Construction

Before questions can be formulated, suitable images first need to be gathered. One way of doing this for radiology is by selecting images from clinical practice. When selecting suitable images it is important to bear a number of points in mind:

- Raw data must be available for the examination
- Each examination selected should preferably feature only one abnormality
- The image must be anonymous

Following the switch-over to digital testing, the software used means that non-conventional question types can be introduced. VQuest was used for both SURF projects. In addition to multiple choice questions with only one answer allowed and multiple choice questions with multiple answers allowed, the programme also offers options for hotspot questions and long-menu questions.

2.3   Test Administration

As an image interpretation test often contains many images (e.g. CT series), the data communication load for this type of test is high. Consequently, it is not currently possible to administer the test in VQuest online. The test data must therefore always be loaded onto the relevant computers before the test. Depending on the speed of the (wireless or otherwise) network connection, the number of computers on which the test will be administered and the size of the server, the tests can be distributed to the computers automatically from a central server.

It is important that the test is administered in a secure environment (no Internet access) and that the answers can be saved securely. In the case of the progress test, a location with around 380 PCs was required. For image interpretation questions it is vital that the images are displayed clearly on the monitor. Darkening the room and tilting the screen if necessary to prevent glare can help to achieve this. For a large-scale test it is essential to draw up guidelines describing all logistical aspects and responsible parties. The first progress test was administered at the University Medical Center Utrecht (UMCU) and Academic Medical Center Amsterdam (AMC) in a large number of small rooms. The second progress test was administered at the VU University Amsterdam (VU) in a large computer room.

2.4   Assessment, Analysis and Evaluation

At the end of the test the answers of all trainee specialists were located on the server. There was a folder for each trainee specialist containing all the answers entered. VQuest was able to read the answer files into the lecturer module, where they were then checked automatically. After the test, the trainee specialists received an evaluation form, followed a few days later by an e-mail stating the answers they entered and the correct answers. Amongst other things, the evaluation revealed that the examinees found the VQuest programme to be very user-friendly.

For digital testing in general, a number of preconditions must be met before a test can be administered. One of the key requirements is an emergency procedure. This procedure describes the steps that will be taken if the test cannot be administered digitally for any reason whatsoever. It must be possible to take this decision both prior to and during the test. The emergency procedure also describes who plays what role and therefore has what specific responsibilities. Comprehensive guidelines are also essential. They must include the following important points: the deadline for supplying questions, allocation of roles and the need for a number of trial runs of the test on site.

3   Conclusion

The two digital tests administered during the project period were entirely satisfactory. The survey revealed, amongst other things, that the trainee specialists feel that digital testing is more consistent with the situation in practice than the conventional testing method. Both digital tests went smoothly from a technical perspective, with the exception of a few minor points for improvement. The first (UMCU and AMC) was a huge challenge in terms of logistics because the around 390 trainee specialists had to be split between 13 rooms. The second progress test at VU, at which there was access to one large room, was therefore a massive improvement from a logistical point of view.

References

1. VQuest, http://www.vquest.nl
2. Ravesloot, et al.: Handbook Digital testing of radiological image interpretation. In: Symposium Digital Testing of Radiological Image Interpretation, Utrecht, pp. 17–28 (2014)

Where Is My Time? Identifying Productive Time of Lifelong Learners for Effective Feedback Services

Bernardo Tabuenca, Marco Kalz, Dirk Börner, Stefaan Ternier, and Marcus Specht

Welten Institute, Research Centre for Learning, Teaching and Technology
Open University of the Netherlands; Heerlen, The Netherlands
{bernardo.tabuenca,marco.kalz,dirk.boerner,
stefaan.ternier,marcus.specht}ou.nl

Abstract. Lifelong learners are confronted with a broad range of activities they have to manage every day. In most cases they have to combine learning, working, family life and leisure activities throughout the day. Hence, learning activities from lifelong learners are disrupted. The difficulty to find a suitable time slot to learn during the day has been identified as the most frequent cause. In this scenario mobile technologies play an important role since they can keep track of the most suitable moments to accomplish specific learning activities in context. Sampling of learning preferences on mobile devices is a key benchmarks for lifelong learners to become aware on which learning task suits in which context, to set realistic goals and to set aside time to learn on a regular basis. The contribution of this manuscript is twofold: first, a classification framework for modelling lifelong learners' preferences is presented based on a literature review; second, a mobile application for experience sampling is piloted aiming to identify which are the preferences from lifelong learners regarding when, how and where learning activities can be integrated.

Keywords: lifelong learning, experience sampling, mobile learning, self-regulated learning, reflection.

1   Introduction

Choosing time and learning opportunities effectively is one of the major challenges for lifelong learners as confirmed by recent statistics of the European Commission [1]. This survey shows that the participation in lifelong learning activities in Europe decreased between 2006 and 2011. Participants in this survey mention access, time, place, and lack of personalization as barriers to accomplish learning activities. Other authors stress the importance of supporting self-direction and self-organization of lifelong learners with regards to using new technologies [2]. Lifelong learners face the challenge that they have to combine their professional activities with learning activities and must engage simultaneously with family time to ensure a balance of adults' responsibilities, overall wellbeing and their personal development. However, finding an appropriate balance between different life domains is neither easy nor instantaneous [3]. We have recently conducted a study concluding that lifelong learner's learning

M. Kalz and E. Ras (Eds.): CAA 2014, CCIS 439, pp. 149–161, 2014.

experiences are disrupted and finding a suitable time slot to learn during the day is the most frequent difficulty reported by participants [4]. Moreover, learners highlight the importance of smartphones to support more constant learning experiences. Hence, there is a need to integrate learning activities in daily life. The European Reference Framework [5] enumerates eight key competences that are fundamental for each individual in a lifelong learning society. One of them is "Learning to learn", being the ability to organize one's own learning through effective management of time and information, and becoming aware of one´s learning.

Providing in-context support and feedback for lifelong learners is key to identify the best learning moments, identify available resources in each context, self-organize their learning day, and set realistic goals. Lifelong learning not only implies setting aside regular time for learning during the day, but also combining learning activities with daily life activities. Mobile devices can facilitate users to keep track of learning preferences in context [6]. Hattie and Timperley [7] differentiate between three different types of feedback and four different effect levels. To provide support for lifelong learners we are currently developing mobile tools and services to provide feed forward feedback (answering the question *"Where to next?"*) targeting the process and self-regulation level. As a method for the development and data collection we have chosen the Experience Sampling Method (ESM).

Sampling of learning experiences in context provides an important benchmark for lifelong learners to identify productive times during the day and to scaffold their learning day on top of these moments. ESM is a method that asks participants to stop at certain times and make notes of their experience in real time and it also allows to gather direct and contextual objective measures and situated subjective measures. A good portion of ESM research has been done exploring both the structure of classrooms as well as students' and teachers' subjective experience in them, by linking variation in attention, interest or challenge to specific instructional practices or conditions [8, 9]. Likewise, contextual ESM has been used to understand daily information needs of people in longitudinal studies [10]. ESM responses measure what the person decides to communicate about his inner states whenever he is prompted a question. It is well known that we tend to be biased and that we edit out responses according to social desirability [11]. For instance, what does it mean if I score 4 in a 5-Likert scale on the question "how busy are you in this moment?" where 1 corresponds to "very busy"? This measure can be quite different depending on the habits or culture of the person who answers. Nevertheless, these reports are significantly more powerful and accurate when they are self-reports (since I only take myself as a reference to measure how busy I am in this moment). Hence, ESM facilitates an intimate and exhaustive account on how people experience their daily existence [11]. Mobile technologies provide an interesting opportunity for users to evaluate situations based on "stimulus variables in the natural or customary habitat of an individual" [12] since they are reported in our own personal device.

This manuscript presents a classification framework that aims to support lifelong learners in their need to model the learning day by instantiating different variations of the ESM. Furthermore, results from a small-scale pilot study are presented to collect experiences and feedback about the chosen approach, the type of the preferred notifications received, and their preferred format when sampling the experiences on a mobile device.

2   A Classification Framework for Modelling Lifelong Learners' Day

In 2003, Consolvo et al. [13] explored the use of the ESM to evaluate regular phones, PDAs, paper booklets or audio recorders ("*ubicomp applications*"). This evaluation contemplates that every instance of the ESM is dispatched in three sequential events (Figure 1): receive a notification; dispatch the question (read, listen, watch); provide an answer.

Nowadays, smartphones are equipped with several sensors that enrich the quality and quantity of the sample with contextual information. Mobile devices enable capturing different context variables and can identify the users' location (GPS), orientation (digital compass), among others. In a first analysis for distinguishing the role of context in mobile learning support, De Jong et al. [14] have identified the main dimensions of context information used in learning applications and further extended to the context taxonomy to the Ambient Information CHannEls model (AICHE) [15] meta-information. The AICHE model addresses context via sensors, artefacts and channels. This model approaches the context of a person or an object defined by five distinct dimensions (Figure 1).

The classification framework presented in this section merges ESM and the AICHE model to provide specific clues on how lifelong learners can model their learning day. This framework instantiates ESM to explore the dimensions of the mobile context and makes use of the features provided by mobile devices in each of the sequential events in the instantiation of the ESM.

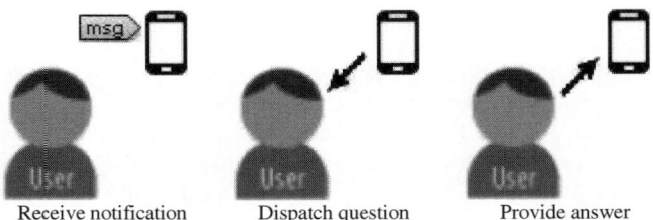

Receive notification   Dispatch question   Provide answer

Fig. 1. Sequential events in an instance of the ESM

2.1   Receive Notification

Notifications can be classified according to two different criteria:

1. Trigger time, this is the rule that identifies the moment in which the user receives the notifications. These notifications can be triggered on three different basis:
    a) Scheduled-based: Notifications are triggered following a time pattern, e.g. *send me a notification every Sunday at 8pm asking me what was the best moment to read during the week.*
    b) Random: Notifications are triggered randomly in time, this is not following any time pattern, *e.g. send me 5 notifications per day asking me how do I feel in that moment.* This type of alerts can be used to identify best occasional

learning moments. The fact of randomizing notifications is not only referred to the timing, but also randomizing the number of alerts sent, or randomizing the order in which a sequence is sent.

c) Event-based: Notifications are triggered on the accomplishment of an event that happened in the context of the user. Hereby, the dimensions of mobile context (Figure 2) are explored with the aim to identify ways to support life-long learners in their goal to organize their own learning towards effective context adaptation:

i) Location. Mobile devices are equipped with capabilities (e.g. GPS or Bluetooth) that make them aware of the current location of the user, e.g. *send me a notification every time I arrive to the University in order to ask me what do I expect to learn today.* Sampling this experience fosters life-long learner´s capacity of reflection [6] and set reasonable goals before starting the learning day.

ii) Identification. Mobile devices are equipped with capabilities (e.g. Near Field Communication readers or Quick Response code reader) that en-able them to identify tagged artefacts in lifelong learner´s context. E.g. *every time I approach with my mobile device the (NFC) tag attached to my German grammar book, send me a notification asking me how many pages did I read today.* Sampling this experience helps the lifelong learner to track his pace of reading while learning the German language and set aside time to learn on a regular basis.

iii) Time. Mobile devices provide calendar functionalities that facilitate the configuration of notifications triggered on the accomplishment of time conditions. E.g. *two weeks before I have an exam-appointment in my cal-endar, send me a notification asking me to rate from 0 to 10 how pre-pared I am for the exam.* Sampling this experience helps the lifelong learner to monitor his perceived knowledge on a subject, and make a plan to prepare the exam with enough time.

iv) Relation. This dimension captures the relation an entity has established to other entities, and describes social, functional and compositional relation-ships. Mobile devices are equipped with capabilities (e.g. social network apps, Near Field Communication) that enable them to identify and/or cluster in groups other entities, and the type of connection they have with the lifelong learner. E.g. *every time my colleagues are online in the cam-pus social network, send me a notification to ask me whether I had any problem making my homework.* Sampling this experience helps the life-long learner to identify drawbacks accomplishing learning activities, and provide direct cues of support to existing drawbacks.

v) Environment. This dimension captures tasks and actions happening in the environment. Mobile devices are equipped with sensors (e.g. compass, GPS) and apps (e.g. forecasting weather or traffic jam) that make them aware of the context in the environment of the user. E.g. *send me a noti-fication when the weather forecast for the weekend is rainy so I can bor-row a book from the library and stay at home.* Sampling this experience helps the lifelong learner to model his week based on the conditions of the environment.

Fig. 2. Five dimensions of mobile context. AICHE model [14]

2. Delivery mechanism. Notifications can happen in the background, when the notification can be dispatched in a different context in which the notification is received. Nevertheless, ESM notifications must happen in the forefront so the sample can capture the specific lifelong learning context when/where they are received. Notifications in the forefront must call user´s attention. Mobile devices feature three main types of delivery mechanisms, namely, visual (e.g. icon, blinking light, adjust brightness, etc.), audible (e.g. beep, tone, etc.) or tactile (e.g. vibration).

2.2   Dispatch Question

The type of question classifies the different ways in which the question can be prompted to the lifelong learner. We distinguish the following criteria as relevant:

1) Prompt format. This is referred to the format in which the question is formulated.
    a) Text. This is the most compatible format across mobile device. They are not only implemented in regular mobile phones (e.g. SMS), but also in smartphones (e.g. chats, online questionnaires) or PDAs.
    b) Rich format. These are extensions of text prompts, but formatted with special font (type, size, colour etc.), images and/or multimedia (audio, video). These features need to be carefully combined so they do not impact the participant's ability to read.
    c) Complex control. Visual environments facilitate the implementation of prompts that aim to describe and collect complex concepts like relations, clusters, orders etc. Instances of complex controls are:
        i)   Multiple/simple choice questions implemented with text and/or images. *E.g. select which learning activity do you prefer to do while commuting to work by bus: (1)listen; (2)read; (3)write; (4)watch videos.*
        ii) Rankings facilitate ordering of items based on a specific criterion. *E.g. based on your current priorities rank your learning goals for the coming month: learn German; iOS development; statistics; research methods;*
        iii) Mapping items facilitate matching of concepts from different groups. *E.g. how much time did you set aside for learning this week? Match your time availability (-commuting to work; -after dinner) to your weekly learning goals (German grammar; C# programming structures for iOS development).*

iv) Sliders facilitate collection of a specific value within a range of them. *E.g. rate your overall progress of the week in statics towards your goal of being able to analyse data with ANOVA test (0 to 100%).*

d) Sensor data facilitates the enrichment of the questions with context data. *E.g. today is a grey rainy day to stay at home, do you feel like posting an entry in your sew blog?*

2) Timeout is the time that the question is available for the lifelong learner to be read. Most of the questions are only significant when they are read within a specific range of time.

3) Question design. [12] contemplate three variables when designing questions in ESM: 1.) order: whether the prompts´ order should be fixed or random; 2.) dependency: whether a prompt is presented depending on what the user reported in a previous question *(e.g. every time I report low learning performance, trigger an instance asking me to report on my regular sport activity so I can see weather there is direct correlation)* and 3.) probability: whether there is a need to assign probabilities that a question will be asked.

2.3   Provide Answer

Answer refers to the externalization of lifelong learner´s experience in a mobile device. We distinguish the following components as relevant for the classification framework.

1) Timeout. The time the user has to answer the question.

2) Answer format. Mobile devices today are equipped with text editors, audio and video recorders or photo camera. Likewise, the proliferation of apps to survey data (e.g. personal response systems, questionnaires) facilitate lifelong learners a wide range of input formats to record their experience. Lifelong learners not only learn by analysing the data answered in subsequent iterations of the ESM, it is also expectable that the single fact of externalizing an answer will trigger a different cognitive process depending on the format of the answer. For instance, reporting an answer with an audio-speech [16] implies a different cognitive process than the one triggered by answering to a multiple-choice-question. Question and answer within an instance of the ESM do not necessarily need to have the same format. Answers reported in an ESM can be:

a) Quantitative. Refers to data that can be quantified in a specific number. Sliders, rankings, mappings and sensor data are instances of items to collect quantitative data. *E.g. report how many hours did you invest this week on physical activities.*

b) Qualitative. Refers to data aimed to collect descriptions, sensations, features or abstract characteristics. Open answers in text, audio or video recordings are instances of items to collect qualitative data. *E.g. every time I pass an exam, record a power video to motivate you for the next one.*

3) Sensor data facilitates the enrichment of the sample with context data so lifelong learner´s report can be correlated with variables that a mobile device can capture. *E.g. every time I run and report a good performance, record the local temperature to find a correlation with weather conditions.*

4) Acknowledgment checks can be used to indicate whether the question was read or an answer was given.

3   Qualitative Study

3.1   Introduction

The qualitative study presented in this section instantiates the framework of the previous section with the aim to make participants aware of their learning preferences, and evaluate which type of questions and answers do they find more suitable in their context. This study took place in a workshop at the Joint European Summer School on Technology Enhanced Learning 2013 (JTELSS 2013) in Limassol (Cyprus). This event offers a learning environment where participants get opportunities to develop research skills, increase their knowledge base, engage in debate, have access to experts in the field. and discuss their own work.

A hands-on workshop presented the ESM as a method of research in the field of lifelong learners, showed existing tools and piloted an app for sampling of experiences. This pilot was guided by the following research question:

1)   What are lifelong learner's preferences, requirements, and needs for ubiquitous support? Including the following sub-questions:
   a)   When do lifelong learners prefer to be alerted to report about learning preferences, requirements and needs?
   b)   How do lifelong learners prefer to be alerted to report about learning preferences, requirements and needs?
   c)   Which formats do lifelong learners find more suitable to report about learning preferences, requirements and needs?

3.2   Method

Participants
The experiment involved 12 voluntary and non-rewarded participants. They were all researchers in the field of technology-enhanced learning, five of them were women and the average age was 29.

Materials
The ESM pilot was developed adapting an existing open-source tool suite for educators, researchers and learners: ARLearn [17] (Figure 3). Two participants used their own mobile devices. The rest borrowed smartphones for the experiment.

Design
All the participants in the experiment had the same treatment. This experiment took place during 90 minutes distributed in the following time slots:

• Lecture. 30 minutes introducing the ESM and showing theoretical framing of the workshop.
• Field trip excursion sampling experiences. 40 minutes of practical experiment where the participants followed the flow given in the mobile app and illustrated in figure 4.
• Questionnaire & discussion. 20 minutes, brainstorming, feedback and data collection

Data was collected in questionnaire about learning preferences that included three questions asking about their preferred sampling method and two more about appreciation of the app.

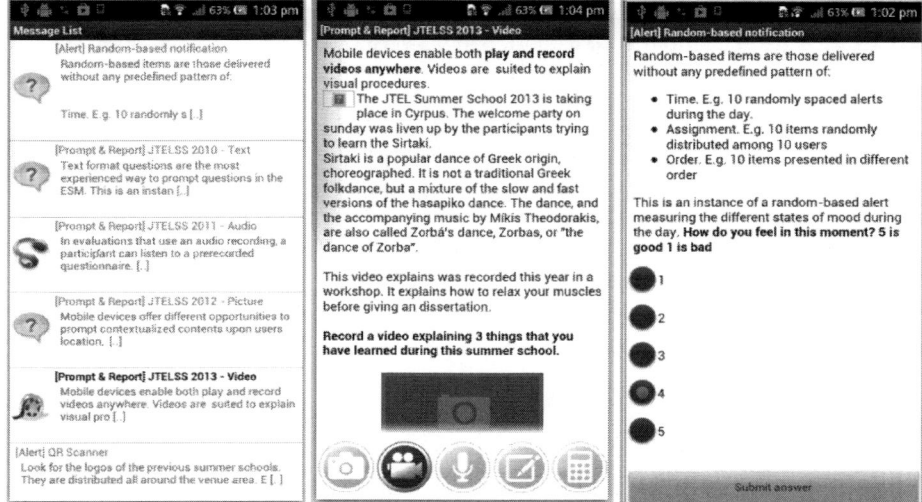

a) List of items   b) Question prompted in video and answer reported in video (qualitative report)   c) Question prompted in text and reported in 5-Likert scale (quantitative report)

Fig. 3. ESM for ARLearn app

Procedure
The lecture presented the guidelines to perform sampling of experiences with mobile technologies. The app whose flow is illustrated in figure 3 was designed so the participants could experience the different type of notifications that can be triggered when implementing the ESM, namely, scheduled-based notifications, event-based notification and random-based notifications. The flow contemplated the following items presented to the participants in the form of notifications:

- App instruction items (See single-lined squares in figure 3). These items teach them on how to navigate within the app, how to record audio, etc.
- ESM instruction items (See double-lined in figure 3). These items were instances of the ESM in the form of notifications appearing in their incoming message box on the following bases: scheduled-based notification came two minutes after starting the app; event-based notifications came after scanning QR codes around the venue (Figure 3a) and, after reading the scheduled-based notification (see dependencies in classification framework); random-based notification came in some moment after the first notification. For these items, participants should read the question given in text, rich-text (Figure 3bc), audio, or video (Figure 3b). After that, they should answer in a required format that could be text, audio, video (Figure 3b), picture or likert scale (Figure 3c).

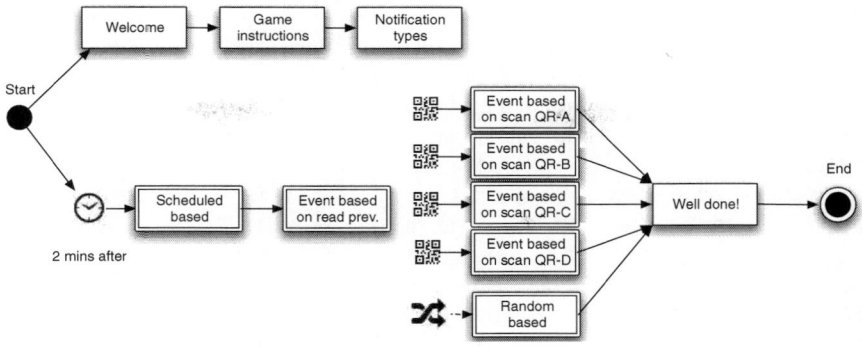

Fig. 4. Flow of the ESM app

3.3 Results

1) Research question 1. Lifelong learning preferences, requirements and needs for ubiquitous support

When participants were asked when they preferred to be notified to report about learning preferences, requirements and needs, event-based notifications were preferred by 92%, scheduled-based by 42% and random-based by 0% of the participants (Figure 5). Participant 1 (P#1) preferred "event-based" and "scheduled-based" arguing that these types of notifications are *"Easier to organize as a learner"*. Some of the participants raised compatibility working aspects in "scheduled-based" notifications. P#4: *"scheduled-based alerts would fit more my working preferences"*. One participant highlighted the bias effect of expecting a question, happened especially in "event-based" notifications, but also in "scheduled-based" notifications. P#3: *"It was logical to expect a question after a particular event"*. As event-based items were triggered by scanning QR codes attached to physical objects, some participants raised the proximity of attaching digital information to physical world objects. P#5: *"Information shown in event-based event seemed to be closer to me"*. P#6: *"event-based notifications are more relevant since they are triggered as a consequence that something in my environment was happening"*.

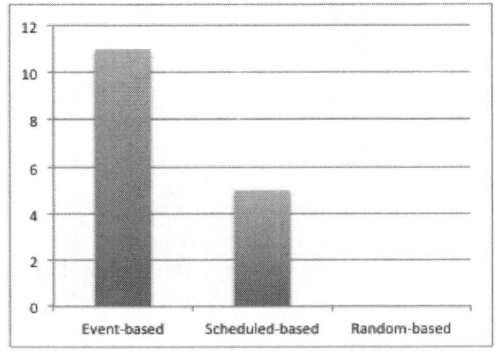

Fig. 5. When do you prefer to be alerted to report about learning preferences, requirements and needs?

When participants were asked how they preferred to be alerted to report about their learning preferences, requirements and needs, the majority of the participants preferred texts and picture formats (Figure 6). Participants that selected "text" and "picture" argued focus on the information and accuracy on the explanation. P#1: *"You get more focused info and it is easier to understand the question"*. Intrusiveness aspects were detected for participants that preferred text. P#2: *"It is the least intrusive way"*. Some participants raised the usefulness of making knowledge understandable to someone and express their impressions with video and picture formats. P3: *"Pictures and videos convey a lot of knowledge in relatively short time"*. Context or environment, were raised as key elements to decide the suitability of the notification, to the extent that some participants did not report a concrete preference. P#4: *"They are all useful media formats depending on the context"*. Suitability of the format text was preferred because of its facility to adapt to be read in different contexts. P#5: *"I can easily adapt my time to read in a suitable moment"*. P#6: *"Text and pictures are better to describe an understanding"*. P#8 preferred text and argued *"The rest of the formats are a kind of 'invasive' mode of communication that might not adapt to the different times of the day, night"*. Pictures and videos were reported as more "catchy" (P#9). P#10 reported text preference arguing that they are less distracting than the rest o the media. When this is about recording feelings and emotions, audios facilitate it. P#12 preferred audios arguing *"personal audio recordings facilitate it in a more personal way"*.

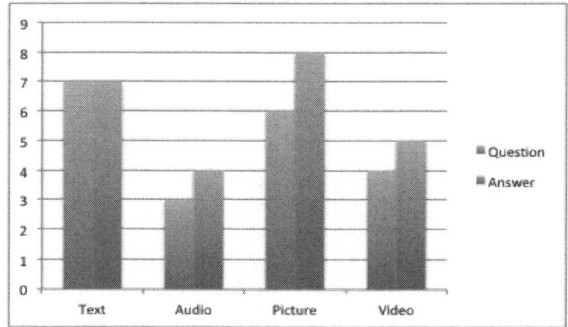

Fig. 6. How do lifelong learners prefer to be prompted? (Question). How do lifelong learners prefer to answer? (Answer).

When lifelong learners were asked which formats they find more suitable to report about learning preferences, requirements and needs, the majority of the participants reported pictures and text as preferred formats (Figure 6). Rapidity on creating the answer was argued as key aspect by some participants. P#1: *"It is faster"*. Likewise as happened in previous question, some participants raised the usefulness of making knowledge understandable to someone and express their impressions with video and picture formats. P#3: *"Pictures are easy to take and again convey a lot of data"*. Participants seemed to be more used to text messaging. Some participants raised were more familiar reporting text samples. P#3: *"Text is the simplest way"*. One participant highlighted that videos are well suited recording of procedures. P#4: *"Video answers facilitate explaining a flow of information"*. Audio recordings were perceived as more natural interventions when reporting. P#5: *"Audio recording is a more natural inter-action interface"*. Pictures seem to be really popular and easy to report method. P#5: *"Taking pictures is a pretty common way to report with a mobile phone"*. Some participants discarded the use of text of notifications because of the difficulty of writing long text messages on the small keyboards of smartphones. Even more remarkable when the smartphones are borrow and they are not the personal ones. P#8: *"Audios, pictures and videos are easier and faster to use"*. P#9: *"I am more used to text and pictures"*. P#10 preferred picture reminding that *"A picture is worth a thousand words"*. Some consider pictures as easier to assimilate information. P#11: *"Text content is easier to process for me"*. Videos are well suited to analyze the participant, gestures, or physical reactions when reporting. P12: *"They are more indicative tow what you like to know from the participant"*.

4   Discussion and Conclusions

The European Reference Framework [5] highlights the ability to organize one's own learning through effective management of time and information, and becoming aware of one's learning (*"learning to learn"*), as one of the eight key competences for each individual in a lifelong learning society. This manuscript presents a suitable approach for introspection and modelling the learning day in lifelong learners. Instantiations of the ESM in personal mobile devices are proposed to foster awareness and to facilitate an intimate and exhaustive data collection on learning habits in context.

Recent work [18] reviews time preferences and availability in e-learning classrooms across a 10-year period in scientific literature concluding that almost all the papers dealt with formal education and quantitatively oriented. The classification framework presented in the current manuscript extends the walls of the classroom in lifelong learners to the mobile context, and proposes a suitable scaffold to identify productive moments exploring not only the quality and quantity of the time, but also the rest of the dimensions in the mobile context (location, relation, environment, artefact) [15].

Moreover, this classification framework is instantiated in a study where a mobile app is piloted with the aim to make lifelong learners record and reflect on qualitative and quantitative learning preferences through the use of different features in smart phones. The experiment resulted in a successful experience where participants where able to report their learning preferences in the specific context of a technology-enhanced learning summer school.

The work presented in this manuscript represents a promising approach for lifelong learners to get actively involved in experiencing their own learning day. The ESM instantiated in personal mobile devices is suited for lifelong learners to explore their own specific context, learning style, and available resources to model each learning moment.

This pilot has raised the following limitations: first, this pilot was tested at the venue of a summer school, which is an exceptional learning context. Real lifelong learning scenarios imply daily routines like workplaces, transitions, etc.; second, the length (in time) of the experiment was too short. Modelling one's lifelong learning day implies a long-term experiment where moments of the day and moments of the week are explored. The analysis on work time and learning activities from Livingstone & Stowe [19] stresses the lack of longitudinal studies especially in job-related informal learning. Likewise, they highlight that initiatives to achieve better work-family balance are most likely to have a positive effect on either quality of work life or workers' learning opportunities, if the full extent of these long hours is recognized more clearly.

Mobile tools are increasingly used for sampling of experiences [10, 20, 21] in the last years where different reports have reviewed existing tools for sampling of experiences [21, 22] classifying them by operating system (iOS, Android, etc.), the price of the app, the project where it was used, or the URL where it can be downloaded. Nevertheless, there is no scientific work reviewing existing apps deepening into the features for experience sampling on mobile devices. In future research, we will extend this work by providing a review of apps for ESM classifying the in accordance to the framework presented in this manuscript and with a special focus on the use of ESM for self-regulated lifelong learning. Likewise, this research will be further extended developing mobile tools and services to provide effective feed-forward feedback targeting the process and self-regulation level.

References

1. Eurostat, Lifelong learning statistics - Statistics Explained (2012) (June 5, 2013), http://epp.eurostat.ec.europa.eu/statistics_explained/index.php/Lifelong_learning_statistics# (accessed June 3, 2013)
2. Kalz, M.: Lifelong learning and its support with new technologies. In: Smelser, N.J., Baltes, P.B. (eds.) International Encyclopedia of the Social and Behavioral Sciences. Pergamon, Oxford (in press)
3. Metzger, L.C., Cleach, O.: White-collar telework: Between an overload and learning a new organization of time. Sociologie du Travail, 433–450 (2004)
4. Tabuenca, B., Ternier, S., Specht, M.: Supporting lifelong learners to build personal learning ecologies in daily physical spaces. International Journal of Mobile Learning Organisation 7, 177–196 (2013)
5. European Commission: Key competences for lifelong learning. An European reference framework (2007)
6. Tabuenca, B., Verpoorten, D., Ternier, S., Westera, W., Specht, M.: Fostering reflective practice with mobile technologies. In: Proceedings of the 2nd Workshop on Awareness and Reflection in Technology Enhanced Learning (2012)
7. Hattie, J., Timperley, H.: The Power of Feedback. Rev. Educ. Res. 77, 81–112 (2007)
8. Leone, C., Richards, H.: Classwork and homework in early adolescence: The ecology of achievement. J. Youth Adolesc. 18, 1989 (1989)
9. Crocker, J., Karpinski, A., Quinn, D.M., Chase, S.K.: When Grades Determine Self-Worth: Consequences of Contingent Self-Worth for Male and Female Engineering and Psychology Majors. J. Pers. Soc. Psychol. 85, 507–516 (2003)
10. Church, K., Cherubini, M., Oliver, N.: A large-scale study of daily information needs captured in situ. ACM Trans. Comput. Interact. 21, 1–46 (2014)
11. Hektner, J., Schmidt, J., Csikszentmihalyi, M.: Experience sampling method: Measuring the quality of everyday life (2007)
12. Hormuth, S.: The sampling of experiences in situ. J. Pers. 54, 1986 (1986)

13. Consolvo, S., Walker, M.: Using the experience sampling method to evaluate ubicomp applications. IEEE Pervasive Comput. (2003)
14. De Jong, T., Specht, M., Koper, R.: A reference model for mobile social software for learning. Int. J. Contin. Eng. Educ. Life-Long Learn. 18, 118 (2008)
15. Specht, M.: Learning in a technology enhanced world (2009)
16. Nielsen, J., Clemmensen, T., Yssing, C.: Getting access to what goes on in people's heads?: reflections on the think-aloud technique. In: NordiCHI, pp. 101–110 (2002)
17. Ternier, S., Klemke, R., Kalz, M., Specht, M.: ARLearn: augmented reality meets augmented virtuality. J. Univers. Comput. Sci. - Technol. Learn. across Phys. Virtual Spaces [Special Issue] 18, 2143–2164 (2012)
18. Gros, B., Barbera, E., Kirshner, P.: Time factor in e-learning: Impact literature review. eLearn Cent. Res. Pap. Ser., 16–31 (2010)
19. Livingstone, D., Stowe, S.: Work time and learning activities of the continuously employed: A longitudinal analysis, 1998-2004. J. Work. Learn. 19, 17–31 (2007)
20. Intille, S.S., Rondoni, J., Kukla, C., Ancona, I., Bao, L.: A context-aware experience sampling tool. In: CHI 2003 Ext. Abstr. Hum. Factors Comput. Syst. - CHI 2003, p. 972 (2003)
21. Conner, T.: Experience Sampling and Ecological Momentary Assessment with Mobile Phones (2013)
22. Khan, V.J., Markopoulos, P.: Experience Sampling: A workbook about the method and the tools that support it, Eindhoven (2009)

Tangible-Based Assessment
of Collaborative Problem Solving

Eric Tobias, Valérie Maquil, and Eric Ras

Public Research Centre Henri Tudor
av. J.F. Kennedy 29, L-1855 Luxembourg-Kirchberg, Luxembourg
{eric.tobias,valerie.maquil,eric.ras}@tudor.lu

Abstract. Using Tangible User Interfaces (TUI) for assessing collaborative problems has only been marginally investigated in technology-based assessment. Our first empirical studies focused on light-weight performance measurements, usability, user experience, and gesture analysis to increase our understanding of how people interact with TUI in an assessment context. In this paper we present three of those studies: a windmill scenario where users can learn about the dynamics of energy generation using wind power; a traffic simulator educating the audience on the impacts of different traffic parameters on its fluidity; and a simple climate change scenario allowing children to comprehend the relation between their family's behaviour and its effect on CO_2 levels. The paper concludes each scenario by presenting assessment methodologies and observed learning outcome.

Keywords: Tangible User Interfaces, Technology-based Assessment, Complex Problem Solving, Collaborative Problem Solving.

1   Introduction

For the last few years, the term 21st Century skill has shown up in scientific literature [1]. These skills include, for example, complex problem solving, creativity, critical thinking, learning to learn, and decision making [2]. A particular 21st Century skill is complex problem solving which encompasses the ability to successfully deal with fuzzy and dynamically changing problems. Despite their importance, assessing these skills with existing technologies poses a challenge. Therefore, exploring new technologies, such as tangible user interfaces (TUI), may prove useful for discovering viable alternatives. TUI offer the possibility to assess collaborative scenarios due to their accessibility to groups. They also allow for using metaphors to imply functionality which can improve understanding and knowledge generation by tapping into the power of human cognition, especially visual cognition.

For each scenario we set up a tangible tabletop system based on the optical tracking framework reacTIVision[1], a toolkit for tangible multi-touch surfaces.

---

[1] http://reactivision.sourceforge.net/ (accessed April 14, 2014).

M. Kalz and E. Ras (Eds.): CAA 2014, CCIS 439, pp. 162–165, 2014.

The worktop has an interactive area of 75 x 120cm. Onto the table we project an image according to the scenario as shown in Figure 1 respectively Figure 2. In addition, for each scenario we create a set of tangible widgets, objects both physical and digital used to interact with the tangible table. The objects are tracked using a camera underneath the semi-translucent tabletop surface. Also located beneath the tabletop, a short throw projector provides real-time feedback as well as the initial scenario context images. The following short sections will elaborate briefly on each scenario before elaborating on the set-up for capturing user data and concluding.

2   Windmill Scenario

The windmill scenario allows exploring and understanding the relation of external variables on the production of electricity in a wind-powered turbine. Users can engage in the scenario by rotating tangibles on the surface to change input parameters. Input parameters such as wind speed or the number of blades are reflected in real time on output parameters such as rotor speed or electrical power output. Because all the tangibles can be moved freely on the table and exchanged, each participant gets a vote and hence collaboration and motivation was expected to be improved.

 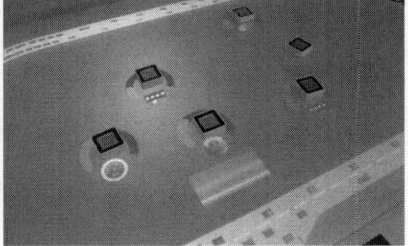

Fig. 1. Windmill scenario   **Fig. 2.** Traffic Simulator

3   Traffic Simulator

The traffic simulator was adapted from an online traffic simulator of the Technische Universität Dresden's Institute for Transport & Economics. The original purpose as well as more information can be found in [3]. The adapted simulator has its interface revamped: all control elements are replaced by the functionality provided by tangibles. Akin to the Windmill simulator, feedback on the input dials is provided in real time but due to the nature of the simulated content, traffic reacts true to the laws of traffic dynamics: forming and dissipating traffic jams as given by the traffic dynamics influenced by the users. The simple scenario (Figure 2 lets users adjust the number of vehicles on the motorway and influx ramp as well as the average speed, and politeness of drivers.

4   Climate Change Scenario

The climate change scenario was build to allow children to understand the relations between causes of climate change and their effect. Special care was taken to expose causes that children of a young age (9 to 12) can relate to. The scenario builds upon the MicroDYN methodology of Greiff et al [4]. The TUI allows using widgets to ask questions to a group of test takers which each can vote on one of the proposed answers. Their votes are fed into a system of linear equations which gives feedback on the effect on climate change. In a second phase, test takers are able to freely manipulate parameters, that is, change votes on questions, to explore the climate model.

5   Experimental Set-up

During experiments, participant behaviour is monitored using video recording from multiple angles. Further, a researcher observes participants and takes notes of the solving strategies and arising usability issues. Afterwards, participants are asked to fill out two questionnaires. The first questionnaire aims to assess the knowledge of the participants gained during the exploration phase, the second consists of questions on the usability and user experience of the system.

The set-up has been tweaked during each experimentation such that for the Climate Change scenario, scheduled to run in 20 sessions in 2014 and 2015, participants will be video and audio recorded during the sessions. Using separate data channels, we prepare for our next iteration of the set-up where we intend to add more data sources and combine them using multi-modal fusion.

Results on a first set of studies using the Windmill scenario are presented in [5]. A detailed description of the Climate Change scenario, the MicroDYN methodology, as well as research questions and expected outcome can be found in [6].

6   Conclusion

Technology-based assessment has the potential to support educational innovation and development of 21st century skills, such as, for example, complex problem solving, communication, team work, creativity and innovation [2]. The multi-dimensionality of TUI: the tabletop and physical objects, the projection and feedback, body language, and speech enable users to benefit from many inputs and learn naturally in a collaborative environment. While the system is not without its faults, mainly due to the spatial limitations of the tabletop, future iterations of the set-up will feature more feedback and information gathering dimensions and enable the use of multi-modal fusion to aggregate data into learning traces. This will in turn enable us to provide better feedback to encourage self-regulating behaviours.

References

1. Better Skills, Better Jobs, Better Lives A Strategic Approach to Skills Policies: A Strategic Approach to Skills Policies. OECD Publishing (2012)
2. Binkley, M., Erstad, O., Herman, J., Raizen, S., Ripley, M., Miller-Ricci, M., Rumble, M.: Defining twenty-first century skills. In: Assessment and Teaching of 21st Century Skills, pp. 17–66. Springer (2012)
3. Treiber, M., Kesting, A.: Verkehrsdynamik und-simulation: Daten, Modelle und Anwendungen der Verkehrsflussdynamik, vol. 1183. Springer, DE (2010)
4. Greiff, S., Wüstenberg, S., Molnár, G., Fischer, A., Funke, J., Csapó, B.: Complex problem solving in educational contexts–something beyond g: Concept, assessment, measurement invariance, and construct validity. Journal of Educational Psychology 105(2), 364 (2013)
5. Ras, E., Maquil, V., Foulonneau, M., Latour, T.: Empirical studies on a tangible user interface for technology-based assessment: Insights and emerging challenges. International Journal of e-Assessment (2012)
6. Maquil, V., Tobias, E., Greiff, S., Ras, E.: Assessment of collaborative problem solving using linear equations on a tangible tabletop. In: Kalz, M., Ras, E. (eds.) CAA 2014. CCIS, vol. 439, pp. 62–69. Springer International Publishing Switzerland (2014)

Author Index